PETER GAMMONS

Beyond the Sixth Game

HOUGHTON MIFFLIN COMPANY · BOSTON
1985

To my mother, Betty. She was the one who wrote down the names so I could find out that the Red Sox got both Bob Chakales and Dean Stone in the deal with Washington that morning, and who took advantage of the Groton public schools' tradition that Opening Day was a legal excuse to leave school early.

Library of Congress Cataloging in Publication Data
Gammons, Peter.
    Beyond the sixth game.

    1. Boston Red Sox (Baseball team)—History.   2. World series (Baseball)   I. Title.
GV875.B62G35   1985   796.357′782   84-25252
ISBN 0-395-35345-9

Printed in the United States of America

P 10 9 8 7 6 5 4 3 2 1

Acknowledgments

Many thanks to the people of the *Boston Globe* who gave me the opportunity to have a job doing something I so enjoyed. First and foremost, Fran Rosa, who took an awful gamble on an undrafted free agent out of the University of North Carolina, and Ernie Roberts, Dave Smith, and Vince Doria, the sports editors who tolerated me. Clif Keane, the late and wonderful Ray Fitzgerald, the late Harold Kaese, Bud Collins (who taught me the art of making out expense accounts), and Will McDonough, who helped me break in, and comrades like Bob Ryan, Leigh Montville, Larry Whiteside, and Mike Madden, with whom I have worked.

I was lucky breaking in, because I was by far the youngest writer on the beat, but the men from the other papers went out of their way to make sure I learned instead of being buried. Unfortunately, all have passed away: Hugh McGovern of the *Worcester Telegram-Gazette*, Fred Ciampa, George Bankert, Jake Liston, Larry Claflin.

My greatest help over the past few years has come from
fellow typists such as Charles Scoggins of the *Lowell Sun,* Joe
Giulotti of the *Herald,* former Quincy *Patriot-Ledger* scoop-
master Bob Finnigan, Gary Santaniello of the *Worcester Tele-
gram,* Dave O'Hara of the Associated Press, and Tommy Shea
of the *Springfield Union.*

Thanks, too, to the Red Sox people, who get over being
ticked off. It was my pleasure to share a glass of champagne — in a Jack in the Box paper cup, no less — in the
back room of the Oakland clubhouse with Tom Yawkey when
they won the pennant in 1975. It's always seemed unfortunate that there had to be such a civil war in that office, for
Dick O'Connell, John Claiborne, and Gene Kirby were mar-
velous people who went out of their way to be cooperative.
Through all the hard times and controversy, Haywood Sullivan, Ed Kenney, Eddie Kasko, John Harrington, and Jean
Yawkey have remained patient and helpful, and from Jack
Rogers to Bill Crowley — who stood up for the media in
ways most of them never appreciated — to Dick Bresciani
and Josh Spofford, the public relations department has been
one of the best. I'd sure hate to have been Helen Robinson
and Mary Jane Ryan answering all my calls over the years.

I think this all started with my late uncle Donald Gammons, and I know my brother, the Reverend Edward B.
Gammons, Jr., never allowed me to forget the existence of
baseball. I'll never understand how my wife, Gloria, put up
with it, or me.

Contents

ONE

1975

THE SIXTH GAME

The established dynasty, Cincinnati's Big Red Machine, meets the dynasty of the future, the Boston Red Sox, and the Red Sox win the most memorable game of the most memorable World Series of a baseball generation.

*B*OSTON, October 22, 1975 — Then all of a sudden the ball was suspended out there in the black of the morning like the Mystic River Bridge. Carlton Fisk broke forward for a step, then stopped and watched. He later remembered none of the clumsy hula dance that NBC made famous, only that "it seemed like the wait for Christmas morning" as he watched to see on which side of the fine line it would land: home run/victory or foul ball/strike one.

When it finally crashed fair off the mesh attached to the left-field foul pole, Fisk raised his fists above his head in applause in the midst of his convulsive leap, and as if conducted by Charles Munch, the reaction unfurled. Fenway Park organist John Kiley boomed the opening notes of Handel's "Hallelujah Chorus," Fisk gamboled his way around the bases, teammates passionately staggered to home plate, and from the bleachers to Presque Isle people looked at one another as the first shock warmed into reality. In Raymond,

New Hampshire, an Episcopal minister named James Smith burst out of his house, ran across to St. Bartholomew's Church, grabbed the rope, and began ringing the church bell about the same time that, in Yardley, Pennsylvania, the wife of another Episcopal minister, Gretchen Gammons, ran across the street to St. Andrew's and did the same.

It had been back in the tenth inning that Pete Rose had turned from his place in the batter's box and said to Fisk, "This is some kind of game, isn't it?" At 12:34 A.M., in the bottom of the twelfth inning, Fisk's histrionic, 304-foot home run brought Red Sox shortstop Rick Burleson running to home plate saying to teammate Rick Miller, "We just might have won the greatest game ever played."

So it seemed at the moment, frozen in time. Judged soberly, rationally, there are undoubtedly dozens and hundreds and thousands of baseball games staged from Old Orchard Beach to Los Angeles that one would have to say had more technical brilliance. But this one had captured all that baseball could be. Fisk's home run had virtually altered the autumnal equinox. By the time the ball had caromed off the screen and thirty-five thousand people had stood to sing "Give Me Some Men Who Are Stout-Hearted Men", as Fisk galavanted across the field to an interview room, the entire emotional scale had been played.

After three days of rain, the Red Sox had begun this fight for survival with a three-run, first-inning homer by wonderchild Fred Lynn. Then they watched in resigned silence as, slowly but surely, the heavily favored Reds chipped away at the mortality of a hero named Luis Tiant. When Cincinnati center fielder Cesar Geronimo homered in the top of the eighth inning, El Tiante left, trailing 6–3, to heartfelt but polite applause that accepted the finality of the situation.

If some clock had been allowed to run out at that point, the sixth game of the 1975 World Series would have been no more, no less than a game from the, say, 1961 World Series or 1969 National League Championship Series. But, turn after hairpin turn, it became the Sixth Game. First, in the bottom of the eighth, Bernardo Carbo hit a stunning two-out, three-run homer that tied it. In the ninth, when Boston had the bases loaded and none out, Cincinnati left fielder George Foster caught Lynn's fly ball and threw Denny Doyle out at the plate to kill what was apparently a certain game-winning rally. In the eleventh, Dwight Evans made a catch that Reds manager Sparky Anderson insisted was "given its significance, one of the two greatest catches ever made" to rob Joe Morgan of a game-winning double, triple, or homer and turn it into a double play. Then, in the twelfth inning, against Pat Darcy, the record twelfth pitcher in the 241-minute game, came Fisk's shot, the cherry on the top of this all-time banana split of a game.

The Sixth Game was an abridgment of the entire splendid series in which Boston led in all seven games and lost the lead in five of them, in which five games were decided by one run, two were decided in extra innings, and two others in the ninth inning. But there was much more to this game, and this series, than statistics, however dazzling they might be. Baseball was coming out of an era of five consecutive vanilla-bland World Series won by teams from Baltimore, Pittsburgh, and Oakland, hardly centers of media excitement. Immediately preceding those five World Series were the years when no one could score runs, which came just a few years after an era in which a team from New York or Los Angeles had been in the World Series for twenty consecutive Octobers. Nineteen seventy-five was the year television coverage of baseball came of age, with the split image of Fisk's rhumba and the ball suspended against the morn, a fitting symbol of TV's ascendancy.

There, too, like a Christmas carol service, at the end of a decade that decried all customs and history, were all the traditions of a sport whose lineage is steeped in history. Cincinnati and Boston, in fact, were the first two professional baseball cities. Fenway Park, with its nooks and crannies and its promise that no two games will ever be alike, is the romanticists' ideal. The matchup of the two teams presented emotional extremes: the IBM image of the Big Red Machine, the best team in baseball, with its short hair and the kind of puissance that earns the Pete Rozelle Trophy, against the Olde Towne Teame, the last great white team, which had come out of nowhere that year with the only rookie ever to be Most Valuable Player (Lynn), an institution (Carl Yastrzemski), a Brahmin New Englander (Fisk), and some characters named Tiant and Carbo and Bill "Space Man" Lee. Riverfront Stadium, which could have been ordered from a Sears catalogue, as contrasted with the idiosyncratic Fenway Park.

The Reds' characters were submerged in and by a team perfection, and in the end, they won the series because they simply played the game more perfectly than Boston, for whom Doyle was the sixth runner in six games tagged out at the plate. It was the Red Sox who did the spectacular in the series, the Red Sox who did so much to bring individualism and personality back into the sport. "When tonight is over," Lee was credited with saying before he pitched the seventh game, "Don Gullett is going to the Hall of Fame, and I'm going to the Eliot Lounge."

What few remember about the Sixth Game was that despite its days of dramatic rainout buildup, it was seven outs from having all the drama of the Astros playing the Giants in August, from a routine conclusion of the Reds defeating the Red Sox in six games. It had begun with Lynn's three-run homer off Cincinnati starter Gary Nolan — who, like all the Reds starters that year, would be gone within three years — in the first inning. That was the final, dramatic blow of what was one of the greatest rookie seasons in baseball history. There was a Joe Hardy air about Lynn, a private, loping kid a year and a half out of the University of Southern California. One week into the season, which the Red Sox had started after a horrible September 1974 collapse, the inability to deal (in the wake of the Yankees getting Bobby Bonds, the Orioles Lee May, and the Tigers Nate Colbert), and a 10–21 spring training, Yankee manager Bill Virdon said, "Don't bother talking about Bonds. Fred Lynn may be the next DiMaggio." Virdon completed his statement with an "I told you so" when Lynn's spectacular diving, bouncing, ninth-inning catch in Shea Stadium in August saved a 1–0 Boston victory that marked the Yankees absent the remainder of the season. Lynn batted .331. He drove in 105 runs, scored 103, rapped 47 doubles and 21 homers, and made one tumblers' catch after another en route to being named both Rookie of the Year and his league's Most Valuable Player. In the fifth inning of the Sixth Game he banged into the center-field fence leaping for Ken Griffey's triple, slid to the ground in a heap, and lay there. The stands fell silent as if witness to a presidential assassination, and Red Sox owner Tom Yawkey turned to scouting director Haywood Sullivan and said, "Those walls must be padded before next season."

For more than a month, it had been Tiant — likened by the *Boston Globe*'s Leigh Montville to the old man in *The Old Man and the Sea* — who had pulled the Red Sox together. El Tiante was listed at thirty-four and rumored to be closer to forty, but he was the central nervous system of the team. He had been sidelined for weeks with a bad back, and when September came (Baltimore manager Earl Weaver kept promising his team's annual comeback and one Baltimore columnist labeled the Red Sox the Boston Chokers), it was Tiant who stepped forth. On September 11, he returned from a three-week absence, took a no-hitter into the eighth, and beat Detroit 3–1. Four days later, with what Red Sox officials later admitted was a crowd in excess of forty-five thousand (prior to standing-room fire laws), he rode the home runs of Fisk and Rico Petrocelli to a 2–0 win over the Orioles' Cy Young Award winner, Jim Palmer, on the night that the chant "LOO-EEE, LOO-EEE" came into being. He shut out Cleveland on the final Friday night of the season to all but clinch the pennant. When the A's began the playoffs as the experienced favorites, he shut them out in the first game and began a three-game sweep. When the Reds began the World Series as heavy favorites, he shut them out, and comically out of place at bat but somehow effective, he started the winning six-run, seventh-inning rally. When, in Cincinnati, the Red Sox were down 2–1 in games, he pitched the game by which he always said he'd like to be remembered: 163 pitches, a 5–4 lead in the fourth, two runners on in each of the last five innings, and a 5–4 victory that was as gutsy as John Garfield in *Body and Soul.*

But this night, El Tiante's marionette abracadabra could carry them no more. A walk to designated bunter Ed Armbrister began a three-run fifth inning that not only broke Tiant's skein of forty consecutive scoreless innings in Fenway but tied the game. Foster made it 5–3 with a line drive off the center-field fence in the seventh, and when Cesar Geronimo angled his homer inside the right-field foul pole leading off the eighth, Tiant left as *Sport* magazine editor Dick Schaap began collecting the MVP ballots in the press box. No one much noticed when the Red Sox got two on leading off the eighth; Cincinnati's prized rookie reliever Rawlins Eastwick III came in and struck out Evans, got Burleson to fly out, and had only to get the pinch hitter, Carbo, to bring the Reds to within an inning of their first championship in thirty-five years.

Bernardo Carbo. He was a cartoon character of sorts, a frizzy-haired kid who traveled with a stuffed gorilla dressed in a Cardinals uniform and named Mighty Joe Young. After running into the bullpen wall to save a home run in the crucial June series with the Yankees, Carbo delayed the game for ten minutes while he scoured the warning track for the chaw of tobacco that had popped out of his mouth; when he found it, he put it back in his mouth and the game continued. Carbo was a streak hitter who, in both of the two years since being obtained from the Cardinals, had hit spectacularly for the

Red Sox until mid-May, then ended up relegated to the bench. He never accepted that, once charging up to general manager Dick O'Connell's office immediately before a game to protest Evans's presence in the lineup. Bernardo always had trouble accepting authority, which is why Sparky Anderson and the Reds had traded him to St. Louis in the first place. He had hardly played at all in the second half of the season, but in game three had pinch-hit a homer, and with two outs in the bottom of the eighth of game six, he got his second chance.

With two strikes, Eastwick threw him a fastball that befuddled Bernardo as if it were the Pythagorean theorem. He pulled his bat up in self-defense, deflecting the third strike off to the left. "That might have been the worst swing in the history of baseball," Fisk would tease Carbo later, but it wasted the pitch. Eastwick came in with another fastball and Carbo drove it into the center-field bleachers. "The crowd willed it up into the seats," claims Rose.

6–6. "Bernie," said Lee, "is the only man I know who turned fall into summer with one wave of his magic wand."

The Red Sox had a chance to win it in the ninth, with the bases loaded and none out. When Lynn lofted a fly ball down the left-field line halfway between third base and The Wall and George Foster settled under it 170 feet from home plate, third-base coach Don Zimmer yelled to base runner Denny Doyle, "No, no."

Doyle, however, thought Zimmer was saying "Go, go." He took off, Foster's throw to Johnny Bench cut him down easily, and the threat passed. Then with Griffey on first, one out in the eleventh, Red Sox reliever Dick Drago pitched to Joe Morgan.

When the series was over, Anderson was to say that the Boston player who had impressed him most was Evans. Dwight was only twenty-three at the time, but his three-year major-league career had been a struggle to approach others' expectations. He arrived in September 1972 with the promise of superstardom, but youth, two serious beanings, and personal problems and insecurities had complicated his baseball life. Once the Gold Dust Twins, Fred Lynn and Jim Rice, arrived in 1975, it was Evans who the media constantly suggested should be traded for a pitcher or a power-hitting third baseman. That only added to his problems. But, whether he hit .223 as he did as a rookie or .274 as he did in '75, Evans never wavered in the field. He was at that point in his career a defensive offensive player and an offensive defensive player, the premier defensive right fielder in the American League, playing the most difficult right field in baseball. In this series it was his dramatic ninth-inning, two-run homer off Eastwick that took the third game into extra innings and to the Armbrister interference controversy.

As Red Sox reliever Dick Drago went into his stretch, Evans tried preparing himself for all possibilities. "In all important situations, Doyle would give me a signal if Drago were throwing a breaking ball to a left-handed hitter so I could be leaning for him to pull," Evans said. "One of the great things about playing the outfield with Fisk catching was that he moved so much you could tell the location of the pitch. Knowing the pitching and seeing Fisk set up, I was thinking that the worst thing that could happen would be that Morgan could pull a line drive directly over my head, so I was mentally leaning in that direction." Morgan indeed smashed the worst, a line drive directly over Evans's head. But, breaking as the ball was hit, Evans scrambled backward, stabbed the ball at full stride as he crossed the warning track, ricocheted off the wall, whirled, and fired back to the infield; Yastrzemski, the first baseman, grabbed the throw halfway between the coach's box and the dugout and tossed to Burleson — who'd raced across from shortstop — to complete the double play. "It probably wouldn't have been in the seats," said Evans, "but it would have been the game." As it turned out, it was a catch that shares a place in World Series history with such other historic defensive plays as Willie Mays's in 1954, Al Gionfriddo's in 1947, and Harry Hooper's in 1912.

Pat Darcy, the seventh pitcher, began the bottom of the twelfth by running a sinker down and in to Fisk's wheelhouse. "He's a lowball pitcher, I'm a lowball, dead-pull hitter, so I was looking for that one pitch in that one area," said Fisk. "I got it, then drove it." He chopped his woodcutter's swing and sent his line drive searing toward the foul pole. The problem was keeping the ball in fair territory, as with that short, chopping swing Fisk had spent much of his career setting unofficial records for foul homers. But this was Fisk's season of retribution — after a knee injury that nearly ended his career in 1974, he had broken his arm in the first exhibition game of 1975 and came back in June to bat .331 the remainder of the season. So he found retribution for game three. That night he impaled his mask onto the screen as Morgan's game-winning line drive soared over Lynn's head and Geronimo danced across the plate in front of him; it had been Geronimo whom Armbrister was trying to advance with his bunt attempt, but after the controversial collision as Fisk tried to pounce on the ball, his off-balance throw to start what could have been a double play sailed into center field to launch what would be a long winter's argument with and torment for home-plate umpire Larry Barnett.

But this twelfth-inning drive crashed against the mesh attached to the foul pole, and as Fisk was madly running and skipping and clapping around the bases, George Frederick Handel echoed across the Back Bay and church bells pealed out for both the New England town team and baseball itself.

No seventh game was really necessary, at least from the romanticist's viewpoint, and that encompassed much of the audience, since so much of baseball and its tradition from Abner Doubleday to Babe Ruth to Fernando Valenzuela is romance. "Instead of playing a seventh game, they should spread tables and checkered tablecloths across the outfields

and just have a picnic, a feast to a glorious World Series, and
toast one another until dawn," suggested television journalist
Clark Booth. There was a seventh game, of course, which
served to put it on the record that the Cincinnati Reds
won — albeit by one run in the ninth inning — and that the
Boston Red Sox still had not been world champions since
1918, when Ruth was their best pitcher and Yawkey was a
fifteen-year-old student at the Irving School in Tarrytown,
New York.

The deciding game was dotted with essences of both
teams. Once again, the Red Sox had a 3–0 lead, forged from
Gullett's sudden wildness in the fourth inning. Once again,
the Red Sox could not put Cincinnati away, either with their
bats (Burleson had struck out with the bases loaded to end
the fourth) or with their pitching or with their defense. Once
again, it was the Hun, Rose, who led their charge, as he'd led
it from the first at-bat of the first game when he snarled,
"Tiant is nothing," a declaration he continued to make for
two weeks.

With his beloved moon staring down over his left shoulder,
Bill Lee had cruised along into the sixth inning with the 3–0
lead. No one entertained America during the series more
than The Space Man, as he happily discussed Vonnegut ("In
nonsense is strength"), organic gardening, violence ("I'd have
bitten Barnett's ear off — I'd have Van Goghed him"), and
Boston politics with any journalist who would listen — and
most of them did. That he was even on the October stage was
surprising: after August 24, when he shut out the White Sox
in the rain throwing Leephus bloopers and had a 17–6
record, he did not win another game, finishing the season lost
in the bullpen until the Boston scouting reports suggested
that his screwball and off-speed stuff would be more effective
against Cincinnati's potent lineup than the conventional hard
sinker–slider repertoire of late-season Reggie Cleveland.
He'd pitched brilliantly in the rain-delayed second game,
coming within an inning of a 2–1 victory that would have

done in the Reds. But Johnny Bench, showing his experience, looked for the screwball, got one inches off the outside corner on the first pitch of the ninth, and drove it into the right-field corner. Then a David Concepcion infield hit and a Griffey double off Drago took the Reds home to Cincinnati 3–2 winners.

By the sixth inning of the final game, Rose was stomping around the dugout like a whiffling Che Guevera. He screamed, hollered, and slapped his teammates, then stomped up to the plate and led off the inning with a single, one of the extraordinary eleven times he reached base in his final fifteen plate appearances. An out later, Bench pulled a Lee sinker into the ground for what appeared to be an inning-ending double play to Burleson. "There are some things you just can't allow to happen," said Rose. "At that moment, a double play was one of them." He sent himself into a kamikaze orbit toward Doyle. "He saw me coming for ten feet in the air," Rose later chortled. "I made sure of it." He wanted his take-out slides to go to Cooperstown with his base-hit records.

Doyle had another problem besides Rose. The baseballs used then were made in Haiti, and once in a while the force of the bat would literally tear the cover off a ball. "The cover had almost entirely torn off when Bench hit it," Doyle revealed the next spring. "When I went to get rid of it to first, it just flew out of my hand." Utility infielder Bobby Heise retrieved the ball in the dugout, an unenviable trophy that Doyle would keep. The only postseason opportunity of Doyle's career was not one bathed in heroics, for he had lost another Bench double-play ball in the whiteness of Bench's uniform in game five.

So, instead of being out of the inning, Lee then had to face Tony Perez. For the first four games, Perez had been mired in a hitless slump. But in game five he walloped two tremendous home runs off Cleveland to provide Gullett the margin for the 6–2 victory. The scouting reports told Lee not to throw Perez, a deadly off-speed hitter, any junk. But The Space Man did what he wanted to do whenever he wanted to do it — which is how he became one of baseball's first and foremost counterculture idols — and he insisted on throwing Perez one of his Moon Curves or Leephus pitches. A blooper ball. He had thrown three earlier, two for strikes, one for a pop-up, and had even thrown one to Perez that was taken for a strike. "Lee was throwing that hard screwball so well, I never thought he'd throw another one of those bloopers," said Perez. "Sure, I was surprised, but I was geared up for the fastball, and that's so slow it's easy to adjust to." Rumor has it that the ball ended up in Kokomo, Indiana, having landed on a truck in the westbound lane of the Massachusetts Turnpike. Fact had the Red Sox lead cut to 3–2, and an inning later Lee developed a blister. "All of a sudden I found myself pitching to Griffey and I couldn't get the ball to go anywhere near where I wanted it," explained Lee, and when he walked Griffey, manager Darrell Johnson had to bring in left-hander Rogelio Moret. Griffey stole second, and after an out and a walk, Rose slapped another single that tied it. Right-hander Jim Willoughby, a tall, floppy sinker-baller who looked as if he were falling out of a tree when he pitched, came on to re- tire Bench with the bases loaded, pitched a one-two-three eighth, and looked forward to the ninth. He had pitched six and a third series innings without allowing an earned run.

After Evans led off the bottom of the eighth with a walk, Burleson failed to put down a bunt, grounding into a double play that would have brought Willoughby, the most effective reliever of the series, to the plate. Johnson sent up Cecil Coop- er. Thus was another link in the chain of Boston's problem- atic baseball legacy forged.

Three months later, a man sat in the Abbeyfeale Café in Inman Square in Cambridge, drinking fifty-cent shots with twenty-five-cent drafts, blankly staring at the television mounted up in the corner of the bar. He had been there for nearly four hours, watching, when he turned for the first time to a group of three men down the bar. "Why," he stammered, "did Johnson bat for Willoughby?"

"Where were you," replied one of the men, "when you heard Denny Galehouse was pitching against the Indians?"

"How," asked another, "could Slaughter have scored from first?"

At the time, Cooper was going through what Gil Hodges had experienced in 1952, and what Eddie Murray and Willie Wilson and Dave Winfield would later have to face. He had gone into a dreadful slump that at that point had reached one-for-eighteen, a dour ending to what had been an emerging (.311) season before he had been hit in the face by a pitch thrown by Milwaukee's Billy Travers September 7.

Manager Johnson, too, was experiencing a public flogging of sorts. Lee, ired at being passed over for the sixth-game start when rain allowed Tiant to come back, said, "Darrell's been falling out of trees and landing on his feet all season." Johnson was a quiet man, whose inability to articulate had made him the butt of press conference jokes by the national media. He'd been the minor-league manager who helped direct most of the extraordinary young talent to Boston, and he'd organized and expertly handled a pitching staff to get as much out of it as one ever could have asked. But Johnson also was nearly fired in June, when, as the team went on a 9–4, job-saving road trip, the front office talked to Detroit officials about luring away Tigers manager Ralph Houk. Second baseman Doug Griffin, replaced by Doyle in mid-June, stated, "We're going to win this thing in *spite* of the manager." Such fragments of disrespect clouded the season. Fisk and Lee walked out of a meeting in the manager's office in Baltimore, claiming Johnson was incoherent. When the Red Sox clinched the division championship the last Saturday, Johnson refused to grant Yastrzemski permission to fly home to Florida and miss the final day of the season and the next couple of workouts prior to the playoffs; Yastrzemski went anyway. When they won the playoffs in Oakland, Johnson never went in and joined in the clubhouse celebration, instead sitting in his tiny office a few feet away, sipping champagne with Oakland outfielder Joe Rudi, his off-season hunting companion.

Replacing Willoughby, Cooper went out, and rookie left-hander Jim Burton came in to pitch the top of the ninth, since Drago had pitched three innings the night before. Burton promptly walked the man he was brought in to face, the left-hand-hitting Griffey leading off. Two outs later, Griffey

---

The Sixth Game, October 21, 1975

Cincinnati	AB	R	H	RBI	Boston	AB	R	H	RBI
Rose, 3b	5	1	2	0	Cooper, 1b	5	0	0	0
Griffey, rf	5	2	2	2	Drago, p	0	0	0	0
Morgan, 2b	6	1	1	1	Miller, ph	1	0	0	0
Bench, c	6	0	1	2	Wise, p	0	0	0	0
Perez, 1b	6	0	2	0	Doyle, 2b	5	0	1	0
Foster, lf	6	0	2	0	Yastrzemski, lf–1b	6	1	3	0
Concepcion, ss	6	0	1	0	Fisk, c	4	2	2	1
Geronimo, cf	6	1	2	1	Lynn, cf	4	2	2	3
Nolan, p	0	0	0	0	Petrocelli, 3b	4	1	0	0
Chaney, ph	1	0	0	0	Evans, rf	5	0	1	0
Norman, p	0	0	0	0	Burleson, ss	3	0	0	0
Billingham, p	0	0	0	0	Tiant, p	2	0	0	0
Armbrister, ph	0	1	0	0	Moret, p	0	0	0	0
Carroll, p	0	0	0	0	Carbo, ph	2	1	1	3
Crowley, ph	1	0	1	0					
Borbon, p	1	0	0	0					
Eastwick, p	0	0	0	0					
McEnaney, p	0	0	0	0					
Driessen, ph	1	0	0	0					
Darcy, p	0	0	0	0					
TOTALS	50	6	14	6		41	7	10	7

Cincinnati	000	030	210	000–6
Boston	300	000	030	001–7

LOB–Cincinnati 11, Boston 9. 2B–Doyle, Evans, Foster. 3B–Griffey. HR–Lynn, Geronimo, Carbo, Fisk. SB–Concepcion. S–Tiant.

	IP	H	R	ER	BB	SO
Nolan	2	3	3	3	0	2
Norman	⅔	1	0	0	2	0
Billingham	1⅓	1	0	0	1	1
Carroll	1	1	0	0	0	0
Borbon	2	1	2	2	1	1
Eastwick	1	2	1	1	1	2
McEnaney	1	0	0	0	1	0
Darcy(L)	2	1	1	1	0	1
Tiant	7	11	6	6	2	5
Moret	1	0	0	0	0	0
Drago	3	1	0	0	0	1
Wise(W)	1	2	0	0	0	1

Tiant pitched to one batter in the eighth. Borbon pitched to two batters in the eighth. Eastwick pitched to two batters in the ninth. Darcy pitched to one batter in the twelfth.
HP–By Drago (Rose). T–4:01. A–35,205

was on second. Burton wisely walked Rose and pitched to the National League's Most Valuable Player, Morgan. It doesn't matter how the ball got out there, that Burton threw a pitch Morgan described as "a breaking ball on the outside corner that two years earlier I couldn't have handled," or that Morgan's bloop barely carried the infield into shallow left-center. The Reds had scored what would be the winning run in the ninth inning of the seventh game, and when Will McEnaney finished off the bottom of the ninth and watched Yaz — who in 1967 had made the last out of his only other World Series — hit a gentle fly to Geronimo, they had completed a task that most everyone in America had figured they'd accomplish with considerably greater ease.

Rose, Morgan, and company had won the 1975 World Series. But when the Sixth Game had ended with that ball suspended out in the black of the morning like the Mystic River Bridge, Carlton Fisk, Bernardo Carbo, Luis Tiant, and the Red Sox *were* the 1975 series.

Baseball had seized the imagination of the entire country; the excitement and color of that World Series marked it im-

Final American League Standings and Red Sox Statistics, 1975

	W	L	PCT	GB	R	HR	BA
EAST							
BOS	95	65	.594		796	134	.275
BAL	90	69	.566	4.5	682	124	.252
NY	83	77	.519	12	681	110	.264
CLE	79	80	.497	15.5	688	153	.261
MIL	68	94	.420	28	675	146	.250
DET	57	102	.358	37.5	570	125	.249
WEST							
OAK	98	64	.605		758	151	.254
KC	91	71	.562	7	710	118	.261
TEX	79	83	.488	19	714	134	.256
MIN	76	83	.478	20.5	724	121	.271
CHI	75	86	.466	22.5	655	94	.255
CAL	72	89	.447	25.5	628	55	.246
LEAGUE TOTAL					8281	1465	.258

MANAGER	W	L	PCT
Darrell Johnson	95	65	.594

POS	PLAYER	B	G	AB	H	2B	3B	HR	R	RBI	BA
REGULARS											
1B	Carl Yastrzemski	L	149	543	146	30	1	14	91	60	.269
2B	Doug Griffin	R	100	257	69	6	0	1	21	29	.240
SS	Rick Burleson	R	158	580	146	25	1	6	66	62	.252
3B	Rico Petrocelli	R	115	402	96	15	1	7	31	59	.239
RF	Dwight Evans	R	128	412	113	24	6	13	61	56	.274
CF	Fred Lynn	L	145	528	175	47	7	21	103	105	.331
LF	Jim Rice	R	144	564	174	29	4	22	92	102	.309
C	Carlton Fisk	R	79	263	87	14	4	10	47	52	.331
DH	Cecil Cooper	L	106	305	95	17	6	14	49	44	.311
SUBSTITUTES											
2B	Denny Doyle	L	89	310	96	21	2	4	50	36	.310
3B	Bob Heise	R	63	126	27	3	0	0	12	21	.214
DH	Tony Conigliaro	R	21	57	7	1	0	2	8	9	.123
3B	Dick McAuliffe	L	7	15	2	0	0	0	0	1	.133
1D	Deron Johnson	R	3	10	6	0	0	1	2	3	.600
2B	Steve Dillard	R	1	5	2	0	0	0	2	0	.400
3B	Butch Hobson	R	2	4	1	0	0	0	0	0	.250
2B	Kim Andrew	R	2	2	1	0	0	0	0	0	.500
2B	Buddy Hunter	R	1	1	0	0	0	0	0	0	.000
OF	Bernie Carbo	L	107	319	82	21	3	15	64	50	.257
UT	Juan Beniquez	R	78	254	74	14	4	2	43	17	.291
OF	Rick Miller	L	77	108	21	2	1	0	21	15	.194
C	Bob Montgomery	R	62	195	44	10	1	2	16	26	.226
C	Tim Blackwell	B	59	132	26	3	2	0	15	6	.197
C	Tim McCarver	L	12	21	8	2	1	0	1	3	.381
C	Andy Merchant	L	1	4	2	0	0	0	1	0	.500

Final American League Standings and Red Sox Statistics, 1975, continued

PITCHER	T	W	L	PCT	ERA	SV
Luis Tiant	R	18	14	.563	4.02	0
Bill Lee	L	17	9	.654	3.95	0
Rick Wise	R	19	12	.613	3.95	0
Reggie Cleveland	R	13	9	.591	4.43	0
Roger Moret	L	14	3	.824	3.60	1
Dick Pole	R	4	6	.400	4.42	0
Dick Drago	R	2	2	.500	3.84	15
Diego Segui	R	2	5	.286	4.82	6
Jim Burton	L	1	2	.333	2.89	1
Jim Willoughby	R	5	2	.714	3.54	8
Steve Barr	L	0	1	.000	2.57	0
Rick Kreuger	L	0	0	—	4.50	0
TEAM TOTAL		95	65	.594	3.99	31

mediately as one of the greatest ever. It seemed inevitable that the Red Sox would dominate their league for years, and that baseball was entering a golden era in which this most traditional of sports would enjoy unprecedented tranquility, prosperity, and popularity.

Instead, the new era was quietly ushered in a few short weeks later in the office of arbitrator Peter Seitz, who ruled that Andy Messersmith and Dave McNally were, as they had claimed, free agents not bound to their respective teams forever through the option clause in their contracts. Though no one suspected it on that glorious October night, the Sixth Game and the 1975 World Series marked the end of an old era, not the beginning of a new one.

TWO

1983

ANOTHER KIND OF GAME

At a spring-training game in Clearwater, Florida, a few alumni of the 1975 World Series gather. Some now wear different uniforms; all now play in a different baseball world.

*C*LEARWATER, FLORIDA, March 10, 1983 — Pete Rose is next to the batting cage, kneeling, leaning on his bat as if he were in the on-deck circle. Joe Morgan is in the cage, hitting off coach Mike Ryan. Tony Perez is standing next to Rose.

"Who is *that* guy?" bellows Rose, pointing to a small, skinny black kid with glasses in a Boston uniform playing catch at the base of the screen behind home plate.

"That's the Can," Perez answers. "Oil Can Boyd. Some players started calling him Oil Slick when they'd get on him, but he's a young kid and throws good. Strike your ass out."

Rose reaches out with his bat and taps the back of the leg of Jim Rice, who is chatting with Morgan and Mike Schmidt. "Jim, do me a favor and bring that Oil Can over here," says Rose. Minutes later, Boyd and Rice come around the cage to where Rose, Morgan, and Perez — 7925 games, 8711 hits, 4729 runs, and seven World Series rings between them — are standing.

"I'll bet you a Coke I get a hit off you," Rose tells Boyd as he shakes his hand, then whirls and hurries to his turn in the cage. Boyd stands with Rice, watching Rose, listening intently to the conversations.

"Where's Yaz?" Perez asks Rice.

"You know the buzzard's too old for these bus trips."

"Do you know Pete keeps telling me, 'You caddied for Yastrzemski last year. How does it feel to caddy for a real player this year?'" says Perez. "By the way, have you heard what Luis Tiant is doing?"

Rice shrugs, then turns to a writer who tells him that Tiant turned down an opportunity to pitch for the Phillies' Portland, Oregon, farm and had gone to Mexico to pitch there for another season. "He'll be back," says Perez. "They told me I was done in Cincinnati in 1976, Montreal in 1979, and Boston in 1982, and I'm still here."

Rose is completing his turn around the bases, sprinting in from third base around the cage toward Boyd. "Not only will I get a hit off you," Rose excitedly tells the rookie pitcher, "but while you're warming up, I'll stand in front of the plate and after two pitches I'll even tell you where I'm going to hit the ——ing ball." Boyd starts laughing and walks away, passing Evans as he comes to join the group.

"What is this, a reunion of the 1975 World Series?" shouts Schmidt. "Was that the only series ever played? These Cincinnati guys here are driving everyone crazy. They keep replaying the '75 series infield drills. Perez says that they wouldn't be wearing the series rings if he hadn't hit Lee's blooper pitch out of the park. Morgan says they wouldn't have the rings if he hadn't had two game-winning hits. Rose just says, 'I hit three-seventy.'"

"If you hadn't made that catch off of me, I'd've driven away in the car," Morgan says to Evans.

It is, in a sense, a reunion, at the appropriate gathering grounds of the batting cage. Evans, Rice, Yastrzemski, and Rick Miller are the only players still with the Red Sox from that '75 series. Rice couldn't play in the series because of a broken wrist suffered that September 21 when he was hit by a pitch in Detroit, and Miller had spent the 1978, '79, and '80 seasons with the Angels, with whom he signed as a free agent. All that are left in Cincinnati are Concepcion, Bench, and Dan Driessen, who in 1975 was a twenty-four-year-old reserve. With Rose, Morgan, and Perez here on a Phillies team that has been tagged The Wheeze Kids and On Golden Pond, the reunion seems to belong here, in the retirement haven of Clearwater, before Philadelphia's first exhibition game of the spring.

Rose, forty-two or forty-four depending on whether you're reading the press guide or his ex-wife's book, was signed by the Phillies at the end of the 1978 season for one reason: to help teach a club that had lost in the playoffs three straight years how to win. In 1980 they won their first world championship. Morgan, thirty-nine, was acquired on December 15 from the Giants in a trade made necessary by a prior deal involving the Phillies' three-time Gold Glove winner at second base, Manny Trillo. "We needed a proven left-handed hitter," manager Pat Corrales is telling a Boston radio reporter. At thirty-eight, Morgan in 1982 had batted .289 with fourteen home runs for the Giants; not only that, but by leading the Giants to a surprising finish only two games behind divisional champion Atlanta, and by culminating his season with a final-day three-run homer that eliminated the Dodgers, he could point to the fact that in his last ten full seasons, in three different uniforms, the teams he'd played for had never won fewer than eighty-seven games or finished lower than third place. Perez, 41 Celsius, signed in late January after being released by the Red Sox. "We needed a right-handed bat off the bench," Corrales is explaining, "and not only was he swinging the bat well in Puerto Rico, but he is a great presence on a ball club. The Reds traded him after winning their second straight World Series in 1976 and never won again. Montreal got him and he turned that club around. Boston never would have made the transition it made when all those players left if it hadn't signed Doggie."

The lineups this windy March afternoon reflected the changes that both the Red Sox and the Phillies had made — in some cases been forced to make — during the off-season. In need of a cleanup hitter, Boston had acquired slugger Tony Armas, sixth in the league in total homers over the previous three years, from Oakland for star third baseman Carney Lansford; they put him in center field. Of course, a major factor in that deal was that Lansford could become a free agent after this season, and the Boston management didn't consider his long-term salary demands ($6 million over five years) to their taste and decided to deal him at as close to 100 percent value as possible, just as they had acquired him from California for Burleson two years earlier under the same circumstances.

Included in the Armas deal was catcher Jeff Newman, batting seventh this afternoon, as the Red Sox had been scrambling for catching since Carlton Fisk was declared a free agent in January 1981 because Boston owner–general manager Haywood Sullivan had failed to send out his contract on time. New England hero Fisk had signed with the Chicago White Sox.

As it turned out, Red Sox manager Ralph Houk wasn't using Boyd for the first three innings, but his starter, a rookie out of double-A named Mike Brown, was his choice to replace the departed Mike Torrez — the most expensive and, next to Ken Harrelson, ballyhooed free agent in the club's history — in the starting rotation. Scheduled to pitch in the last two innings was John Henry Johnson, who management hoped could replace fellow left-handed reliever Tom Burgmeier, who was allowed to leave as a free agent and signed with Oakland.

The Phillies are using Morgan in the second spot behind Rose. Corrales explains that right fielder Von Hayes, acquired from Cleveland for five players (including Trillo) the previous December, can only pinch-hit because of a bad shoulder. Part of the reasoning behind the megadeal with the Indians was that Trillo would be a free agent at the end of the '83 season, and that the Phillies have a twenty-year-old phenom named Juan Samuel that they presume will be ready as soon as Morgan steps down. Morgan and left-handed reliever Al Holland were acquired a week after the Hayes trade, mainly because the Giants were in a contract stalemate with Morgan and Holland was to be a free agent at the end of the season. Even Perez was a contractual free agent of sorts: partly Houk felt that he couldn't keep two over-forty designated hitters (Perez, Yastrzemski) who couldn't play the field, but more important, the option in the final fourth and fifth years of Perez's $350,000 contract belonged to the club.

The crowd of nearly four thousand is fascinated by Boston's batting-practice pitcher. He is Mark "The Bird" Fidrych, in second spring of a comeback from the serious shoulder injury that forced the Detroit Tigers to release him at the end of the 1981 season. It has been seven years since The Bird captured America as a twenty-two-year-old kid, winning nineteen games, leading the American League in earned run average, talking to the baseballs he threw so brilliantly, and becoming an overnight celebrity. He hurt his knee the next spring, then his shoulder, and has won only ten games since, that last victory coming in September 1980. He is in spring training as a nonroster invitee, principally because of Houk, his manager in Detroit, and Boston team physician Dr. Arthur Pappas, who supervised his rehabilitation program the last two winters. As he walks off the mound at the end of his fifteen-minute stint throwing batting practice, he is treated to a small, enthusiastic ovation. Fidrych and some fans still cling to the dream that The Bird will fly again.

Between the 1975 World Series and Fidrych's great 1976 season, Andy Messersmith and Dave McNally had broken ownership's control over players by taking the reserve clause to court, where it was invalidated, thus freeing the players and forcing the owners into agreeing to a new free-agent system with the players. Fidrych didn't understand all that when he was turning twenty-three at the end of his fabulous rookie year, but he certainly wasn't alone: no one completely foresaw the scope of the changes that would sweep through the game in the wake of the Messersmith-McNally decision. By 1983, personnel moves — Perez, Trillo, Lansford, Morgan, et al. — are dictated as much by contract as by talent. Fidrych, his career having faded just at the outset of the long-term, big-money deals, is throwing batting practice simply trying to prove that he can actually again be considered as personnel.

The Phillies pitcher is Cy Young Award winner Steve Carlton, at the age of thirty-eight still the premier left-hander in the game. This is Philadelphia's first (Boston's third) exhibition of the spring, and it is likened by Schmidt to a "stretching exercise." Carlton pitches as if he's throwing batting practice, loosening his arm by throwing fastballs and only a few of the hard, angular sliders that most nights make him virtually unhittable. He walks Evans, the second hitter, then throws a fastball right down the middle to Rice, which is sent towering into a biting crosswind. The ball lands thirty feet past the left-field fence, and as Rice's home-run trot takes him around third, Schmidt tells him, "With the loft you're getting, you ought to hit forty homers this year."

Rice nods. "It's about time." The strike-shortened 1981 season and 1982 as well have been disappointments to the thirty-year-old Rice, between nagging injuries and, since the departure of Lynn hitting behind him, the opposition constantly pitching around him. Getting Armas into the cleanup spot theoretically will get Rice pitches to hit. Given that, and given good health in the hitters' months from June 15 to August 15, Rice hopes to forget the (for him, sub-par) .284 and .309 averages and 17 and 24 home-run totals of the last two years and return to the awesome form he showed in 1977,

'78, and '79, when he *averaged* .320 with 41 homers and 129 RBIs.

In the third inning, Evans hits a low, outside Carlton fastball to right field and watches as the wind carries it into the screen to make it 3–1 for the Red Sox. This is not a happy spring for Evans. Two weeks before he was to report to Winter Haven, Evans called a press conference and demanded to be traded, citing internal ownership problems that made him "concerned about the long-term stability of the club" and its refusal to approach what he and his agent felt was his fair market value. Evans's contract expires at the end of the 1984 season, but Sullivan's practice with his stars has been to trade them a year before they are free agents so he can get some return on the player. He did it with Burleson, dealing him to the Angels for Lansford, relief pitcher Mark Clear, and Rick Miller. He tried to do the same with Lynn, sending him to the Dodgers for three players, only to have Lynn and agent Jerry Kapstein refuse to sign anything more than a one-year contract until then–free agent Dave Winfield established his market value. He did it with Lansford.

Evans says he would rather go now and work out a deal with some other club. He knows that second baseman Jerry Remy is the only one of the last thirteen potential free agents to have been kept. Burgmeier is the most recently gone, signing with Oakland. "This club is going to be like the Minnesota Twins," Evans has stated.

"Sullivan says they can't pay anyone above their 'salary ceiling,' but their salary ceiling is predicated on 1979 prices. This is 1983." And, with each passing year since the Messersmith decision, salaries have increased at a minimum of 25 percent.

Rice follows Evans's homer with his second hit, a line-drive single to right field, but before he can even chitchat with Rose at first, Armas hits the first pitch to shortstop Ivan DeJesus for a double play that finishes Carlton's first outing. It is the seven-year, $4.9 million contract that Rice signed in

January 1979, following his MVP season, that has been the ceiling to which Sullivan has stuck. When Rice signed it, he was one of five players making that much; now, some seventy players make more than he does.

That contract is up at the end of the 1985 season, but he, too, is concerned about his future and the direction of the team. "What's happening with Dewey [Evans] is important to the future of this franchise," he had said off the record to a reporter the night before. "Are they going to refuse to whip out their wallet and let Dewey go, then let Dennis Eckersley go, let Armas go, and let me go? What are they going to do for players then? Because they refuse to go out and sign any free agents or trade for players making more than a couple of hundred thousand, our talent is dangerously thin right now. I don't know what I'm going to do, but I don't want to end up being pushed away like Burleson, Lynn, Fisk, or Lansford, and I don't want to stay around here on a sixth-place team. I want the money I've got coming to me, but I also want to win. I don't know what I'll do. If I have a big year and they're letting Evans and Eckersley go, I guess I'll demand to be traded."

Rice and Evans, thirty-one, have become the elder states-men of the Red Sox, as Yastrzemski, going on forty-four, is more of a ceremonial figure than anything else. It is Yaz's last spring training, and he has been slow to get going because of ankle and leg problems. He promises he will play in the field no more, admitting that his attempt to play center field and first base at the end of July made him ache for the entire month of August, during which he batted .144 with five RBIs. Yastrzemski weighs now what he weighed in 1975. He is grayer. He also has a friend named David Mugar, a Boston communications baron, who is trying to help him buy 43 percent of the club. "Owner, huh?" Rose said to Evans when they were together at the bag in the first inning. "Now *that* sounds old."

The Phillies had scored their run off Mike Brown in the

first inning when the rookie started off nervously. Rose hit his
first pitch to rookie second baseman Marty Barrett, who let
the ball go right between his legs. Brown then walked Morgan and Gary Matthews to load the bases with no one out.
But shortstop Glenn Hoffman sneaked in behind Morgan and
Brown picked him off second base, and when Bo Diaz hit a
high hopper to Hoffman and was thrown out at first,
Matthews tried to go from first to third and was thrown out
by first baseman Dave Stapleton to end the inning. Brown
works through the next two innings with ease, then gives way
to a succession of two-inning shutout performances by Steve
Crawford, Boyd, and Johnson that completes the 3–1 Red Sox
victory.

Rose does get an at-bat against Boyd, but is walked on five
pitches and leaves the game as Perez takes his place at first
base. With his three-at-bat, five-and-a-half-inning 1983 debut
completed, Rose walks down to a roped-off area in front of
the clubhouse to talk to two writers. "How old is that
Brown?" is his first question. "He pitches like he's thirty. I
like the arm speed on Trash Can, or whatever his name is.
They're all right. At least they throw a fastball once in a
while. It used to be that you wouldn't see a breaking ball
until the third week of spring training. Now some of these
guys throw one fastball each at-bat, which is one more than
they'll throw once the season starts." On he rambles about
baseball.

Rose has played more games, been to the plate more times,
and had more hits than anyone in National League history.
He hasn't missed a game since he signed the original four-
year, $3.2 million contract with the Phillies, and he says that
if he misses one before he gets the 324 hits he needs to pass
Ty Cobb, it won't be by his choosing.

He admits that it was partially at his insistence that they
got Morgan. He admits he was pushing for Perez a year ago,
when Houk and the Red Sox were trying to deal him. The

original deal would have sent Perez to the Dodgers for outfielder Mark Bradley, but Perez, exercising his contractual
right, refused the trade. "I was going to be sitting behind
Steve Garvey. Do you think I'd have ever played?" Perez
asked. Rose called him, and Perez told Houk and Sullivan
he'd go to Philadelphia, but when the Phillies refused to part
with outfielder Dick Davis, no trade could be worked out.
Davis eventually fell out of favor and was traded to Pittsburgh for forty-year-old Bill Robinson.

"I will never understand why Ralph [Houk] made up his
mind that I was all done," Perez says after the game. "I had
done the job in 1980 [25 home runs, 109 RBIs]. I was starting
to hit when the strike came in 1981. Then when we came
back to work, he didn't play me. Maybe it was impossible to
keep me and Yaz, since he thought we were DHs who can't
play in the field anymore. But I don't understand why he
gave up on me. That's why I worked so hard in winter ball,
ran every day on the beach, got myself in such good shape,
and swung the bat good all winter."

By January, Perez had shown enough so that a half-dozen
teams contacted him. As Corrales — not coincidentally, a
Cincinnati teammate of Perez and Rose's in the 1960s — and
Rose kept pressuring him, Phillies general manager Paul
Owens kept checking with scouts and players in Puerto Rico.
"Our young players kept telling me that Perez kept winning
games with big hits," Owens told reporters.

"With big leaguers, there are certain guys you know can
win. Rose is one. Morgan is one. Perez is one. They create an
atmosphere where all the players think they can win. And
Perez may be the greatest in that regard. Ask Sparky Anderson. Ask any of those players. They'll tell you that Perez was
the heart and soul of those great Reds teams. The other guys
always got the headlines, then somewhere in the story it
would read, 'Cincinnati won the game on a hit by Tony
Perez.'"

Owens had given this speech to a group of New England reporters before the game. Afterward, Morgan is giving virtually the same speech. "Pete and I won the MVP awards, but Tony was just as valuable, especially in the clubhouse and on the airplanes," Morgan is saying. "When they traded him before the '77 season, I was upset. So were a lot of the players. All season, we kept waiting for Doggie to bail us out, but he was in Montreal. There's no doubt that if he'd still been with us in '77, we'd have won three straight World Series."

Rice had left the game after the sixth inning and watched the last three innings from a runway leading to the bus. "I look at Rose and Morgan and Perez and think back to '75," Rice says, "and it frustrates me that we didn't stay together. Pete, Joe, and Doggie in 1975 were in the same stage of their careers that Dewey and Freddie and Rooster and Cecil and I are now. Look what those guys in Cincinnati had. What we never had. In a lot of ways, I envy them. We've got the money, but they've got something money can't buy."

What they had was the experience of playing with what may well have been the last *great* baseball team. The 1976 Reds were the only modern team to lead their league in home runs, stolen bases, and runs. They had five regulars who eventually accrued two thousand hits, and when they had finished winning 102 games, they became the first and last team to sweep through the postseason undefeated in seven straight games.

"We had absolutely everything, and it's not worth insulting anyone else by comparing them to that club," said Sparky Anderson, who managed them. They hit .280 as a team, stole 210 bases, hit 141 home runs, scored 857, and slugged .424. They had the best catcher of his era, Johnny Bench, another Hall of Famer at third in Pete Rose, and a man who deserves a place in Cooperstown at first base named Tony Perez. Rose was Cincinnati, the local kid from Western Hills High School who hustled and scrapped his way to stardom.

Bench was the superstar, good-looking, durable, and consistent at a position that physically wore down so many of his peers.

But it was Little Joe Morgan who personified that team. He was the league's Most Valuable Player in both 1975 and 1976, another near-certain Hall of Famer, and he was also the forerunner of a generation of multidimensional offensive players in the middle infield (such as Robin Yount, Garry Templeton, Dickie Thon, Alan Trammell, Cal Ripken, Julio Franco, Juan Samuel, Tony Fernandez) that began to dominate the 1980s. He came to the end of the 1983 season tenth on the all-time list in stolen bases; Rogers Hornsby was the only second baseman ever to have hit more home runs (277 to Morgan's 273); Eddie Collins was the only man ever to play more games at the position; and he earned five Gold Gloves for defensive excellence.

After the Reds acquired him in an eight-player trade with Houston to start the 1972 season, Morgan stole 58, 67, 58, 67, and 60 bases, more than anyone else in either league during that time. In those five years he also averaged 22 homers, 113 runs scored, 85 runs batted in, and 119 walks per season, numbers that would be of all-star caliber for a left fielder, first baseman, or designated hitter, much less a second baseman with better-than-average range and ability to turn the double play.

Little Joe somehow was buried in the images of Rose and Bench. Perhaps it was because he came in from the outside, and when he escaped Houston — where he was labeled a troublemaker — for Cincinnati, somehow there was the public perception that it was the atmosphere of the clean, all-American Big Red Machine that brought the greatness out of Joe Morgan rather than vice versa. Time and facts changed that perception, however, for not only did the Reds win their division four of the first five years Morgan played for them, but in the first twelve full (not including strike-shortened 1981) seasons after Morgan got out of Houston, Morgan did

not play for a team that won fewer than eighty-seven games
or finished lower than third. When he returned to Houston in
1980, the Astros not only won their only divisional championship but came within an out of beating the Phillies out of a
pennant. The '83 Phillies team he helped take to the World
Series was the sixth first-place finisher in that eleven-year
span, and that Giants team in 1982 was his only third-place
finisher, a mere two games behind division champion Atlanta. In the first three full seasons after Morgan's departure,
not once did the Reds finish ahead of the club for which
Morgan played.

There was no doubt about Morgan deserving the MVP
awards he won the two years the Reds were world champions. He got on base nearly 550 times over the two seasons,
and that was magnified by the 58 doubles, 11 triples, 44
homers, and 127 stolen bases he ran up. Not only that, but in
1976 he became the first second baseman since Hornsby to
lead his league in total bases. "Just the way he stood at the
plate, flipping his left arm like a penguin, riled opposing
pitchers," Perez maintained. "He drove them absolutely
crazy. He was cocky as hell, and they always wanted to knock
him on his behind, only they knew he was so tough he could
never be intimidated. He had that small strike zone, and from
the side you could see pitchers trying to work him. If they
were careful, they'd walk him, and the way he could steal,
that meant at least one stolen base and all the disruption that
went with it. If they simply tried to throw it over to his tiny
strike zone, he could hit the ball all over or out of the ballpark, and they knew that Bench, George Foster, and I were
right behind him. I don't think I ever saw a player who
disrupted pitchers more than Little Joe. Put Pete in front of
him, with all that act of his, and pitchers were really screwed
up!"

As Morgan grew older, the injuries increased and all the
years of playing on the artificial turf began to dull and
tighten his legs. He began drifting, going from Cincinnati to

Houston to San Francisco to Philadelphia to Oakland. Part of the reason for the drifting was the subtle clashes he had with managers. Bill Virdon openly disdained Morgan's propensity for talking about himself in the third person. Frank Robinson in San Francisco privately called him "one of the more selfish players I've ever encountered." Less than halfway through his first year with the Phillies, Pat Corrales was fired, and he fingered Morgan as one of the prime reasons for the loss of his job. Oakland's Steve Boros was dismissed two months into the 1984 season, which led to immediate speculation that Morgan was involved.

Little Joe would talk about himself anywhere, anytime, and journalists would always listen because he is an articulate man. People who run baseball teams want players to talk in the first person plural, but there is a thin line between the selfish and the team player. After he was forced to watch his California Angels teammates in the 1982 American League playoffs from the stands following a shoulder operation, Rick Burleson explained that he couldn't help a feeling deep down that rooted for the Brewers to beat the Angels, that something inside him wanted to be needed. "I know exactly how you felt," Jerry Remy told him. "When I was out with the bad knee in 1979 and 1980, I felt the same way — to a degree. It's an inherently selfish game. You do your job, everyone else does his job, and the game rolls on. But you have to know how to control it. Like everything else, there's a right way to be selfish and a wrong way, and, for instance, the wrong way is to refuse to do what the manager tells you or start pulling injuries to protect your average."

Joe Morgan was never that way. At the end of 1983, in Philadelphia, he didn't want out of the lineup even though his average was below .200 and his range reduced from yards to inches, because in his mind he was convinced he could still help them win. When he and Perez didn't play, they second-guessed Corrales, or they rode young outfielder Von Hayes, for whom the Phillies had traded five players in the off-

season. Morgan and Rose nicknamed him Five-for-One and
Norman Bates. Morgan, Rose, and Perez were used to winning together, and they were hard-liners who didn't accept
frailty. But, like Carl Yastrzemski a few hundred miles away,
Morgan also was trying to deny age. "I've gone two or three
weeks struggling before, and I was left in the lineup and
came out of it," he said after one Corrales benching in May.
"What's so different now? They got me here because I did
the job last year. What's a year? I can't come out of it and
help this team sitting on the bench. I'm being criticized behind my back for the same kind of drive that helped make the
Reds so good. Egos. You don't think egos drive men?"

In late August 1983, Phillies owner Bill Giles told the
media that Morgan had one week to prove he could still play
or phenom Juan Samuel would be brought up and handed the
job. "That was wrong," Morgan said. "I deserve more respect
than that. I proved it, too."

Now, admittedly, the threat of asylum closing in on athletes makes them lash out. As early as 1977, Luis Tiant began
having problems with Don Zimmer. The Red Sox manager
had wanted to use a five-man rotation for a number of reasons, most of them having to do with the ability of his other
starters to bounce back, but Luis wanted to go every fourth
day. Zimmer refused. Twice Tiant took himself out of games,
citing his inability to find his control caused by the lack of
work. Tiant always believed that he could and should be
there as the ace, steadfastly refusing to give in to any other
suggestion; in 1980, he punted his glove into the stands when
relieved by Yankees manager Dick Howser, only where Zimmer took the heat and eventually agreed with the decision to
allow him to leave after the 1980 season, Howser laughed,
hashed it out with Tiant, and stroked him as much as he
could. Yastrzemski was the same way right to the end, refusing even to admit that he was retiring his last time around the
league, because he felt to give in to such an admission would
be to give in, period, and he believed that much of his career

was built on pure, hard-rocked will. When Perez was first platooned by Dick Williams down the stretch in 1979, on the days he wasn't starting, he would stand in center field before the game and stare at Williams, and when he left Boston three years later, he bore a hard grudge against Ralph Houk for not playing him except on a platoon basis. "Managers worry too much about that —————," says Morgan. "They shouldn't listen. They should use it, so that when the player gets in there, he has the burning desire to produce."

"Egos were a big part of that team in '75 and '76," Sparky Anderson says. "There was a great deal of competition within the team, but that's healthy. Rose was trying to outdo Morgan, Perez was trying to outdo Bench, and they drove the younger players like Davey Concepcion and Foster. Morgan had a burning desire to be recognized over Rose, who had a burning desire for recognition, period. That's healthy. They had the same thing in Boston when Lynn and Rice had their heydays." Indeed, Rice and Lynn had played for a year and a half in Bristol, Connecticut, and Pawtucket, Rhode Island, en route to the major leagues, and Rice had been the league MVP both seasons. But as rookies, Lynn excelled and Rice always held a feeling of competitive jealousy, openly taunting Lynn for not playing when hurt. In 1979, the one other year when each excelled, the competitive factor between the two was clear to everyone around them. Most years, however, it was not in Lynn's nature to respond to Rice's obvious challenge.

"Morgan and Rose," says Anderson, "were two of the greatest who ever lived when it came to challenges." Not many urban blacks make it to the baseball big leagues. Baseball is not a city game, and the everyday, accountant mentality it so often requires runs contrary to the upbringing of the ghetto. But there are some who feel that when you can find the city player who can put his environment aside and adapt to baseball's own law, then you have a player who really knows the measure of the word *tough* and, unlike most professional ballplayers, has never had to be pampered in any way. Frank Robinson and Eddie Murray come to mind, and perhaps Toronto's Lloyd Moseby can become that kind of player.

Morgan was born in Texas, but moved out to Oakland for high school (McClymonds, the same as Robinson and basketball's Bill Russell), and he knows what it's like to be a city kid. "Joe Morgan knew what it took to beat the other guy," says Anderson. "And he loved doing it."

In 1976 the Big Red Machine hammered the Phillies out of the playoffs in three straight. In the second game, they were being no-hit by Jim Lonborg into the sixth, trailing 2–0, and turned a walk, two infield hits, and their speed into four runs before reliever Gene Garber could get the second out. They went by the Yankees in the World Series as if the Bronx Bombers were standing still. Only the second game, when they had to score a run in the bottom of the ninth off Catfish Hunter to win it, was close, and for four games the armless New York outfielders fruitlessly tried to keep the Cincinnati speed from circling the bases at will.

The flaw in the Reds was their arrogance. Not arrogance of the players, although they certainly were cocky, but of the front office and ownership. In 1972, Anderson made it seem as if the World Series were being played between Oxford and the University of Huns, with the Reds' clean-cut, Wall Street image as opposed to the bearded, long-haired A's, who celebrated their playoff victory over Detroit with a fistfight between Vida Blue and Blue Moon Odom. In 1975, the Red Sox resented the Reds' arrogance, particularly their dismissal of Luis Tiant ("He showed me nothing; he wouldn't win five games in the National League," said Rose). Even in '76, Anderson infuriated Thurman Munson by saying, "Please don't embarrass Munson by comparing him to Bench."

There was the constant air of superiority, coupled with the military school mentality. In the community, it was marketable, for Cincinnati is one of the nation's most conservative cities, the only major metropolitan area that Franklin Roosevelt failed to ever carry. "Players on those clubs were taught discipline in the old-fashioned sense," Anderson recalls, fondly. "They had to do what they were told or be gone, and they respected that. They respected authority." Problem is, when Messersmith and McNally put an end to the reserve system, they took the hammer out of the owners' hands. All of a sudden, players were on equal footing with management, although, like most clubs and players, the Reds didn't fully comprehend the impact at that time. Reds president Bob Howsam and general manager Dick Wagner scoffed at agents, but as Perez and Don Gullett and David Concepcion began hiring them, the era changed. Jerry Kapstein, as the Red Sox knew from spring training onward, saw something happening, and although he couldn't fully make it out, he held many of his clients to a hard line.

There were twenty-two players in the first November 1976 free-agent pool. Of the thirteen biggest free-agent packages, ten of them belonged to the Kapstein stable. That included Gullett, who, when he threatened to take the free-agent route, was told to take a hike. Perez had hired Kapstein at the end of the '75 season, so when Dan Driessen stepped in as the first National League designated hitter in the 1976 World Series and batted .357, Perez was coldly shipped off to Montreal at the end of the season for a relief pitcher named Dale Murray. Privately, Rose and Morgan chided the decision, which was made by Wagner. Rose realized that baseball does not begin at 7:35, it begins at 3:30 in the clubhouse — and Perez was the heart and soul of the Cincinnati clubhouse, besides being a man who knocked in a hundred runs a year. As it turned out, injuries that shortened Gullett's career made the decision to let him go seem like good business, even if Gullett was their only quality pitcher. Perez, solely from a positional standpoint, seemed a logical man to trade, what with Driessen available. But while the Reds had put together a team of unrivaled talent and character, whose roots went back to the early 1960s with Frank Robinson and Lee May (both of whom became cornerstones of the Baltimore Orioles "magic"), Vada Pinson, Rose and Perez, the Dick Wagner front office didn't understand that. Wagner was a businessman; Perez's value could not be measured by any bottom line, and so when at the same time they declared that they wouldn't accept being held for ransom by Gullett and Kapstein, they also declared that their values were those of a cold heart and a large profit. Three years later, the Red Sox did the same thing when they allowed Luis Tiant to go to the Yankees after their high-water season of 1978; similarly, under the guise of "fiscal sanity," they dealt with the new open-market world by neither retaining their own players nor signing new free agents. After the first line of refugees — Perez, Gullett, and, the following June, Rawley Eastwick, another Kapstein client — departed, the Reds would not be in the World Series again. Within six years, they went from what might have been the best team of the modern era to the worst team in baseball, with Morgan, Rose, and Perez watching from a distant site in Philadelphia.

Their slide from greatness was sad, but even sadder was the tragicomic demise of their 1975 World Series rivals from Boston. The Cincinnati dynasty at least had its years of glory. The Red Sox dynasty ran into serious trouble right from the start of the free-agent era.

THREE

1976

A NEW AGE
NOW BEGINS

The Boston dynasty experiences bumpy beginnings in the first season after the epochal Messersmith-McNally free-agency decision.

*T*HEY WERE SITTING somewhere near the rear, Lynn in one row, Burleson in another. The bus was leaving an hour after the game, taking the Red Sox to Logan Airport for a thirteen-game road trip that was to begin in Minnesota, move on to Oakland and Anaheim, and end in Baltimore. As it began pulling out of the Fenway parking lot and onto the street, first Burleson, then Lynn, began singing. "Good-bye Fenway, good-bye Fenway." They sang, rowdily, laughed, and a few teammates joined in the laughter. In the front seat, manager Darrell Johnson stared straight ahead, sullenly.

The year was 1976. It was June 10, which meant that it was five days from the trading deadline, and Californians Lynn and Burleson and even the New England patrician Fisk had heard threats and rumors that they might be traded before the deadline passed. By then, they'd been tagged the Kapstein Connection, the three Red Sox clients of Providence-

based agent Jerry Kapstein, the first three serious holdouts
ever against Tom Yawkey.

The previous October, they had been starry-eyed wonder-
children, romanticized and lyricized as the up-the-middle
heart of the next dynasty, a dynasty that turned out to have
lasted only from the sixth to the seventh game of the World
Series.

When Andy Messersmith and Dave McNally put an end to
the reserve system only weeks after the 1975 World Series,
Kapstein, more than any other agent, immediately comprehended the ramifications. Under the system that had
originated in 1879, the reserve clause effectively bound a player
and his rights to one club as long as that club wished to exercise its option, traditionally interpreted as being automatically and indefinitely renewable. There had been prior
challenges, one by a Yankees minor-league outfielder named
George Toolson in 1953, the other by St. Louis outfielder
Curt Flood in 1969. The former ended up having the
Supreme Court reaffirm baseball's antitrust exemption; the
latter ended up with a nondecision that for baseball management was the decision it wanted to continue with the
status quo.

Messersmith and McNally did not sign their 1975 contracts
with the Dodgers and Expos, Messersmith because the club
would not give him a no-trade provision in his contract
(curiously, when Messersmith went back to the Dodgers in
1979 at the age of thirty-three, he got that provision). Their
respective clubs therefore exercised their options and renewed their contracts, but at the end of the season the players filed grievances claiming that the reserve clause that read
"for a period of one year" meant exactly that. Under the
grievance arbitration procedure established in the 1970 Basic
Agreement, the case then went to baseball's independent arbitrator, Peter L. Seitz, who ruled — and his decision was up-
held by the courts — that the reserve clause was *not*

renewable and was good for only one year. Whereas management had always held the gun and been able to tell a holdout player that if he didn't like his contract he could go become a hod carrier or, like Vida Blue in 1972, a plumbing executive, now the players held an equally powerful gun. The entire system under which the game had operated was suspended until a new Basic Agreement was signed, and Kapstein knew precisely what it meant: if a player didn't sign for the 1976 season, he could be free to sign with anyone at the end of the season.

In Oakland, Kapstein had Joe Rudi, Rollie Fingers, Ken Holtzman, Gene Tenace, and Bert Campaneris unsigned. In Baltimore, he had Wayne Garland, Bobby Grich, Doyle Alexander, and Don Baylor. In Philadelphia, Dave Cash. In Cincinnati, Don Gullett. And, in Boston, Lynn, Burleson, and Fisk. Kapstein later said he didn't know where the market would take these salaries, only that the $44,000 average salary in 1975 would jump dramatically.

New England fans didn't comprehend what was happening with the game and these players. Neither did most of the media, some of whom castigated Kapstein and his clients for the audacity of insulting Yawkey, who was hospitalized with pneumonia. Not long after Yawkey died on July 9, one columnist suggested that Kapstein, Lynn, Burleson, and Fisk helped break his heart and were a factor in his death. The other Red Sox players had all been signed by spring training, but then the other players didn't have Kapstein.

What Kapstein also knew was that Lynn right then had more market value than any other player in the game. So did John Claiborne, who had been hired by Dick O'Connell as his assistant general manager after stints with the Mets, Cardinals, and A's. O'Connell had moved Haywood Sullivan from the upstairs executive suite of offices where he had the title of player personnel director and replaced him with the ambitious Claiborne, as O'Connell realized that they were

entering a new, complex era. "The open-market value is
greater for a younger player," Claiborne said, "and no one
anywhere is in a greater position than Lynn."

Rice was brute strength and a potential Jimmie Foxx, but
Lynn was Boston's DiMaggio, the apparent successor to Ted
Williams and Carl Yastrzemski. He loped with such grace
that everything he did seemed held in freeze-frame. His
swing had the arc of an architect's compass, he played center
field with grace and daring, and he could throw. He had
given a glimpse of his extraordinary talent in September
1974, fifteen months out of the University of Southern California, when in a late-season look with the Red Sox he hit
.419 in fifteen games. Then in 1975 he became the first player
ever to be both Rookie of the Year and Most Valuable Player.
He batted .331 and led the league in runs (103), slugging percentage (.556), runs produced (187), and doubles (47, a rookie
record); he hit 21 homers, knocked in 105 runs, and won a
Gold Glove for his defensive excellence. Rice, who hit .309
with 22 homers and 102 RBIs before being injured on September 21, was simply overshadowed. Lynn made the spectacular diving catches, such as the one he made in the first
game of an August 1 doubleheader in New York off Graig
Nettles — diving to snatch away a sure triple, then bouncing
and rolling over to the warning track in left-center — that
saved a 1–0 Bill Lee victory that effectively eliminated the
Yankees for the season. He hit dramatically, as on the night of
June 18, when he hit three homers and knocked in ten runs in
a game in Detroit.

For Yastrzemski, baseball was "always a struggle," one
that entailed batting practice at 6:00 P.M. after games or 9:30
A.M. before them. So, too, was it for a Burleson, or even Fisk,
who in 1973 lost thirty-seven pounds during the season. But
for Lynn the game seemed uncommonly easy. "I guess it has
something to do with my style and personality," Lynn would
say years later, "because people would always say I could do
anything I wanted to. I wish it had been that way."

It often seemed that it was that way, though. One night in 1979, the year he put on twenty pounds of upper body strength pounding Nautilus machines all winter, he walked into the cage for batting practice and, on suggestion, hit ten straight pitches for home runs, beginning with one into the screen inside the left-field pole and going right around Fenway Park to the right-field foul pole. As players on both teams stopped and stared, Lynn calmly walked out of the cage to the dugout, put his bat in the rack, and went up the runway to the clubhouse.

He ran with grace and instinct. In the first game of the memorable August 1, 1975, doubleheader in Shea Stadium that effectively eliminated the Yankees, he reached first base on shortstop Jim Mason's error with two out in the top of the ninth against Catfish Hunter and promptly stole second base, from whence he scored on Rick Miller's single. "The base had to be stolen," he said with a shrug afterward, and in the bottom of the ninth inning, he made a tumbling catch in left-center off Graig Nettles that saved Bill Lee's 1–0 win and would be remembered for years as one of the finest defensive plays made by any Red Sox outfielder. He could throw, so well that he was the Yankees' third draft pick out of high school as a pitcher.

And he was born for Fenway Park. He had been a dead-pull hitter all his life, known more as an all-around outfielder and power hitter than an average hitter. He had batted only .273 and been benched against certain left-handers in his last (junior) year at the University of Southern California, and after signing with the Red Sox hit .259 and .282 at Bristol and Pawtucket, far outshadowed by his teammate Rice, who was at the same time leading those Eastern and International leagues at .317 and .337. "One of the first times I took batting practice in Fenway, I was fooling around and slapped an outside pitch to the opposite field, and the next thing I knew I heard this 'CLANK,' " Lynn recalled. "I could hit the ball into the screen, off The Wall . . . and any time I'd come back

The Fenway Effect

	BA	SP	HR	RBI	
Wade Boggs, 1982–83	.382	.531	6	87	Fenway
	.329	.402	4	64	Road
Dwight Evans, 1972–83	.279	.517	122	426	Fenway
	.254	.413	82	339	Road
Carlton Fisk, 1971–80	.298	.523	90	330	Fenway
	.271	.440	72	297	Road
Fred Lynn, 1974–83	.350	.603	69	303	Fenway
	.270	.437	55	220	Road
Rico Petrocelli, 1963–76	.272	.489	134	369	Fenway
	.230	.354	76	284	Road
Jim Rice, 1974–83	.327	.577	153	446	Fenway
	.284	.486	123	377	Road
Carl Yastrzemski, 1961–83	.306	.503	237	994	Fenway
	.264	.422	215	822	Road

off the road in a little slump, I'd just go out for a couple of minutes of early batting practice, clank a half-dozen balls off the fence, and I'd be set for two weeks." When Lynn was finally traded, his lifetime average in Fenway was .350; his average on the road was an even .270. It took him nearly a year and a half — in 1981 batting .219 with five home runs in seventy-six games with the Angels — before he learned to get along without Fenway's thirty-seven-foot friend that rises beyond shortstop. "I simply had to get used to the fact that outside of Fenway, I can't hit for power and average. In Anaheim, I think I'm probably best off hitting two-eighty with thirty homers and batting in the middle of the order."

Freddie was never the type to chew tobacco or talk ball ("outbleepingstanding"). He'd breeze into the clubhouse in cut-off shorts and a T-shirt, in from a day spent at the pool or out fishing. Even as a kid, his father and his Little League coach nicknamed him Loose, a name that, while it didn't stick, could have. Like Ken "The Hawk" Harrelson, he could style with the best of them, with eyeblack and two and sometimes three colorful wristbands crawling up each arm.

He never really let too many people other than Jerry
Remy, Carlton Fisk, and fishing partner Tom Burgmeier
know him, and because he was so polite, seldom cursed, and
had an air of grace about him, older writers such as Clif
Keane of the *Globe* adopted him as the all-American boy next
door. Which he was, to some degree: he was the only player
to call Don Zimmer when he was fired as manager in 1980,
despite Zimmer's oft-open contempt for his willingness to
play; and he and his wife, Dede, were always the first to send
flowers or cards to any ill member of a family in any way
connected to the ball club. Yet there was also an air of outra-
geousness about him: he used to say that his favorite song
was "The 'Fish' Cheer / I-Feel-Like-I'm-Fixin'-To-Die Rag"
(which contained the line "Be the first mother on your block
to have your son come home in a box") by Country Joe and
the Fish; and once in Detroit, when he spotted some of his
playboy teammates in the Sunday Bible-reading session, he
asided, "John Lennon was right — God wrote one book and
has been living off the royalties ever since." Some feel that
Lynn was the most intelligent player of this Red Sox generation, one who let you know of him exactly what he chose to
let you know, one who always seemed to have baseball in
perspective rather than letting baseball define him. "Royalties are life-and-death matters," he once said, "not baseball
games." That from a man who got an $875,000 bonus and a
five-year, $1.7 million contract in 1976 and another four-
year, $5.3 million deal when that ran out, without once play-
ing more than 150 games.

There was no reason to believe Lynn was anything but a
superstar capable of virtually anything. Sure, the Messersmith decision was a big deal, but no one conceived of the
Tom Yawkey Red Sox having any problems signing players.

"When we won that final playoff game in Oakland in '75,"
O'Connell recalled, "there were four or five of the A's players
in Darrell's office — Fingers, Rudi, Bando, and Jackson
are the ones I remember — pleading with him to find ways to

get them to Boston. I remember Jackson saying, 'The Red Sox represent what players want to play for.'" Theoretically, the free-agent system would, if anything, just feed this budding dynasty.

After all, O'Connell that November had beaten a number of teams to Ferguson Jenkins, heisting him away from the Texas Rangers for utilityman Juan Beniquez, two minor leaguers, and some of Yawkey's money. O'Connell had been trying to get Jenkins for years, in 1971 actually completing a deal involving Reggie Smith going to the Cubs for him, only to have Cubs general manager John Holland back out on the deal at the last moment. In 1974, when the Rangers finally got him from the Cubs, he had won twenty-five games, and even in 1975 had been 17–18 for a team that encountered serious internal problems in Billy Martin's second season. Adding him to a starting rotation of postseason heroes Tiant and Lee, plus nineteen-game winner Rick Wise and potential star Don Aase, seemed to assure a formidable staff, especially considering the talent in the field. Tiant had averaged twenty wins a season for the last three years, Wise had just won twenty (including the playoff pennant clincher in Oakland), Lee had averaged seventeen wins in 1973, '74, and '75, and Aase was proclaimed their finest pitching prospect since the 1965 arrival of Jim Lonborg.

In January, the *Boston Herald American* ran a series on Johnson entitled "Why We'll Win in '76." While they gave Dick Drago, their best reliever down the stretch in '75, to California in a flimsily disguised player-to-be-named-later completion of the key deal for Denny Doyle, getting Tom House from Atlanta for Rogelio Moret was supposed to cure all their left-handed woes (ah, Jim Burton) in the bullpen. When House and Jim Willoughby went the entire spring training without allowing a run, the departure of Drago was forgotten and the emerging significance of the role of the great short reliever could be ignored.

The beginning of spring training was delayed until March

19 when the owners announced on February 23 that they would lock out the players until a new Basic Agreement was signed. Because of the Messersmith decision, there was virtual anarchy in the rules and structure of the game. Players' Association director Marvin Miller, after a decade of fighting for such gains as grievance arbitration (which eventually ended the reserve clause) and salary arbitration, was fighting the owners broadside, trying to give in as little as possible from the outright one-year free agency that Seitz had granted.

On March 17, the Players' Association voted to reject the owners' final offer — that players who didn't sign their contracts could be free agents, à la Messersmith, after eight years of major-league service — but there was a crack. The vote was only 17–5, the first indication of a split in the ranks of the players. To this day, then-members of the Player Relations Committee, such as Clark Griffith of the Twins and Frank Cashen of the Orioles, claim that Miller was under tremendous pressure from the players, and that within a week or two he would have had to give in and agree to virtually what had been turned down on the 17th. But here Commissioner Bowie Kuhn stepped in.

Right after the announcement of the players' vote, Kuhn ordered that the lockout be ended. "Because I think it is now vital that spring training get under way without further delay, I have directed that the camps be opened by the earliest possible time," Kuhn announced, and the players' fear of not having a way to put bread on their tables was eliminated. PRC members felt that Kuhn took the hammer away from his employers, the owners, and forced management into a Miller-dominated agreement signed at the All-Star break in Philadelphia on July 12. Had the new system been put in place in March, Lynn certainly wouldn't have taken until August or Burleson and Fisk until late July to sign. None of the trade rumors involving the trio would have so dominated the first two months.

But few Red Sox followers anticipated that March that the glory ride would ever stop. Even when they got to Baltimore and lost the opener, it only seemed to encourage everyone more. Jenkins lost that opener 1–0 to Jim Palmer, but his Boston debut was a three-hitter lost when Burleson made an errant throw after fielding a routine Lee May ground ball, Bobby Grich hit a single off the end of his bat into center, and Lynn's throw to Rico Petrocelli hit a hole in the baseline and caromed over the third baseman's head. "I've never had an experience quite like catching that man," Fisk said after the game. A dazzling running catch by the Orioles' peerless Paul Blair robbed Rice of a double immediately preceding a Yastrzemski double to seal the victory for Palmer.

When House and Willoughby gave up runs in the eighth inning and wasted seven shutout innings by Wise the next day for another loss to the Orioles, 5–1, nothing seemed fatally off. El Tiante, the stopper, rode Lynn's homer to a 6–2 victory on Sunday, and they returned home for a 7–4 home-opener win over the Indians in which Cleveland left fielder Charlie Spikes lost several one-on-one encounters with the wind.

On April 23, Tiant won 9–2 in Chicago to put them over .500 (6–5) for the first time, and everything seemed to be going as it was supposed to. Lynn was leading the league at .432. Fisk had three homers, Yaz and Rice two apiece. Petrocelli was among the league-leaders in RBIs. Tiant was 3–0, 1.88, Jenkins was only 1–2 but had a 2.42 ERA for twenty-two and a third innings, and Wise was 1–1, 2.84. "Most of us had won in our first or second years in the big leagues and we thought that was the way it was going to be," Burleson later remembered. "We just took it for granted that we would win. We believed what we read and heard."

By the time the Red Sox next won a game, five Democratic candidates had dropped out of the presidential race, seventeen days had passed, and Channel 4 had sent a witch to try to revive them in Cleveland. First came four rainouts. The afternoon after Tiant's 9–2 Chicago win it rained, and the next morning it began snowing so hard that the game was postponed by 9:00 A.M. and Red Sox traveling secretary Jack Rogers had the team at O'Hare Airport for an 11:30 flight to Kansas City. Problem is, the snow started canceling flights, so they sat around for nearly ten hours before flying out to Kansas City. Monday was warm and sunny, but it was also a scheduled day off. Tuesday and Wednesday were cold and wet, so those games were postponed until the series after the All-Star break. Again, there was an airport problem. Rogers couldn't get a charter in until nearly 11:30 because of the severe storms, so again they sat around an airport, this time for five hours. When the plane finally got up in the air, an officious stewardess walked up to Yastrzemski in his usual front-of-the-plane bridge game and told him he couldn't sit there if he was going to smoke.

For most of his career, Yastrzemski sat in the same area playing the same card games on every club charter. His partners varied greatly over the years, from John Curtis to Bob Burda to Mike O'Berry to Mark Clear, but he and three others always sat as a foursome in two rows of seats near the right front of the cabin, playing cards, drinking beer, and smoking one cigarette after another the entire flight. But this one stewardess didn't know who Carl Yastrzemski was, and couldn't have cared less. She demanded that he put on his seat belt and put out his cigarette. "Who put you up to this prank?" Yaz laughed.

"This is a designated nonsmoking area. Either desist smoking or move," she replied.

"Jack, since when has a charter ever had a nonsmoking area? Is this a joke?"

"This is no joke. I determine where you can smoke and where you can't."

Yastrzemski turned away and went back to his card game. The stewardess then grabbed the cigarette out of his hand and put it out. Rogers tried to explain to her that team charters do not have smoking and nonsmoking areas. "If that man lights another cigarette in that place, I'll report him and have him arrested," she threatened loudly.

Yastrzemski lit another cigarette, took a sip of his beer, and laid down a card. "When we land," she told Rogers, "I'm having him arrested."

Yaz was not arrested, of course, but the incident was another omen, another example of unexpected hassles plaguing the dynasty-to-be, and when the Red Sox finally started playing in Texas the next Thursday, they began the descent into the ten-game losing streak. They lost four straight in Texas, a series culminated that Sunday when Tiant took a 3–0 lead over nemesis Gaylord Perry into the fifth inning, only to give up a solo homer to Tom Grieve, which was followed by Mike Hargrove's two-run, game-tying homer in the sixth, and finally, Jeff Burroughs's three-run shot in the eighth. For the Rangers, it was a wondrous weekend stomping the poster boys, and Jim Piersall, who worked for Texas owner Brad Corbett on a personal services basis, came racing into the press box ranting, "World Series, my ass. Take that." Red Sox publicist Dick Bresciani caustically mumbled, "Yeah, see me in August," and Piersall jumped Bresciani and had to be pulled off by two writers.

They returned home and lost five in a row to Kansas City and Texas, then went to Cleveland and gave Jenkins a 3–1 lead in the seventh. Poof! With one swing, catcher Alan Ashby hit a two-strike, two-out, three-run homer and the streak was ten. The next night, witch Laurie Cabot arrived, escorted by a Channel 4 crew. Bernardo Carbo put his hat on Cabot's head, but most players avoided the stunt. "I think it's weak, and we don't appreciate making a joke of the game," said Fisk. "Nothing's funny right now."

The next night Reggie Cleveland and House pitched ten shutout innings of relief, Yaz broke the tie with a chalk-line bloop double, and the Red Sox won 6–4 in twelve innings. That started them on another streak, this time winning seven out of eight, and they took a 9–2 win replete with three homers by Yastrzemski from Detroit to Yankee Stadium for their first showdown series with the Yankees in their renovated park. New York, led by newly acquired speedsters Mickey Rivers and Willie Randolph at the top of the order, was off to a 19–10 start, and led the Red Sox by six games. But the Red Sox had been able to beat the Yankees when they had to for years: in 1973, when they trailed by five and a half games, they won four out of five over the July Fourth holiday and swept them in August; in 1975, when the Red Sox moved into first place for good, they took three out of four from New York in Boston the last weekend in June and did the same in late July. The Yankees hadn't won a series from Boston since 1971.

The series, which would draw the largest four-game crowd in The Stadium since 1947, was vital to Boston's getting back in the race. "We've got a lot of guys around here who think we're just going to catch up automatically," said Yastrzemski, "but eight or ten games is a lot to make up. If we do worse than break even, we may never get close again."

The first night, May 20, Bill Lee, who was 0–3, 9.27 in five starts and hadn't won a game since the previous August 24, finally pitched his first strong game of the season. He trailed Yankee starter Ed Figueroa 1–0 in the sixth when Otto Velez singled with Lou Piniella on second base. Piniella, naturally, tried to score, but Evans uncorked a perfect throw to the plate that was in Fisk's glove strides ahead of Piniella's arrival. The throw had skidded, and Fisk had some trouble gripping it, which Piniella noticed, and knowing he had a chance to knock the ball away from Fisk, Piniella went into the kneeling Red Sox catcher with cleats and knees. Fisk took umbrage and came up swinging.

Lee came charging in from the mound, firing punches, and in the melee that ensued, Rivers was spotted on television jumping over the pack throwing blind punches ("Look at those cheap shots," shouted Boston telecaster Dick Stockton).

Lee ended up under one pile, got up, and when Yankee Graig
Nettles tried to hold him off, the two began throwing
punches at each other. Nettles wrestled Lee to the ground,
where he landed on his shoulder. "I could tell immediately
that it was hurt," said Nettles. "He had tears in his eyes, and
was screaming." Nettles tried to hold Lee down, which Lee
claimed amounted to lying on his injured shoulder. Then,
after peace was restored, Lee ran around to Nettles and
began screaming at him.

"I'll get you," Lee shouted, adding a number of obscenities.
Nettles dropped him with another punch to the eye, and
after they were separated Lee was led off the field by trainer
Charlie Moss with torn cartilage and torn capsule in his left
shoulder. The next day, in a press conference in the Eliot
Lounge, Lee, in a sling and sporting a black eye, promised to
"get the Yankees," called Billy Martin a "Nazi," and referred
to the Yankees as "Steinbrenner's Brown Shirts."

Still, the Red Sox had come back that night. Burleson hit
a two-run homer in the seventh, then when the Yankees tied
it back up at 2–2, Martin brought in left-hander Tippy
Martinez to pitch to Yaz and the Captain hit a towering
two-run homer. When Yastrzemski hit yet another homer in
the ninth off a rookie named Ron Guidry to finish a four-run
rally and the 8–2 win, he had hit a record five home runs in
two games. "That," said Yastrzemski, "is the first will to win
I've seen on this team since the World Series. I think the fight
did it."

But other than losing the club's only left-handed starter,
the effects of the fight lasted just that night. On Friday, the
Yankees tied it in the ninth off House and won it in the
twelfth 6–5 off Willoughby. The hero? Someone named
Kerry Dineen, who at 5:55 P.M. was taking batting practice in
Syracuse with the Yankee farm club, took American Airlines
flight 184 to New York, was picked up by a limousine, and
arrived in the fifth inning, in plenty of time for his dramatic
appearance. The next night Catfish Hunter shut out the Red

Sox 1–0 in eleven innings, and only Burleson's perfect relay saved a 7–6 split on Sunday.

Other than the injury to Lee, the most significant part of the weekend in New York might have been Yastrzemski's statement about the club's will to win, since the two victories only postponed the inevitable. The sighting of Kapstein and Claiborne sitting in different sections of Fenway became as much a part of the press box routine as watching the games, and rumors of major trades echoed around the park. O'Connell one night said, "We could make a one-for-one, a two-for-two, or a five-for-five," and assorted reports continually cropped up: Fisk to California for Nolan Ryan, Lynn to California for Frank Tanana, and so on.

When the Orioles and Yankees took turns coming into Fenway and winning two out of three from May 28 to June 3, it prompted Boston to make their first move. They traded Carbo, who had played in only seventeen games behind the "best outfield in baseball," to Milwaukee for pitcher Tom Murphy and outfielder Bobby Darwin. Murphy was playing out his option with the Brewers, and the Red Sox felt they could sign him. Also, he was a right-handed reliever, something they desperately needed without Drago. With Rice off to a slow start and Petrocelli no longer hitting for power, getting Darwin was taking a flyer. He had once been able to hit home runs.

The Carbo deal was announced after an 8–2 victory over the Yankees, but Bernardo had showered, dressed, and gone out the clubhouse door before Johnson could find him to tell him. In the parking lot, Channel 4 reporter Jimmy Myers ran up to Carbo's four-wheel-drive vehicle to ask him for his reaction to the news. "I got traded?" Carbo shouted. Myers said he had been traded to Milwaukee.

Carbo slammed his foot on the accelerator and bolted out of the parking lot, scattering the circles of fans that hang around the gate nightly. As he went around the gate, he drove directly into a hot dog wagon, knocking it and the cus-

todian over and sending soft-drink cans, hot dogs, and kiel-
basa flying as he screeched around the corner onto Jersey
Street. It eventually took him a week to report to Milwaukee,
where he didn't last long. At the end of the season, when the
Red Sox and Brewers were completing the George
Scott–Cecil Cooper trade, Milwaukee general manager Jim
Baumer told the Boston delegation, "We don't make the deal
unless you take Carbo back." Which they did, gladly.

There weren't many characters like Bernardo Carbo. Yawkey found that out three months after Carbo joined the Red
Sox in 1974 in a deal with the Cardinals. Yawkey came down
to the clubhouse most every afternoon, dressed modestly in
baggy pants and a Windbreaker. Often when players came in
for early hitting, they sent clubhouse boys or clubhouse attendant Pete Cerone out for food. One June afternoon, Yawkey walked over to Carbo, who was sitting in front of his
locker. Bernardo saw him coming, reached into his locker,
handed Yawkey a five-dollar bill, and said, "Go get me a couple of cheeseburgers."

Yawkey introduced himself. "Sorry," replied Carbo. "I
thought you were Pete Cerone."

Don Zimmer had managed Carbo at Knoxville in the Cincinnati system in 1967. The team won only thirty-five games
all season, and one time was in a twelve-game losing streak
when Carbo hit a one-out triple in the bottom of the ninth.

"Tag up on a fly ball," Zimmer, coaching third at the time,
told him, and sure enough, Hal McRae followed with a four-
hundred-foot fly ball to straightaway center. The ball was
caught, and Zimmer turned to watch Carbo score easily.
When he turned, there was Carbo, right foot on the base,
back turned to the outfield, staring at Zimmer.

"What are you doing?" Zimmer screamed.

"Waiting for you to tell me when to go," Carbo answered.

When Zimmer threw his hands in the air in frustration,
Carbo took off and was thrown out by fifteen feet at the

plate. Knoxville lost in the twelfth and lost six more in a row.

In 1974, losing 5–0 in Detroit, Darrell Johnson couldn't figure out why Carbo tried to steal second and was thrown out. So he called him over in the dugout. "I got the steal sign," Carbo told him.

"What is the steal sign?" Johnson asked him, figuring Bernardo had forgotten.

"Any combination adding up to five," answered Carbo, referring to Johnson's system of adding the value of two signs together to get a number that signified the specific sign.

"What was the value of the first sign?" asked Johnson.

"Two."

"What about the second?"

"Two," Carbo snapped.

When he came to the Red Sox, Carbo had brought along a large stuffed gorilla named Mighty Joe Young, a gift sent to him by former Cardinals teammate Scipio Spinks (later Oil Can Boyd's college coach). Bernardo seated him over his locker, took him on trips, and one time ordered him milk in a Dallas hotel coffee shop. Carbo also bought a gold-plated statue of Buddha, which he called Weaver, "because he looks like Earl Weaver." Soon thereafter in a game at Fenway, someone threw a dummy into the Orioles dugout and Weaver kicked it out, saying, "I thought it was Carbo."

Carbo hit only .249 in his first year with Boston, but became the first player to take the Red Sox to salary arbitration, or "arbistration," as he called it. Right into 1978, he thought Dick Stockton, the well-known announcer who did the Red Sox games, was Dick Woodson, a former pitcher with the Minnesota Twins. One day he was at the batting cage when someone came out with a bat made by the Worth Company of Nashville, Tennessee. "Hey, Fort Worth," exclaimed Carbo, "that's where they keep the gold." Carbo was stationed at Fort Knox in the army.

On an off-day workout in Kansas City in April 1976, Carbo

hadn't shown up. Lee, Willoughby, and House all tried calling his room from the clubhouse and got no answer, so the
manager announced a fine. Late that afternoon, his teammates found him and asked him where he had been. "In my
room," replied Carbo. Asked why he didn't pick up the
phone, he said, "I only answer the phone when it's my wife
calling."

When he returned in 1977, he hit a grand slam off Mariner
left-hander Mike Kekich in the Seattle Kingdome. When the
game was over and reporters asked him about the grand slam,
Carbo looked at them in amazement. "Grand slam?" he
asked. He hadn't known the bases were loaded.

Then he was asked about the last time he had hit a home
run off a left-hander. "Now I know you guys are pulling my
leg, because he was right-handed," Carbo replied. "Zim
would never let me hit against a left-hander with the bases
loaded."

Eccentricities aside, Carbo was traded because the Red
Sox desperately needed bullpen help. With the Angels and
the A's following the Yankees into Fenway, the rumors about
the Kapstein Connection sprouted everywhere. When California was in town, catcher Ed Hermann said he'd been told
that Ryan was going to Boston for Fisk. When Oakland was
in town, Johnson and Claiborne sat in the stands and talked
to Rudi and Fingers, heightening speculation.

O'Connell talked to California general manager Harry
Dalton, but later staunchly maintained that he had no inten-
tion of trading Lynn, Burleson, or Fisk. "We thought we
would sign them one way or another," O'Connell said. Five
years later, when Lynn, Burleson, and Fisk all left because
they were unsigned, Haywood Sullivan and Jean Yawkey
claimed that the hospitalized Tom Yawkey didn't want them
signed in 1976 and that he had insisted they be traded.

"That," O'Connell maintains, "is simply not true. He knew
what we were trying to do in terms of signing them, and he

never said a thing. His reaction to what we did on the fif-teenth told us where we stood."

O'Connell was talking to Oakland owner Charlie Finley between two and six times daily. The discussions actually had started at the end of the previous season, when O'Connell, Johnson, and Yawkey talked to Fingers, Rudi, Jackson, and Bando in the manager's office following the pennant-clincher in the Oakland Coliseum.

"They were all telling us that they wanted out of Oakland and wanted to come to Boston," O'Connell remembers. "Yawkey stood there and talked to them for an hour."

By March 1976, Finley had realized that he was going to lose the heart of his three-time world championship club at the end of the season. Before the season opened, he traded potential free agents Jackson and Ken Holtzman to Baltimore for another potential free agent, Baylor, as well as twenty-game winner Mike Torrez and young right-hander Paul Mitchell. By May, he and O'Connell were talking constantly. Finley wanted to trade Rudi, Fingers, Blue, Tenace, and Bando for Lynn, Fisk, and a couple of young players. Then, on June 10, as Lynn and Burleson chanted "Good-bye Fen-way" after the Red Sox finished a 5–7 homestand by blowing a 5–2 lead in the eighth and losing 8–5 to Oakland, O'Connell and Finley were close to a deal. They were so close, in fact, that that afternoon Johnson and Claiborne had met with Rudi and Fingers and asked them what they wanted to sign. Rudi and Fingers named their prices. Claiborne reported back to O'Connell, and O'Connell told him to be ready to fly out and get them signed.

On Friday, while the Red Sox were playing in Minnesota, Finley asked O'Connell if he'd give him Rick Miller and Andy Merchant for Fingers. "Done," said O'Connell. Finley told him he'd check with his people. "You don't have any people," O'Connell chided him. The next morning Finley backed off.

The next night, Finley talked about Miller, Merchant, Willoughby, a minor leaguer, and cash for Rudi and Fingers. Then he backed off. He told O'Connell that he didn't want any charade, that he wanted the cash: $1 million a player. O'Connell and Vice-President Gene Kirby jumped on a plane Sunday, June 14, and flew out to San Francisco. When they got to DiMaggio's Restaurant, O'Connell phoned Finley, who told him he wanted to unload Blue, too. O'Connell called Claiborne and told him to get on the 9:00 A.M. flight ready to sign either Rudi or Fingers or both. He then grabbed Kirby. "I wanted to get to the airport to meet our flight from Minnesota to talk to Darrell and see if he'd agree to take Blue instead of Rudi," O'Connell remembers. "But what happened when we got to our rental car? It didn't start. By the time we got a cab to the Oakland airport, we'd missed Darrell, and he'd gone to Pinole [thirty-five miles north of Oakland]. We called for four hours and couldn't reach him."

By the time the frantic night was over, O'Connell had agreed to give Finley $2 million apiece for Fingers and Rudi. "I told Charlie that I'd buy all three because I didn't want Blue going to the Yankees. He told me that Blue was going to Detroit, so I didn't want to screw [G.M. Jim] Campbell. Then I found out that he called Steinbrenner and told him that Blue would cost him one point five million. Steinbrenner paid it."

O'Connell believes that had Finley kept his word, the deals would have been accepted. The agreement was to wait for any announcement until late afternoon, to give Claiborne a chance to get to Rudi's house to sign Rudi and Fingers. "But Charlie called all over the place boasting about getting three and a half million for three players, and we were already in trouble. The worst part of it was that he called Rudi and Fingers and boasted about what he got for them. They called Kapstein and he told them not to sign anything."

June 15, 1976, was the day the world realized that baseball had been uprooted. Finley, unable to sign most of his players, had sold off three of them for $3.5 million. Orioles G.M. Hank Peters, unable to sign pitchers Ken Holtzman (whose deal to Kansas City had fallen through over the weekend because he refused the Royals' offer) and Doyle Alexander, traded them along with reliever Grant Jackson, catcher Elrod Hendricks, and minor leaguer Jimmy Freeman for Rudy May, Tippy Martinez, catcher Rick Dempsey, pitcher Dave Pagan, and a minor leaguer named Scott McGregor. The Cardinals, unable to satisfy slugger Reggie Smith, sent him to the Dodgers for catcher Joe Ferguson and cash. The Braves and Giants swapped potential free agents Darrell Evans and Willie Montanez.

"This all seems too strange. I haven't really had time to think about it," Johnson told reporters. "They say, 'Do you want Joe Rudi?' Hell, yes, I want Joe Rudi. It's as simple as that. No players given. All of a sudden we have one of the best everyday players and the best relief pitcher in the game. The Yankees all of a sudden have Blue, just the way they got Hunter. It's all beyond my comprehension."

O'Connell and Claiborne realized the lack of logic in acquiring Rudi instead of Blue. The win by rookie Rick Jones in Minnesota the previous Saturday was the first by a left-handed starter all season, and with Lee and, at Pawtucket, Aase — who after starting off 4–0 with a one-hitter and a two-hitter hurt his shoulder — out for the season, they desperately needed pitching. Acquiring Rudi meant putting Cecil Cooper, who was hitting .292 coming off a .311 season, on the bench and making Jim Rice, who was working hard to become a dependable defensive left fielder, the DH. "I'm no dummy, I'm going to be the one who gets dumped on. I always am," Cooper said, disgusted.

Cooper had fallen out of Johnson's favor early in 1975 when, upset at not playing regularly, he refused to play first base in the ninth inning of a blowout game when Yastrzemski wanted to leave early; Bob Montgomery had to go out instead. Johnson even told Tigers manager Ralph Houk that he could have Cooper at the end of the season, something his strong finish and clutch play the entire second half of the season made impossible. Rudi, on the other hand, was a close friend of Johnson's. They lived near each other. They hunted together several times during the off-season. When the Red Sox won the pennant in Oakland, it was Rudi with whom Johnson sat in his office, talking for more than an hour instead of being with his own players.

"In that kind of situation, you like to give the manager what he feels he wants," said O'Connell. "If we'd have gotten hold of Darrell Sunday night, we'd have probably been able to convince him to take Blue." O'Connell feels that if Finley had not started calling people to boast of getting $3.5 million, Rudi, Fingers, and Blue would have remained in Boston and New York because Rudi and Fingers would have been signed and the figures wouldn't have gotten out until it was too late.

What would have happened had Johnson played Rudi and Fingers that first night? Johnson claimed that they both asked for the night off, because they were emotionally exhausted. All the two players had to do physically was move their equipment from the A's clubhouse down the hall to the visiting clubhouse and put on their Boston uniforms, Fingers taking Zimmer's 34 (Zimmy took 21) and Rudi wearing number 28. They worked out, and each later claimed he could have played. Fingers threw in the bullpen late in the game, right before Jenkins gave up his second homer of the game to Gene Tenace in the eighth for a 3–2 Oakland victory. Then when A's manager Chuck Tanner brought in left-hander Paul Lindblad to pitch the ninth, Johnson could have used Rudi as a pinch hitter for Cooper leading off the inning.

The next day, Kuhn called for a meeting in New York of the Yankees, Red Sox, and A's officials, and declared Rudi, Fingers, and Blue ineligible until the hearing; Tanner tried to get Johnson to go along with a prank to come up to home plate with a Red Sox lineup that included Rudi in left and Fingers pitching, while he'd hand in a card with Rudi in left

and Fingers pitching, but they didn't do it. The meeting was
Wednesday, and that night, after the Red Sox finally won a
game, 8–3, they flew to Anaheim without Rudi and Fingers.
They were told to wait and catch a noon flight from Oakland
to Orange County Airport.

Rudi and Fingers never did arrive. Citing article 1, section
4, of the Major League Agreement of 1921, which states,
"The Commissioner may take such steps as he may deem
necessary and proper in the interest and morale of the players and the honor of the game," Kuhn voided the sales. "The
whole game," Rico Petrocelli lamented, "has gone completely crazy."

Naturally, the parties involved were upset. Finley filed a
$10 million lawsuit against the commissioner. Steinbrenner
was outraged. Boston officials protested. "Who tells me if the
player's batting average is bad enough, or that the price is
low enough?" asked O'Connell. "Who are we supposed to
check with?" O'Connell then added that the Red Sox would
not pursue the matter in court. The Red Sox didn't wish to
undermine baseball; it wasn't their way. But Yawkey, who
had made these kinds of deals involving Jimmie Foxx and Joe
Cronin and Lefty Grove forty years earlier, was not, as some
claimed, unhappy with the moves. O'Connell and treasurer
John Harrington claim that when they called him Monday
afternoon and told him they'd bought Rudi and Fingers for
$1 million apiece, the first thing Yawkey said to them was
"How come you didn't get Bando?"

But Sullivan claims it wasn't that way, and that week's
dealings are what eventually got O'Connell fired and gave
the club to Sullivan. "Mr. Yawkey was undergoing chemo-
therapy at the time the club left for the Coast," Sullivan
maintains, "and he was so sick and tired of the way things
were going — the way they'd refused to negotiate early, then
the way the agent used the three as a package — that he told
O'Connell to trade Lynn and Burleson before the deadline;
he figured that Fisk, being a local guy, could eventually have

things worked out. They'd talked to some people, too. But not only did Dick not trade them, he went and bought these other two Kapstein clients. Yawkey called me up at home at seven-thirty the next morning. 'Do you know anything about this?' he bellowed. I told him I didn't. He was outraged, and O'Connell was gone from that point on."

Red Sox history is dotted with endless questions and "what if?" situations. What if Hughson, Ferriss, Lonborg, and Santiago hadn't hurt their arms? What if the Indians hadn't twice reneged on deals for Gaylord Perry during the 1973 World Series and winter meetings? What if O'Connell hadn't been blocked by the Yawkey Estate trustees from dealing Wise for Torrez in early 1977? What if Winfield had signed ten days earlier and the 1980 Lynn deal to the Dodgers (for outfielder–first baseman Mike Marshall and pitchers Joe Beckwith and Steve Howe) had stood? But the Rudi-Fingers speculations are especially fascinating. Having Rudi would have avoided the Cooper–George Scott deal made that winter. Fingers had 177 saves from June 15, 1976, to September 1982, when he hurt his arm, thrice leading the National and once leading the American League in saves and winning both the Cy Young and Most Valuable Player awards for the Brewers in 1981. In the November 1976 free-agent market, instead of Bill Campbell, the Red Sox would then have probably centered on Grich to play second base. How many pennants would they have won? Maybe 1977, maybe not; getting Torrez a year too late cost them one pennant there. If they'd had Fingers in 1978, they certainly would have won, and the same may be true of the second half of 1981.

FOUR

1976, Continued

THE ASCENT OF DON ZIMMER

After the signing of Lynn, Fisk, and Burleson, the firing of Darrell Johnson, and the death of Tom Yawkey, the Red Sox regroup.

*A*MIDST all the second-guessing, the only thing that can be said for sure is that the whole crazy affair was no help to the already troubled and turbulent 1976 Red Sox season. Of course, the Red Sox didn't need any outside agitation; their season was a mess long before Rudi and Fingers came and went. Two days before the Rudi-Fingers purchase, Darrell Johnson sat in the visitors' dugout in Bloomington, Minnesota, rubbed his fingers through his hair, and quietly muttered, "I hope this all is just the contractual thing, because everyone's on edge, no one's himself — on and off the field."

The night before, Johnson had seen his team fall behind 6–0 in the first inning of a 10–4 beating by the Twins. More important, he and Fisk had been at each other all night. In the first inning, with Rod Carew on second and Butch Wyne-

gar on first, Johnson told Fisk to throw to second should
Carew take off for third; Fisk argued that Carew usually runs
on his own and that chances were Wynegar wouldn't be
going. That was one argument. There were two or three ex-
changes about Fisk's selection of pitches called, and at the
end of the six-run first, Johnson shouted at Fisk, "I don't want
any more of your lip." When Fisk struck out in the sixth inning and returned to the dugout, Johnson, at one end of the
dugout, asked Fisk, "Have you had enough?"

"You're ——ing right I've had enough," bellowed Fisk,
and with that he fired his helmet down the dugout in Johnson's direction. It skipped off a step and struck the manager,
and Fisk stomped down the steps into the runway and
walked up to the clubhouse. "He's been second-guessing me
all season," Fisk said hours later over a drink in Duff's. "He
got all over me in Texas for a couple of pitches, one of which
Burroughs hit out off Tiant. Every time someone gets a hit off
us, it seems that Darrell's blaming me for calling the pitch.
It's been going on all year and I'm sick and tired of it. I'm
sorry in one way, because it hurts the team, but it was bound
to open up. I thought after my knee, the groin, the broken
arm . . . I thought that I'd be able to just go and play and
everything would be the way baseball's supposed to be. But
this has turned out to be the worst year yet."

It was nearly 3:30 A.M. when Fisk got something to eat in a
little all-night Minneapolis spot called the Blue Ox. He was
sitting there, waiting for his sandwich, when two girls sat
down at the table. Twenty minutes later, Fisk had pulled out
his wallet and lined the table with pictures of his children.
The two young ladies, uninterested in the Fisk children, po-
litely got up and left. "Right now," he said, "my family is the
only stability I know. Everything else seems out of kilter."

Fisk did not get to the park until an hour before that Saturday afternoon game, missing batting practice and accepting
the fine that went with it. Johnson said, "When he tells me
he's ready to play again, I'll put him back in there," but

without Fisk saying anything, he was back in the lineup the next day for the final game of the Minnesota series. Johnson didn't fully understand the scope of what was going on around him, but he knew that the Red Sox had somehow lost their driving wheel, and that at the root of the problem was the fact that Fisk, Lynn, and Burleson were the first holdouts in the history of the franchise. And they were as confused at the eye of the storm as anyone feeling the backlash.

No one with the team — not the three holdouts, not veterans like Carl Yastrzemski or Rico Petrocelli, not the manager or coaches — understood what was going on. The gravitational force that had held baseball together so simply for a century had been eradicated by the Messersmith decision. It wasn't until Fisk brought in Kapstein in 1973 that O'Connell had even *talked* to an agent. The usual procedure was to come in, sit down and shoot the breeze, and agree on some figure. Players didn't exactly hold much of a hand; Yastrzemski and Bob Woolf tried to create a hedge in 1972 by claiming Yaz might jump to Japan, but Yastrzemski later said, "My usual contract discussions consisted of going to lunch with O'Connell, drag it on, hope he had three or four drinks, and sign by four o'clock." It was always player on one hand, general manager on the other, and in the case of the Red Sox, there was always the kindness of Tom Yawkey hovering above. Tom Yawkey didn't have holdouts or contractual problems.

"All this stuff has definitely affected my concentration, and I'm certain it's affected Rooster [Burleson], Freddie, and probably some of our teammates," Fisk said that night. "I'm trying to play. My arm's killing me. Darrell's on my case. And there's Claiborne coming around talking to me. I'm just completely ——ed up."

Fisk, Lynn, and Burleson were suddenly more than young men in their twenties being paid to do what they'd always done, namely, play baseball. The gradual, traditional steps up the game's ladder now had become a glamorous, high-speed elevator ride, and they were commodities as well as people, commodities whose values were being argued like pork bellies or gold bullion by hired guns named Claiborne and Kapstein. "They brought in a guy who only saw us play in the playoffs and World Series last year and he's the one evaluating what we're worth," Burleson constantly complained. But on talk shows and in newspapers, Kapstein was treated as some sort of treacherous shyster. Haywood Sullivan, who'd been demoted by O'Connell to scouting director when Claiborne had been hired the previous fall, leaked some of Kapstein's asking prices on the three players to radio talk show host Clif Keane that June. Keane had a legitimate exclusive, but as he railed against Kapstein for asking "insane" numbers, neither he nor the players' teammates (who privately were very critical of the trio) comprehended what the open market was going to mean to baseball.

Some of baseballs' conservatives did. "The most important thing in baseball right now is the Boston situation with the three unsigned players," Twins owner Calvin Griffith said that June weekend in Minnesota in discussing what was going on around Fisk's head. "Let's face it, people in my situation have always considered the Red Sox the team that screwed things up for everyone else the way they pay. Now, if they hold the line and don't sign the players for the sake of signing them, the entire structure of the game will be saved."

O'Connell seemed to comprehend how complex this era was going to be. In restructuring his front office, he had moved Sullivan downstairs, in effect taking him from the number-two spot in the hierarchy to a developmental post. There seemed to be a constant struggle for power under the Yawkey umbrella between the two. O'Connell, however, had been a successful top dog since Mike Higgins and his "Sound and the Fury" regime was toppled in September 1965. Sensing the importance of the electronic media and going to a hundred-game UHF television schedule, O'Connell hired an electronic media authority named Gene Kirby. That rankled

the Red Sox traditionalists in the front office, particularly
when Kirby would show up for work at 8:00 A.M., but Kirby
and O'Connell appreciated that the radio and television
broadcasts are a club's most important public relations vehicle. They brought the skilled Dick Stockton and Ken Harrelson together for TV and the legendary Ned Martin and Jim
Woods for radio; few radio teams ever had a greater effect on
any market than Martin and Woods. Late in the '75 season,
Claiborne began showing up scouting the Oakland club —
for which he'd worked for four years — and at the end of the
World Series moved in with treasurer John Harrington to an
assistant general manager's position that between the two of
them was to cover both baseball and business. O'Connell respected Sullivan, but only in terms of judging talent. Privately, he felt that Haywood was "slow" and "incapable of
making a decision." While he demoted Sullivan by putting
him in charge of the scouting department, O'Connell had
also put him in the position he felt he was best equipped to
handle.

Claiborne, in his late thirties, looked far younger. He'd
started out in the Mets organization as an assistant farm
director, moved to St. Louis with Bing Devine, and taken the
Oakland player personnel job with Charlie Finley in 1972.
That, as far as Claiborne was concerned, was a great opportunity, for he'd had to run the scouting, farm-system, and
major-league contracts by himself. He'd also had the opportunity to go head-to-head with Kapstein on more than a
dozen arbitration cases involving the A's players, something
O'Connell was very much aware of, realizing the power
Kapstein might have with Fisk, Lynn, and Burleson. Claiborne was a deeply religious midwesterner from St. Louis,
but he was also highly motivated and energetic; when he was
out of a job because of the changeover in ownership in 1978,
Weston businessman Martin Stone gave him the opportunity
to try to run a failing business in Texas, and Claiborne, in
Stone's words, "did an astounding job righting it." Many

within Boston's "members only" organization resented Claiborne's working hours; often he would be at Fenway in the afternoon and Pawtucket or Bristol at night.

Kapstein at the time was thirty-two, and had risen to notoriety in less than three years since Fisk and Pittsburgh's Richie Zisk became his first clients. He is the son of a Providence attorney, a kid who at nine or ten "kept all the box scores — I loved math and I loved statistics," a passion that earned him the nickname Jerry Statstein as a Harvard undergraduate. He was well known to TV people, be they local in Providence or national (like Keith Jackson at ABC, who credits Kapstein with suggesting several statistical categories now used on the network's broadcasts), and when he got out of Boston College Law School he was so obviously headed for sports that he never did bother to pass the bar. Kapstein was such a workaholic that it eventually ruined his first marriage, but it earned him the respect of his players. "No one knows more baseball than Jerry Kapstein," Fisk maintained during the negotiations, a claim echoed by Rudi and Fingers, whose cases he argued in arbitration against Claiborne in Oakland. In June 1976, he represented nineteen of the nearly sixty players who could become baseball's first pure free agents at the end of the season, and Finley so feared the power he had to dismantle his great team that Kapstein believes he had his phone tapped, one of the many bizarre spying and espionage attempts against Kapstein that eventually turned him into an eccentric hermit.

O'Connell, Claiborne, and Harrington saw what was happening, and had more than half of their players tied to long-term contracts by the end of spring training. Kapstein, however, was the one agent who read the market perfectly, and he, the brazen easterner, and Claiborne, the quiet midwesterner, were off on three months of nonstop contract negotiations that were in another galaxy from the contracts signed by the other Red Sox players. They'd be spotted seated together in box seats down the first-base line, or in a coffee shop across the street, talking and talking and talking. Claiborne was trying to cling to some semblance of the old salary structure in which $100,000 meant a player was something special. Kapstein was talking five years and millions.

Sullivan claims that Yawkey never wanted the trio signed, not at the prices they were demanding, not at what they might cost the game. O'Connell and Claiborne vehemently deny Yawkey opposed their signing at all. In any case, his absence — he had been in the hospital the entire season — added to the impersonal, hard-line business sense of the negotiations.

Of the three players, Fisk took the months of haggling hardest. He grew up in the heart of Red Sox country, and was available in the January 1967 draft to them because, as one Baltimore scout said, "everyone knew that he'd only play for the Red Sox." He looked so much the part of the hearty, square-jawed WASPish New Englander, getting up at 6:00 A.M., chopping down trees on his farm, and being willing to defend New England's team with his fists, his bat, and his body. He had come to believe in that role for himself, and was convinced that he really *did* hate the Yankees.

His disillusionment with the romance of the game had actually started after he tore up his knee trying to block home plate in Cleveland in June 1974. He had been hurt before; in October 1973, he nearly sheared off the top of a finger in his garage door, then the next March in spring training was hit by a foul tip in the groin area that sidelined him for nearly a month. But this time he felt that the Red Sox had neglected him, and he accused them, Dr. Thomas Tierney, and their staff of not bothering to give him a rehabilitation program ("The doctors told me the tear was worse than the one Gale Sayers suffered") or bothering to check how he felt. Then, in 1975, after a winter of intense work on his own, he got to spring training and in his second exhibition game was hit by a pitch by Detroit's Fred Holdsworth that broke his forearm.

Ironically enough, it had been Fisk who, in 1972 and 1973,

when Eddie Kasko was still the manager, was Darrell Johnson's greatest booster. Johnson knew Fisk well, and appreciated that "a lot is going through his mind that sometimes
may have left his thinking a little fuzzy." In 1976, as the Sox
stumbled through the early season, Johnson thought his pitch
calling was obviously fuzzy. Fisk was hitting under .250. And
when the fans started booing him, he was totally confused, so
confused that one night after striking out to Gaylord Perry,
he made an obscene gesture to the stands. Afterward, he
called over a reporter and asked him to make an appropriate
public apology in the papers, but the damage had been done.
"I can't win," he lamented, "whether I get what I want or
not. I've been criticized everywhere for not sitting down
with the club, but every day in spring training or early in the
season it seems I was talking to Claiborne and that took my
thinking away from baseball."

Then came the trade talks. Rumors had him going to California for Nolan Ryan. Or to Oakland in a five-for-five package. "I'd never thought of being anything but a Red Sox,"
said Fisk. "All of a sudden I was threatening to leave and become a free agent, the club was threatening to trade me, and
I was up in the air." The rumors of deals unsettled everyone
from May 15 until the wild Finley fire sale in Oakland a
month later.

In June, Burleson was still hitting in the .230s and was near
the bottom of the league's shortstops defensively. His problems became so acute that he was occasionally benched in
favor of Steve Dillard. He was growing increasingly loud in
his criticism of the ball club. He would rave about letters
he'd receive. "I got one from a doctor who wanted to know
how I have the nerve to ask for more money," he hollered
one day in the clubhouse. "I feel like writing him and asking
him how he could charge his patients so much money."

Fisk and Burleson kept claiming that Lynn was the one
who cared the least whether he stayed or went, but he, too,
was clearly affected. "For the first time in my life," he said in

late June, "baseball isn't fun. It was always easy to play a game. This is hard. I get these letters about surfing and California. One read, 'This is Rick Miller country, and if you don't like it here, go back to California.' Why write stuff like that? I'm kinda disappointed in the fans." While Kapstein threatened that the attitude of the fans had changed Lynn's thinking about staying in Boston, they rode him unmercifully about his Aqua-Velva commercial. They rode him about not playing every day. The fans were not alone, either, for all of a sudden, as Lynn came up with back spasms, leg cramps, nagging injuries, seemed more cautious in the outfield, and had only six home runs in half a season, his teammates began to doubt him, too, and began openly talking about him on buses. "He's the most gutless ———— I've ever seen," one veteran said loudly on a bus one night, loud enough for Lynn to hear.

Fred Lynn was twenty-four years old at the time, and the only experience he had in the major leagues was being the Most Valuable Player and going to the seventh game of the World Series. Now he was faced with being a commodity with probably more open-market value than anyone in the game, but he was being dissected by his peers and his public. "The story that began in *Boy's Life* thus concludes its *Business Week* phase . . . The Red Sox have bought themselves one slightly dented Frank Merriwell," wrote the *Globe*'s Leigh Montville when he finally signed. "Which," Lynn later reflected, "is a heckuva change to undergo. That adjustment those three or four months when we were negotiating and playing was far worse than the jump from triple-A to the majors."

No one knew Fred Lynn then. Later, he would be called Fragile Freddie and miss a lot of games because of his injuries. He was not a Rod Carew, one to duck certain pitchers; when he enraged Don Zimmer by limping off the field and missing the last two games of a crucial September 1978 series in Yankee Stadium, he had played against Ron Guidry and missed two of his favorites, Catfish Hunter and Jim Beattie. He often was hurt crashing into fences or diving after fly balls. Amateur psychologists among his teammates theorized that since he grew up solely with his father after his mother left when he was two, he had had to play the roles of both mother and son, and had learned to mother himself. Others felt that like Orioles superpitcher Jim Palmer, he is of such high intelligence that he knew when he was doing damage to his body and refused to adhere to the tradition of "playing with pain" that left so many athletes crippled by middle age or, sometimes worse, addicted to the drugs and alcohol that deadened the pain. All this was nothing new, either. Although he demonstrated as a collegian the kind of ability that sends scouts' eyes into a spin-dry cycle, he had lasted until the end of the second round of the draft out of USC because of concerns about his attitude (one Royals report claimed that he didn't hustle after balls hit into the alleys, for instance).

"With the talent we have on this team, playing .500 is a disgrace," Yastrzemski said the day — July 5 — they finally got there, with a half-dozen potential all-stars hitting a collective .251. They had inched to within one game of .500 eight previous times and every time had lost the next game. Four days later, Yawkey died.

Despite the genuine outpouring of grief for Yawkey, the full effects of his death were not then realized. Since the team went into the hands of the Yawkey Trust, represented by his widow, Jean Yawkey, a Palo Alto attorney named James Curran, and estate official Joseph LaCour, there seemed no reason for the traditional Red Sox style not to continue. Most of the speculation centered on O'Connell putting together a group with Dominic and Joe DiMaggio — which is what he was discussing the night of June 14 — and possibly Jack Satter of Colonial Provision Company, but no one appreciated how crucial a role Jean Yawkey would come to play.

The team, meanwhile, dragged its heels for the rest of the week to head to the All-Star break at 40–40, nine and a half games behind the Yankees. The two rookies who'd exploded into stardom the previous year, each hitting .300 with more than a hundred RBIs and runs, had had dismal halves: Lynn had six homers, Rice was hitting .243. Fisk was hitting .255, Petrocelli .228. Johnson got to manage another American League loss in Philadelphia, and if that wasn't bad enough, he and the other Boston representatives — Lynn, Yastrzemski, Fisk, Tiant, Bill Lee (there for the Players' Association meetings that produced the new, historic Basic Agreement), and Johnson's trusted bullpen coach, Don "Bear" Bryant — stayed at the Bellevue-Stratford Hotel. Three weeks later, they would all get calls from federal health officials. The American Legion convention was also at the hotel, and it was in those three days that numerous guests came down with the infamous Legionnaires' disease. "Maybe," Lynn surmised after being told about the disease, "that's what got Darrell."

After the All-Star Game the Red Sox opened a six-game, four-day series in Kansas City that turned out to be Johnson's last hurrah. It didn't help to begin the second half of the season pitching Dick Pole and Rick "Tall Boy" Jones in Thursday's twinighter, although Jones's 2–1 victory turned out to be the only win they'd have in the series. They were swept 5–1, 2–1 on Friday night, and when Tiant was beaten 2–1 Saturday afternoon by George Brett's ninth-inning home run, the club sat in fifth place and Johnson sat stoically in his office, staring at a cold piece of pepperoni pizza. He was still in his office when the team bus left, and Yastrzemski and Petrocelli were still in the clubhouse, so the manager called them in and closed the door.

"Do you think my resigning would help?" he asked the players.

Both Yastrzemski and Petrocelli said no. "Quitting isn't going to solve anything," Yastrzemski answered, "particularly what's wrong with this team."

That night, however, O'Connell was making plane reservations to fly to Dallas, the team's next stop. They finished the five-out-of-six burial on Sunday afternoon with another 6–3 loss and flew to Texas. O'Connell called Johnson early in the morning, boarded a plane, and sat down with him that noon. "We had to do something right then," O'Connell would later recall. "We probably should have done it earlier, but after all, Darrell had won the pennant the year before. I'd have loved to have brought in an experienced, name manager — a Weaver, Martin, Houk — but I didn't have time. I liked Zimmer, and he was the only person available." So, the next afternoon, O'Connell announced that Zimmer was the manager and Johnson was not.

Thus ended a curious career for Johnson. He won a pennant, which is more than any Red Sox manager since World War I except Joe Cronin and Dick Williams can say. He handled and laid out the pitching staff well in 1975, staying with his best starters — Luis Tiant, Rick Wise, Bill Lee — and using Dick Drago and Jim Willoughby in such a way that the Red Sox had a hot short reliever most of the season. He also had played an important role in the development of most of the young players that came through their farm system in the early 1970s, like Fisk, Burleson, Cooper, Ben Oglivie, Juan Beniquez, Rick Miller, John Curtis, Lynn McGlothen, and Rogelio Moret. Fisk and Curtis, for two, felt that he had been a major force in their step from double-A to major leagues, as an instructor, manager, and psychiatrist.

Fisk always said that Johnson was a different man in the major leagues. The pressure might have been part of it. Part of it might have been the fact that he was inarticulate, starting every answer off with clichés ("Well, Ray, as you and I both know"; "First of all . . .") that made him the butt of media jokes during the 1975 series. He certainly got carried away with his own importance in his first managerial season in 1974, constantly telling writers, "I'm a winning sonava-bitch."

Johnson was then a drinker, not any worse than a lot of baseball people, but because he managed between the strait-laced Eddie Kasko and Don Zimmer, his habits and the problems he had drinking — constant bickering with broadcaster Ned Martin, one time showing up at the park in Baltimore at 7:00 A.M., once arriving at Fenway with a black eye — stood out. He sometimes did bizarre things; when he "rested" Carl Yastrzemski and Dwight Evans and put Bob Montgomery at first and Beniquez in right in the opener of the big July series against the Yankees in late July 1975, Yawkey called O'Connell from his hotel room and wanted him to go down to Shea Stadium and have Johnson fired. Seven weeks earlier, he almost was fired, as after a poor homestand and two terrible beatings by the Texas Rangers in early June, the club was .500 and in the middle of the pack and off on a thirteen-game road trip that took them to such places as Kansas City, Detroit, and Baltimore. O'Connell had already contacted Tigers general manager Jim Campbell about the possibility of their letting Ralph Houk go at that time, but Campbell put them off. Former Indians manager Ken Aspromonte was called. But a series of circumstances rallied the players together. There was the infamous "Frankly, The Sox Are in Trouble" column by the *Globe*'s Bob Ryan, which suggested that Doug Griffin and Dwight Evans might not be stars and that Diego Segui and Reggie Cleveland should take a flight with Amelia Earhart. That column became the center of an antimedia rally led by broadcaster Ken Harrelson so strong that Petrocelli later said, "It was the single most important thing that turned us around." There was the release of the extremely popular backup catcher Tim McCarver, a move the players claimed was based on Johnson's fear that McCarver might get his job. Then, too, the talent of Lynn, Rice, Yastrzemski, et al. began coming through, and Griffin's "We're going to win this thing in spite of the manager" became the team's slogan. Whatever the cause, they won nine of thirteen on that trip, came home and beat the Yankees three out of four to move into first place on June 30, and went on to win the pennant.

When he had been Dick Williams's pitching coach in 1968 and '69, Johnson had been accused by the media of being something less than honest. The *Globe*'s Clif Keane was told by Jim Lonborg that Johnson had told the pitchers to lie to the press in response to medical questions, which Keane rightfully attacked. Darrell then didn't help himself on a Friday night in late August 1974 by insisting that the Red Sox had no interest in picking up McCarver (Fisk was out for the season) on waivers, then the next morning telling a writer who hadn't asked to tell "the guys" that they'd acquired McCarver. Three days later, in losing a Labor Day doubleheader in Baltimore 1–0, 1–0 in their collapse that took them from a seven-and-a-half-game lead to finishing eight games out in five weeks, Johnson explained that he hadn't played Tommy Harper against Mike Cuellar — whom Harper hit well — because Harper had a pulled hamstring. The next morning, Harper called a writer's hotel room. "If Darrell says he didn't play me because I'm hurt, he's a liar, because I'm one hundred percent healthy," Harper announced.

Griffin, for instance, learned that if he'd go in and demand to know why he wasn't playing, he could get himself back into the lineup because Johnson would want to appease him and keep controversy out of the newspapers. The Saturday they clinched the divisional championship on the last weekend of the '75 season, Yastrzemski went into Johnson's office and told him that since they weren't playing for a week, he was going to Boca Raton, Florida, for a few days. Johnson told him he couldn't go, that they had one more game, then they would be working out during the week. The next morning Griffin poked his head into the manager's office and said, "Yaz said to tell you he had to go to Florida — his back's bothering him."

What symbolized Johnson's distance from the players best

was what happened after they won the championship series in Oakland. While the players sprayed champagne and celebrated, Johnson looked in immediately after the game, gave a cursory "way to go, guys," and stepped into his office across the hallway, where he sat for two or three hours drinking beer with Rudi.

While the Reds were rolling up the best record in July 1976, right around the time the Red Sox tried to cure their own floundering by firing Johnson, significant history was unfurling. On July 12, three days after Tom Yawkey died, owners and players agreed in Philadelphia on a new union-management Basic Agreement, establishing the specific guidelines for the new free-agent system. Less than four weeks after that, Fisk, Burleson, and Lynn ended their holdouts, signed five-year contracts, and passed up the opportunities to see what they could do on the open market.

Yawkey's death was not a bolt out of the blue. He had been hospitalized for nearly two months, and had actually not been well since the night the Red Sox clinched the pennant in Oakland the previous October. There, he went off the wagon for the first time in more than a decade, sipping champagne from a Jack in the Box paper cup, and a week later was so sick that he had to watch the third, fourth, and fifth games of the World Series from his hotel suite in Cincinnati. The day he died, Dick O'Connell responded to questions about the future of the ball club by quoting Yawkey as saying, "I want to own the Red Sox until the day I die; then I'll decide what to do with them." No one knew exactly what would happen to the team or who would own it. Yawkey had provided only that it be run by his estate — the trust headed by Jean Yawkey, James Curran, and Joe LaCour — and eventually be sold to someone else. The immediate speculation centered on two principal parties: Yawkey's nephew Billy Gardner, who had owned their Louisville farm club until it folded in 1971 and was a long-time hunting buddy of Yastrzemski's; and O'Connell, who was thought to be able to assemble a group that would have included both Dominic and Joe DiMaggio and insurance man Bernard Baldwin. "It will be at least a year before there is any change," O'Connell said the night of Yawkey's death. "Things will pretty much be carried on as usual." It had been so long since New Englanders were accustomed to anything but the lavish, extravagant style of Yawkey that they assumed nothing would change. Other owners felt the same way; two weeks after Yawkey died, Calvin Griffith, in defending Bowie Kuhn's cancellation of the Rudi-Fingers-Blue sales, said, "Somehow the game has to be saved from the big-money teams like the Red Sox and Yankees buying up everyone in sight and buying — not building — pennants."

So when the Basic Agreement was signed three days after Yawkey's death and the Kapstein Connection of Lynn, Fisk, and Burleson agreed to their five-year deals weeks later, the public perception was that the Red Sox would continue to be run as Yawkey had run the club for years, buying whatever players were necessary (from Jimmie Foxx to Joe Rudi).

The Basic Agreement spelled out a clear new order of rules: that any player with six years' major-league experience could opt for free agency and put himself on the market, subject to selection by a maximum of twelve (after the 1977 expansion, thirteen) teams. The agreement was to take effect August 9, and players signed before that would still have the option year at the end of the contract; those signed afterward — hence under the new agreement — would not. The Red Sox rushed to get Fisk and Burleson signed on August 3, and after a few wrinkles, they signed Lynn one day before the deadline. Months later, it came out that Lynn received a staggering deal that included a signing bonus of $875,000 as part of a five-year total of $1.65 million, that Fisk received a total package of nearly $900,000 and Burleson $600,000. At that time, everything seemed normal.

"Now we can return to the business of getting back to the World Series where we belong," said Don Zimmer after the final signing. "This has been a screwed-up year, but, remember, after the Reds won the first time in 1970, it took a few refinements to make them the team they are." The feeling that the Red Sox were the next great team still prevailed. "At that point," Carl Yastrzemski would say in his final 1983 season, "I couldn't believe we wouldn't win at least two and possibly three or four world championships."

No one, not Yastrzemski, not even Kapstein or Players' Association director Marvin Miller, could foresee the spin cycle baseball would soon be in. Kapstein knew from the way Yankees owner George Steinbrenner had traded for and signed Ken Holtzman on the June 15 trading deadline and had hinted about Lynn and Burleson that some of the owners would trip over themselves trying to get players while giving up nothing but money. "However," Kapstein later admitted, "I really had no way of knowing where salaries would go. The game had operated under the old [take-it-or-leave-it] system of salary negotiations and its structure for so long, it was impossible to conceive of what would happen." Miller simply reiterated his famous line that the reserve system was "simply a means of protecting owners against themselves," and that he was "curious" to see what would ensue in a free-market system. What he didn't realize was that the salary arbitration he had won in lieu of free agency in 1972 and the minor clause in the 1976 Basic Agreement that allowed a player traded in the middle of a long-term contract to opt for free agency at the end of that season would both tie in to free agency to create such a spiral that the average major-league salary would multiply sixfold in the first seven years of the new system.

It took Zimmer nearly two months to restore what he felt was the discipline that had been lost both under Johnson and because of the diversities of the contracts, as well as the Oakland deal and Yawkey's death. He closed one era and tried beginning another by benching Rico Petrocelli and bringing up Butch Hobson to play third base, and by mid-September

Hobson had raised his average from the mid-.100s to .234. He
cracked down on rules he felt were being ignored, and rookie
left-handed pitcher Rick "Tall Boy" Jones was the one who
felt Zimmer's wrath first. Jones was a twenty-one-year-old
kid from Jacksonville who the season before had pitched in
Winston-Salem and Bristol, and when Johnson — on Zimmer's advice — kept him over seventh-game loser Jim Burton
at the end of spring training, he went north with the club to
Baltimore, claiming that the night's stay at the Holiday
Inn–Baltimore would be the occasion of his first ride in an
elevator. When he missed a curfew or two, management
blamed older players, particularly Willoughby and Bill Lee,
citing their wilder influences on this hayseed. But no one had
to lead Tall Boy — so named by Willoughby after the Schlitz
Tall Boy sixteen-ounce can and the fact that Jones was six-
foot-five — astray. His high school buddies were three members of the rock band Lynard Skynard; the band was named
after Leonard Skinner, their high school athletic director and
football coach, who had suspended Jones and the band members from the athletic program. By midseason Jones had
taken the injured Lee's place in the starting rotation, and the
day Lynn signed his contract, August 8, he was 4–1 and had
the staff's best earned run average at 2.84. That Sunday afternoon's game with the Brewers had been rained out, and
the club was scheduled to fly to California at 6:00 P.M. Jones
missed the flight. The next morning, he was spotted by one
club official walking through Kenmore Square, but when he
arrived in California, he called Zimmer to tell him he had
gone home to Florida to visit his sick father. To compound
his problem, he arrived in Anaheim Monday night, left Zimmer a note, then missed curfew. When, on Thursday night,
he called Zimmer in the dugout in the third inning of the
game with the Angels and told him he was delayed because
he was on the phone with his father, Zimmer sent him to
Pawtucket. Tall Boy unfortunately was ahead of his time as
far as getting himself into trouble, and while he would return

in September for a brief stay before going to Seattle in the expansion draft, he threw away what appeared to be a promising career. The Red Sox were ahead of their time as far as being concerned about the use of drugs, for that September they put private detectives on the road with the team for two road trips.

Under Zimmer, they managed to win fifteen of their last eighteen games, which fanned the flames of optimism. Rice came out of his four-month struggle around .250 to finish the year with an eighteen-game hitting streak, Luis Tiant streaked to finish 21–12, and with Hobson's finish and the promise that the contractual problems were behind Lynn, Fisk, and Burleson, they took their record 1,895,846 attendance and set off toward replacing the Reds as baseball's premier team. When the first free-agent draft was held at the Plaza Hotel in New York November 4, the Red Sox and Yankees were the most visible presences. John Claiborne announced their first selection as Minnesota relief pitcher Bill Campbell, and within ten hours had created history. Claiborne went upstairs with Campbell and his agent LaRue Harcourt, swapped figures and concepts, and by 10:00 P.M. had reached an agreement that made Campbell not only the first player signed through the new system but the first instant millionaire, as his five-year deal was worth $1,050,000. "Honestly, I couldn't believe what was happening," said Campbell. "A million dollars? No one's worth that, but if they want to pay me, I'm certainly not going to turn it down."

Campbell had refused to sign with the Twins when owner Calvin Griffith refused to budge from his offer of $22,000 toward Campbell's request for $27,000. Griffith immediately screamed when Claiborne signed the ace reliever so quickly, and so did others, including Baltimore general manager Hank Peters and Haywood Sullivan from within Fenway Park's own walls. Sullivan felt that the Lynn-Fisk-Burleson deals and the Campbell signing did as much as any other club's ac-

Final American League Standings and Red Sox Statistics, 1976

	W	L	PCT	GB	R	HR	BA
EAST							
NY	97	62	.610		730	120	.269
BAL	88	74	.543	10.5	619	119	.243
BOS	83	79	.512	15.5	716	134	.263
CLE	81	78	.509	16	615	85	.263
DET	74	87	.460	24	609	101	.257
MIL	66	95	.410	32	570	88	.246
WEST							
KC	90	72	.556		713	65	.269
OAK	87	74	.540	2.5	686	113	.246
MIN	85	77	.525	5	743	81	.274
CAL	76	86	.469	14	550	63	.235
TEX	76	86	.469	14	616	80	.250
CHI	64	97	.398	25.5	586	73	.255
LEAGUE TOTAL					7753	1122	.256

MANAGER	W	L	PCT
Darrell Johnson	41	45	.477
Don Zimmer	42	34	.553

POS	PLAYER	B	G	AB	H	2B	3B	HR	R	RBI	BA
REGULARS											
1B	Carl Yastrzemski	L	155	546	146	23	2	21	71	102	.267
2B	Denny Doyle	L	117	432	108	15	5	0	51	26	.250
SS	Rick Burleson	R	152	540	157	27	1	7	75	42	.291
3B	Butch Hobson	R	76	269	63	7	5	8	34	34	.234
RF	Dwight Evans	R	146	501	121	34	5	17	61	62	.242
CF	Fred Lynn	L	132	507	159	32	8	10	76	65	.314
LF	Jim Rice	R	153	581	164	25	8	25	75	85	.282
C	Carlton Fisk	R	134	487	124	17	5	17	76	58	.255
DH	Cecil Cooper	L	123	451	127	22	6	15	66	78	.282
SUBSTITUTES											
3B	Rico Petrocelli	R	85	240	51	7	1	3	17	24	.213
UT	Steve Dillard	R	57	167	46	14	0	1	22	15	.275
2B	Doug Griffin	R	49	127	24	2	0	0	14	4	.189
DO	Bobby Darwin	R	43	106	19	5	2	3	9	13	.179
3S	Bob Heise	R	32	56	15	2	0	0	5	5	.268
DH	Bernie Carbo	L	17	55	13	4	0	2	5	6	.236
1B	Jack Baker	R	12	23	3	0	0	1	1	2	.130
OF	Rick Miller	L	105	269	76	15	3	0	40	27	.283
OF	Deron Johnson	R	15	38	5	1	1	0	3	0	.132
C	Bob Montgomery	R	31	93	23	3	1	3	10	13	.247
C	Ernie Whitt	L	8	18	4	2	0	1	4	3	.222
C	Andy Merchant	L	2	2	0	0	0	0	0	0	.000

Final American League Standings and Red Sox Statistics, 1976, continued

PITCHER	T	W	L	PCT	ERA	SV
Luis Tiant	R	21	12	.636	3.06	0
Rick Wise	R	14	11	.560	3.54	0
Ferguson Jenkins	R	12	11	.522	3.27	0
Reggie Cleveland	R	10	9	.526	3.07	2
Dick Pole	R	6	5	.545	4.31	0
Rick Jones	L	5	3	.625	3.38	0
Jim Willoughby	R	3	12	.200	2.82	10
Bill Lee	L	5	7	.417	5.63	3
Tom Murphy	R	4	5	.444	3.44	8
Tom House	L	1	3	.250	4.30	4
Rick Kreuger	L	2	1	.667	4.06	0
TEAM TOTAL		83	79	.512	3.52	27

tions to accelerate the inflationary spiral, and at that point Sullivan helped get the ear of the Yawkey Estate in putting a hold on the expenditures of the O'Connell administration. O'Connell had authorized the Campbell signing without checking with the operating ownership, and when Claiborne set off in pursuit of their allotted second free agent — either second baseman Bobby Grich or pitcher Don Gullett — the message came abruptly to O'Connell that there were to be no more signings. In the next year, O'Connell and Claiborne would be stopped from making a number of deals involving cash outflow. In 1977 spring training, they had a deal with Oakland that would have sent Rick Wise for Mike Torrez, and Claiborne even worked out the contractual agreement with agent Gary Walker for five years in the vicinity of $1 million. It was vetoed, Torrez ended up with the Yankees for three players, and signed at the end of the season with Sullivan and the eventual new ownership for $2.7 million. Claiborne reached an agreement with Rice's agent Tony Pennacchia on a ten-year, $2 million deal that was similarly vetoed; Rice signed in 1979 for $4.9 million.

But that all reflected an internal struggle involving a front office that had the politics of Boston's City Hall. As far as the public was concerned, the Red Sox were on their way back. In December, they made their big off-season deal, reacquiring George Scott and Carbo from the Brewers for Cecil Cooper. Cooper never had found favor in Boston, not with Eddie Kasko, not with Darrell Johnson, not with Zimmer. Johnson was so down on him in June 1975 that he told Tigers manager Ralph Houk he could have him at the end of the season, and, of course, it was Cooper who was to be benched after Rudi was acquired. Zimmer thought so little of him that he bet minor-league manager Joe Morgan that Cooper wouldn't hit .270 in Milwaukee. And, Zimmer rationalized, they needed right-handed power. Hobson wasn't proven, Rice hadn't quite emerged as a superstar, Fisk was coming off a mediocre (.255, 17 home runs, 58 RBIs) season, and good left-handers were eating them alive. Scott, who'd won two home-run titles for the Brewers after being traded by the Red Sox at the end of the 1971 season, would be the panacea.

"Scott," predicted Claiborne, "will do for us what Reggie Jackson will do for the Yankees. The acquisitions offset one another." It didn't quite work out that way. Though the horrible stumblings of the 1976 season would not be repeated, the next couple of seasons had new things to teach the Red Sox about frustration.

FIVE

1977

THE CRUNCH BUNCH

Boston sets home-run records and returns (for a while) to the top of the standings, finally finishing just behind the hated Yankees.

*C*HARLESTOWN sits on the New Hampshire side of the Connecticut River, up where the Connecticut is just getting started. It is a *New Yorker* cover of a New England town, with the white tower of the Congregational church augmenting the village green and the people's center of gravity. Charlestown has had to struggle to keep its thousand residents, but it's done so; they drive the twenty-five-mile commute to Keene, or farther down the river to Brattleboro, Vermont. For generations going back to the Allen brothers and their land granters who settled the valley, they have had to be hard, self-sufficient people. Carlton Fisk remembers one of the old-timers in Charlestown telling the story of how a guy with New York plates pulled through town ("probably trying to finding Woodstock"), rolled down the window, and asked an old-timer if he knew how to get across the river and over to Route 5. "Yup," answered the old-timer and kept on walking.

The Red Sox are not the Boston Red Sox. They are the

Olde Towne Teame because they are sport's first and fore-most regional franchise, the *New England* Red Sox, for whom winning and losing involves a kind of chauvinism that has its roots in the traditions of town team baseball that began in the 1860s and '70s. That New Englanders are such traditionalists is part of the reason that the Townies occupy so much of the lives of small-town New England, as they did even in the days of Speaker or Williams. Part of it may be that there are so few other complications in the people's lives — no theater, no concerts, no lectures, no anti-nuke demonstrations. But as one drives the back roads of northern New England and slides across the radio dial, one small station after another fades in and out with Red Sox baseball, stations that for gen-erations have made Curt Gowdy, Martin and Woods, and now Ken Coleman voices as familiar as those of the ministers at the Congregational and Episcopal churches. Up the road some fifteen miles from Charlestown is Claremont, and it has a station that broadcasts the Red Sox games. Across the wooden bridge and ten miles into Vermont is Springfield, and you can get the games on that town's station, and during the day the stations in Keene and Brattleboro come in with them.

Charlestown is how Carlton Fisk grew up, with his father Cecil and mother Leona listening to Gowdy and Martin. She grew up in Minnesota and was later a star woman on a men's softball team in Charlestown. Motivation was a dominant force in the family, as one brother and one sister are Ph.D.'s, younger sister Janet (who married teammate Rick Miller) was a championship athlete, and Carlton, the third of the six chil-dren, was about the best athlete the state ever had. In bas-ketball, as a six-foot-one sophomore, he had forty points and thirty-six rebounds in a state tournament game against Con-toocook and six-ten Craig Corson (who was good enough to play at the University of North Carolina), and when they lost by one point, all Cecil told his kid was "You missed four free throws." He was good enough in basketball to get a scholar-ship to the University of New Hampshire and lead the freshman team to its best record in the school's history, but all along he was going to play baseball. He had starred as a pitcher and shortstop for Charlestown High School and the Keene American Legion team, and when the late Red Sox scout Jack Burns went up to see him catch on the Legion team, he said, "The kid was raw, didn't catch too well — but he had a great arm. He had good hands in the infield and tremendous power. They kept showing me places where he'd hit balls out beyond the field." By the time the January 1967 draft came around, there was no question in anyone's mind that he was going to be the Red Sox catcher. "The family had made it very clear that he'd play for one team and one team only," said veteran Orioles scout Frank McGowan, who'd selected Fisk on a lark when he graduated from high school in 1965. "All the other clubs just sort of stepped out of the way and let the Red Sox take him, as if it were one of those regional selections." After a year in the service, Fisk was hitting .338 in Waterloo, Iowa, and the following spring training opened Dick Williams's eyes "because he wasn't afraid to go tell off the pitchers."

In the hearts and minds of New Englanders, Fisk was "one of us." He wasn't afraid to say what was on his mind, no matter how much trouble it got him into. He stood up for what he believed in and fought for it; no modern catcher was in as many home-plate fights as Fisk, with players such as California's Alan Gallagher and Frank Robinson and the Yankees' Thurman Munson, Gene Michael, and Lou Piniella. He was stubborn, and bristled at what he felt was "open questioning of the roots from whence I came" (one of his favorite expressions), which led to sorties with managers Darrell Johnson, Don Zimmer, and Tony LaRussa, as well as Red Sox owner–general manager Haywood Sullivan. He came from a place where one's word is good enough, where they don't have lawyers, and so when, in 1976, he and Jerry Kapstein were told, "If anyone else renegotiates, you can renegotiate," and then when Sullivan effectively renegotiated Rice's contract and told Fisk, "Show me in writing where you were told you could renegotiate," the final blow to a strained relationship had been struck, a bastinado that ended in a bitter parting in 1980.

Fisk was the kind of small-town New Englander who abhors New York and all it symbolizes. "There are more people on that block than there are in Charlestown," he once marveled during a cab ride up Madison Avenue through the 130s en route to Yankee Stadium. "And more rats and pollution on that block than in the whole state of New Hampshire." If there is one common strain among Red Sox fans, it is hatred of the Yankees, an Athens-Sparta rivalry (in their eyes) that has been carried on for nearly a century. No Red Sox player of his era carried the gauntlet of hatred for the Yankees more than Fisk: from the night in September 1971, when in full catching array he beat Munson down the line for a — rarest of rare — 3–6–2 double play, to the fights, to the "Fisk Eats Rice" T-shirts that sold by the thousands outside The Stadium, to angry New Yorkers smashing in his window on the team bus outside the ballpark in 1976.

No player better exemplified the Red Sox era, from the rebirth of the Boston farm system that began with his arrival in September 1971 with Kasko's Kiddie Corps. As a rookie in 1972, he nearly led them to the Eastern Division title; then, when they got into first place for the first time in 1974, it was his severe knee injury at the end of June that eventuated their downfall. His return in June 1975 coincided with their explosion that pulled away from the Yankees and made that year so glorious right down to his memorable home run in the Sixth Game. He was one of the three members of the Kapstein Connection involved in the long, much publicized holdout in 1976; then it was he who for all of 1977 until he broke down physically in August 1978 enjoyed the finest one and two-thirds seasons of his career — like the team.

When in March 1981 he signed as a free agent with the Chicago White Sox, that signaled the end of the era, an end dramatized that Opening Day by his returning in one of those sailor-boy White Sox uniforms wearing the number 72 and hitting an eighth-inning homer to beat his former teammates.

Despite his raw skills graced by movie star looks, it wasn't easy for Fisk. Once he got beyond the Midwest League and got to double-A and his first confrontation with breaking balls, he struggled through two horrid years. He batted .243 in 1969 in Pittsfield, and the next year found himself back in double-A, this time in Pawtucket, and slid all the way to .229. "I found out," he said, "why so few hitters ever come out of northern New England. You get a few pitchers, and an occasional glove man like Mark Belanger, but it's pretty tough going into professional baseball when most of the guys you're playing against had more games in one year than I played in my entire life." But in Louisville in 1971, he met and became close to Darrell Johnson, whom he credited with teaching him about calling games and applying himself to every game. A shoulder he separated in a home-plate collision limited his average to .263, but he hit .313 that September and in 1972 was the American League Rookie of the Year. It never was easy, because even as a kid, he didn't know how to pace himself and fought a losing battle to retain weight. In 1973, he started spring training at 218 pounds and finished the season at 191, and in the process saw his average swoon from .320 in June to .246.

Fisk had his detractors. It was his nature to be slow, be it dressing, getting up in the morning, or walking out to the mound. It got so that in 1980, his last year with the Red Sox, their times of game were the longest in the league; in 1981, '82, and '83 the White Sox played the longest or second-longest games in the league. Red Sox traveling secretary Jack Rogers used to announce bus departure five or ten minutes earlier than he intended just to get Fisk on board on time. Some pitchers, notably Dennis Eckersley, felt that Fisk's slowness and frequent trips to the mound destroyed the natural rhythm they needed to pitch. Fisk and Lee used to have public shouting matches on the mound, both over Fisk's penchant for strolling to the mound and over pitch selection.

What probably got Fisk in the most trouble was his bluntness. Ask him a question and he answered it. "I'd grown up being taught to be honest and forthright." In July of his rookie season, making a personal appearance in western Massachusetts, when someone asked him about the leadership of Carl Yastrzemski and Reggie Smith, Fisk said they weren't providing any leadership. "How was I to know that some off-hand remark would end up in headlines?" he later asked. The next day he was in Eddie Kasko's office, explaining to Yastrzemski and Smith what he'd said. When Kasko was fired and Smith traded at the end of the 1973 season, he infuriated Kasko supporters by publicly stating that he thought it was for the best because Kasko was "aloof" from some of the younger players, and added that "the loss of Reggie's bat will be outweighed by the loss of anxiety and disrupture that Reggie occasioned." That, in turn, resulted in tirades from Smith, who before a St. Patrick's Day spring-training game in St. Petersburg the next year called Fisk a "backstabber and a crybaby" in an emotional outburst that stunned his new teammates. It was in that game that Fisk took the foul tip in the testicles, and as Fisk writhed on the ground, Smith began shouting at him so wildly in the dugout ("I hope you die, you ——er") that one veteran Cardinal told him to calm down and be quiet.

He upset American League officials after the 1973 All-Star Game by admitting that California's Bill Singer had thrown Pete Rose a spitter. After his knee surgery, he accused the Red Sox medical staff in the winter of 1974–75 of failing to provide him with even a skeleton rehabilitation program. "They could have at least given me some idea of what to do," Fisk said. "Everything I did, I did on my own, so it's a miracle that I came back." He spoke his piece during the 1976 contractual battle, and in November 1977, when controversy was swirling around the attempted purchase of the club by Buddy LeRoux and Haywood Sullivan, Fisk came right out and not only criticized their selections in the free-agent draft but said that the unsettled ownership situation could have an adverse effect on the players. "I'm concerned about the involvement of the bank because of the clause in the loan which puts a ceiling on the raises a player could get," Fisk told the *Herald American*'s Bill Liston. So when he also openly questioned the dumping of Ferguson Jenkins, Bill Lee, and Luis Tiant in the next twelve months, the sensitive Sullivan was already enraged by the time Fisk confronted him about the Rice negotiation and an offhand Sullivan remark that "Rice's contract is bothering him more than his elbow" when he couldn't throw during 1979 spring training. Fisk didn't whimper after Sullivan's comments hit the papers; he charged into Sullivan's Winter Haven office, slammed the door, and offered to have it out. Sullivan called a press conference and apologized.

He was never afraid of fights. On August 1, 1973, with the Yankees and Red Sox tied for first place and tied 2–2 in the ninth inning with Munson on third, Felipe Alou on first, Gene Michael batting, and one out, New York manager Ralph Houk attempted a suicide squeeze. Michael missed the John Curtis pitch but tried to get in Fisk's way as he stepped forward to tag Munson. Fisk brushed Michael aside with one swipe of his left arm, then absorbed Munson's kamikaze cross-body block. When Munson lay on top of Fisk (with Alou rounding second), Fisk kicked him off to look for the remaining runner and the two bitter rivals started throwing punches. Michael jumped Fisk from behind, and they went to the bottom of the pile, but Fisk managed to pin Michael's neck to the ground with one arm and flail away at Munson, also on the ground, with his right fist. Houk had to crawl underneath the pile to pull Fisk's elbow off Michael's throat and restore breathing.

Fisk fought Alan Gallagher after a home-plate collision,

and he got into it with Frank Robinson over a Bob Bolin
brushback pitch before starting the famous May 1976 New
York brawl with Piniella in which Lee separated his shoulder.
"He's the most disliked player in the league because of the
way he struts that walk and the way he won't give in to anyone," said Robinson. Munson's dislike ran deeper. Munson
was short, almost dumpy, dirty, and hardly a model; Fisk was
tall, clean, angular, and patrician. Munson was just getting
his due when Fisk arrived and was an instant all-star. Fisk
had beaten him down the line on the double play in September 1971 to ignite the feud; then Munson later said, "He
never talks to anyone behind the plate." To that, Fisk replied, "Aren't I supposed to want to beat whoever's at the
plate?" Fisk openly talked about pitchers throwing inside to
opposing hitters, then never said anything when he got
drilled enough to lead the league. It's worth noting that aside
from leading in triples in his rookie year, being hit by pitches
is the only offensive category in which Fisk has ever led the
league.

That is a statement about Fisk's career. Through 1983 he
had driven in more than a hundred runs once, more than seventy-one only three times. He batted .300 over a full season
once, and scored more than ninety runs twice. He wasn't a
Bench, and he might not have been a Munson, either. Injuries
and background had something to do with that, for it wasn't
until 1977 that something wasn't in the way: the loss of
twenty-seven pounds, the knee, the arm, the contract. In

Catchers with 100 Runs Scored and 100 RBIs

CATCHER, YEAR	TEAM	BA	R	HR	RBI
Johnny Bench, 1974	Cinn.	.280	108	33	129
Yogi Berra, 1950	Yankees	.322	116	28	124
Roy Campanella, 1953	Brooklyn	.312	103	41	142
Mickey Cochrane, 1932	A's	.293	118	24	112
Carlton Fisk, 1977	Boston	.315	106	26	102
Darrell Porter, 1979	K.C.	.291	101	20	112

1977, he became one of six catchers (Mickey Cochrane, Yogi Berra, Roy Campanella, Bench, and Darrell Porter were the others) to ever score and drive in one hundred runs while batting .300 in the same season, and he was on his way to another .300–100–100 year in 1978 when he cracked his ribs; he was hitting .301 on August 1, and, in hitting .255 the last two months as he blew out, finished at .284 with eighty-eight RBIs and ninety-four runs scored. From that August, when he was hurt and playing every day because "my name was in the lineup," he was never the same. Neither were the Red Sox.

When, at the end of the 1982 season, the fans overwhelmingly voted him the catcher on the Red Sox all-time team, it wasn't so much that he'd run up the kind of numbers Bench accumulated, although the only American League catcher to hit more home runs was Yogi Berra. Carlton Fisk, of the Charlestown Fisks, was one of them, and when they reached their emotional peak in October 1975, it was he who brought them to their feet, madly. When they reached their wild, crazy, home-run and attendance peak in 1977 and 1978, it was Fisk — next to Rice — who was their best player. And when the dream turned sour, it was Fisk who said, "The direction is hopeless," and left.

No season had been more pure, unadulterated fun than 1977. "We were a team of extremes," Zimmer lamented at the end, for it was the extremes that caused the Red Sox to finish tied for second place with Baltimore, two and a half games behind the Yankees. But it was the extremes — indulgent, wild, simple home run–or–nothing extremes — that made this team so enjoyable. They could go through a stretch in which they hit 33 home runs in ten games, beat the Yankees and the Orioles seven straight, then turn around, get swept in Yankee Stadium, and go on a nine-game losing streak that took them from five games in front to one game behind. They could win eleven in a row on the West Coast, then turn around and fall out of first place by losing seven in succession. They not only hit 33 homers in ten games, but

they hit five or more in one game eight times; one day against
the poor expansion Blue Jays they hit eight in one game —
and struggled to win 9–6. They had three players with 30 or
more homers (Rice, 39; George Scott, 33; Butch Hobson, 30)
and two more with more than 25 (Yastrzemski, 28; Fisk, 26),
but not one starting pitcher won as many as the thirteen
games won by reliever Bill Campbell. At the age of thirty-
eight, Yastrzemski hit .296, knocked in 102 runs, played left
field so well that not only did he not commit an error, but he
led the league in assists, and to top it all off, he stole eleven
bases and was thrown out but once. Yet the epitaph for
the season may have come from two left-handed relievers'
lines:

   Ramon Hernandez: Walk, balk, walk, single, L. 0–1.
   Rick Kreuger: Four pitches — 0 2 2 2 0 0, L. 0–1.

   The season opened with a banner hanging atop the center-
field bleachers that read, "SELL CAMPBELL, BRING BACK
$1.50 BLEACHERS." That was the last strain of romanticism
for the purists who frequented the purist ballpark. They had
demonstrated against the installment of the electronic megaboard the previous April, as well as the advertising that went
with it. The 1975 World Series had shown what baseball can
be at its pure best, but after 1975, the flow of both players
and dollars was no longer in the hands of the owners. No
longer was it as easy as writing down forty names on a yellow
legal pad, then swapping names around and making trades.
In 1975, sure, people made money, but it was still a game. By
1976, it was evidently a business, and if the megaboard was
good for $500,000 in revenue as well as an entertainment
factor, then it was a good investment. Tom Yawkey never
had to think that way, but Tom Yawkey had owned the Olde
Towne Teame in another era. The free-agent bidding wars
and detailed reports of contracts helped fan baseball enthusiasm — first, because it kept baseball in the news all winter
for the first time, second, because, as lawyer-agent Arthur
Kaminsky pointed out, "Americans are fascinated by money.

They love to see and hear the figures these guys sign for, then try to translate those figures into dollars per hit and things like that. Reggie Jackson was always a *star*, but if he hadn't been the *highest-paid* star in New York, he'd never have been the name he became."

The fans who put up the "SELL CAMPBELL" sign weren't opposed to Campbell. They just didn't like the cold, hard reality that went into the signing/price equation. Perhaps there was a perception that despite the forty-three years of the Yawkey bankroll, Boston would never be able to wholly compete with the big-money cities. New Yorkers, Texans, and Los Angeles types bought what they wanted; New Englanders don't deal in such crass values. Maybe the fans saw the weakening of baseball's centrifugal forces, longed for the order that existed before arbitrator Peter Seitz invalidated the reserve clause on December 23, 1975 (which all current players should annually honor as their own Bastille Day). But on Opening Day 1977 there was a curious edge of expectation and bitterness. "Everyone in the starting lineup is making a hundred thousand dollars, the fans know it, and I guess we're going to see fans take a produce-or-else posture towards us," observed Yastrzemski. "There was a funny feeling out there, one I've never felt before." When Campbell lost a 4–2 lead in the ninth by giving up a two-run homer to Cleveland's Buddy Bell and the Red Sox lost 5–4 in the eleventh, the booing turned vulgar, and when Campbell and a cast of others gave up thirteen runs in the eighth inning of a 19–9 loss the following day, the crowd got very ugly.

Fans forgive and they forget, and the Red Sox went on to break their season attendance record by putting 2,074,549 into Fenway. Fans love home runs. And just as kids got out of school and the summer began, the Red Sox went off on one of the most tempestuous home-run tears in baseball history: thirty-three in ten games, including sixteen in a three-game series against the Yankees, which in turn included four in one inning off Catfish Hunter. It began on June 14, in Fenway, against the White Sox, when George Scott belted a 430-foot shot into the center-field bleachers. Two pitches later, Bernardo Carbo lined another one over The Wall, and in the eighth inning Scott iced the 7–1 victory with another three-run blast. The next day Scott and Rice each hit his fifteenth of the season, but Boston's six-game winning streak ended with a 7–3 loss to the White Sox. Enter the Yankees and . . .

June 17. Burleson led off the bottom of the first inning against Hunter with a line drive into the screen. Lynn followed Burleson and sent a towering drive beyond the Red Sox bullpen into the bleachers. Two outs later, Fisk cleared The Wall, the screen, and perhaps even the Charles with a moonshot of his own, and no sooner had Billy Martin returned to the dugout from trying to reassure the great right-hander than Scott hit the next pitch out. By the time the game was over, not only had Fisk hit another and Yastrzemski the sixth Boston homer of the day, but the Boston starter — in this case, Lee — hadn't been able to get through the third with the initial four-run lead, so Bob Stanley and Campbell had to work six and two-thirds innings for the 9–4 win.

June 18. The Yankees got two runs in the top of the first off Reggie Cleveland. In the bottom of the inning, Burleson singled, Lynn singled, and after a ground-out, Yastrzemski jumped on a Mike Torrez fastball and sent it screaming into the center-field bleachers for a 3–2 lead. This day's total would be five homers — another by Yaz, two by Carbo, and Scott's seventeenth — but it would also be remembered by a national television audience as the day Martin yanked Jackson out of right field for misplaying Rice's sixth-inning fly, which resulted in the two having to be separated in the dugout. To win 10–4, Campbell had to pitch another three and two-thirds innings.

June 19. In the fourth inning of a 1–1 tie, Denny Doyle — who hit as many homers in his career as the Red Sox would on this weekend — hit a three-run homer into the Boston bullpen off Ed Figueroa. Soon thereafter, Carbo hit his third screen job in two days, Scott hit another into the center-field bleachers, Yastrzemski and Rice made it five for the day, and Ferguson Jenkins had an easy 11–1 romp for the sweep. In the three games, the Red Sox slugged .917, outscored the Yankees 30–9, outhomered them 16–0, and had ninety-nine total bases to New York's thirty-five. Not only that, but they went from half a game behind the Yankees to two and a half games in front as they blew Baltimore away.

June 20, Baltimore. As Rick Wise pitched a two-hitter, Hobson kept the streak alive with an eighth-inning homer to dead center off Rudy May to cap off a 4–0 victory.

June 21, Baltimore. Tiant followed Wise's two-hitter with a two-hit shutout of his own, but after Rice broke a scoreless tie in the fourth with a rising shot to left-center and an out later Scott hit a two-run job off Dennis Martinez, it was the ninth-inning pitch with which Martinez hit Scott that caused the furor of this game. Scott took off for the mound and chased Martinez into the outfield (and, it turned out, right out of the game). Needless to say, Scott never caught the Baltimore pitcher, which prompted Bob Ryan to suggest in the *Globe* that the Boomer be saved for short-yardage situations.

June 22, Baltimore. They had hit four homers off Jim Palmer in Fenway June 9, then hit four in one inning off Hunter on the 17th. Palmer went into the seventh this night with a 4–1 lead when Rice and Fisk cut it to 4–3 with solo homers. Then in the ninth, after Rice led off with a double and Yastrzemski popped up, Fisk launched another fly ball to the left-field fence. "The Reverend" Pat Kelly leaped and could have caught the ball, but it hit the heel rather than the pocket of the glove and deflected over the fence for a three-run homer. Before the inning was over, Palmer, who'd never allowed more than three home runs in a game prior to his Fenway engagement June 9, served up his fifth of the night to Butch Hobson, and the Red Sox won 7–4. Scott's solo blast in the second made him the first player in the majors to reach the twenty plateau. Buried beneath the headlines created by this remarkable binge was the news that Dwight Evans — who was leading the team in homers with thirteen when he suffered a pulled hamstring on May 22 — had torn cartilage in his right knee, needed an operation, and would probably be out the remainder of the season. It didn't seem important then, but it would at season's end — the Red Sox got their regular lineup on the field for only three games the entire rest of the season.

June 23, Baltimore. The *Globe* headline the next morning read, "SOX HIT 'ONLY' 1 HOMER—WIN 7TH STRAIGHT 7–3." Only one homer, a Butch Hobson drive over the center-field fence off Mike Flanagan for a 1–1 tie in the second. As his teammates completed the four-game sweep in Memorial Stadium, with nine homers, thirty-seven hits, and twenty-five runs, Ferguson Jenkins pitched a six-hitter. As it turned out, this was the last win Jenkins would get in a Boston uniform against a .500 team, and the next time the Red Sox were in Memorial Stadium, Jenkins would be involved in the infamous bullpen nap that got him given back to the Rangers. No one saw ahead then, however; all they saw were the Yankees and Orioles in the rearview mirror, five and six and a half games behind, respectively.

The last night of the home-run tirade was the next night, June 24, in Yankee Stadium. It would eventually turn out to be the most important game of the season, but for then, it seemed nothing but a little blood returning to the Yankees' face. Yastrzemski and Hobson homered in the second off Hunter, and when Scott hit his twenty-first off Catfish in the fourth, it seemed that the 5–3 lead would be enough. Campbell was rushed in to start the sixth and held the lead until there were two out and none on in the bottom of the ninth, when Willie Randolph hit a triple that Yastrzemski overran in left. Roy White then homered to tie the game, and when

The 1977 Red Sox in Perspective

Most Home Runs by One Team in One Season

	TEAM	YEAR	HR
1.	New York (AL)	1961	240
2.	Minnesota	1963	235
3.	New York (NL)	1947	221
	Cincinnati	1956	221
	Minnesota	1964	221
6.	Milwaukee	1982	216
7.	Boston	1977	213

Highest Team Slugging Percentages

	TEAM	YEAR	SP
1.	New York (AL)	1927	.489
2.	New York (AL)	1930	.488
3.	New York (AL)	1936	.483
4.	Chicago (NL)	1930	.481
5.	Brooklyn	1953	.474
6.	New York (NL)	1930	.471
7.	St. Louis (NL)	1930	.471
8.	Philadelphia (NL)	1929	.467
9.	Boston	1977	.465

Campbell finally gave out from the exhaustion of five innings' work, Zimmer turned to Hernandez.

No one knew how old Ramon Hernandez really was. Some said forty-five, some thirty-nine. Zimmer had once kicked him off his club in winter ball with a final shout — "Take your guns and knives and get the hell outta here" — but he'd also seen the sidearming left-hander get some left-handed hitters out in the National League. Zimmer had gone through Jim Burton and Tom House, and in late May decided to chance that Hernandez could trick a few batters the first time around and dealt Bobby Darwin to the Cubs for him. The worth of that gamble was summed up by walk/balk/

walk/single of his eleventh-inning entrance in this game. He faced three left-handed batters, walking Graig Nettles on four pitches, balking him to second, walking Mickey Rivers intentionally on four pitches, and giving up the game-ending single to Jackson on the first pitch. Eight balls, one balk, two walks, one strike, one base hit; Yankees, 6, Red Sox, 5. The Yankees won the next day 5–1, won Sunday 5–4, and were right back in the race while the Red Sox were off and running on a nine-game losing streak that took them from five games up to a game back.

There were close to a hundred home-run records that the Red Sox pursued in that voyage into space. Rice went thirty-one for fifty-seven in a fourteen-game stretch, Hobson hit five homers in six days, and Carbo hit the screen three times in six at-bats. But no one personified the home run–or–nothing style of this team more than Scott. The Boomer was, in reality, a tragic figure. He came to the big leagues in 1966 with magnificently instinctive talent. He knew the game, and between his hands, range, and instincts played first base better than any man of his generation. But the Boomer had to be a showoff, with his gold teeth (one had a gold "B" for Boomer) and shopping sprees. He had to go out and, as he once did in Seattle, buy $5500 worth of suits, or buy each new Cadillac model as it came out. Before he turned forty, Scott would be managing in Mexico, in the off-season hanging around Boston trying to sell his Cadillac and begging people at the ballpark for a job. Boomer wasn't smart. Dick Williams once said, "Talking to Scott is like talking to a cement wall," but while that was exaggerated, Boomer's failure to listen to anyone caused him to hit .171 in 1968 (and then go in and demand a raise). Weight had always been a problem for him, and by 1977 he'd steadfastly refused to listen to those who warned him that he was eating himself out of the game; Clif Keane and Larry Claflin, two former newspapermen who had the popular "Clif 'n' Claf" radio show on the Red Sox flagship station, had nightly roasted Scott for what Keane claimed was "devouring buckets of chicken wings" in spring training, a roasting that would continue as Scott made twenty-four errors, 50 percent more than any other first baseman in the league. All the noise about his waistline caused Scott to stop talking to the media; instead he sat in front of a tableful of salad each night in full view of the media, although that didn't last long. Boomer loved to talk, although understanding him was another matter. He had a high, squeaky voice, and interjected "muddafukka" every third or fourth word.

As the Red Sox went into the eighth game of the nine-game losing streak in early July, Scott told reporters, "We may be down now, but we'll bounce up off the campus." When he hit two line drives to the second baseman, he said, "I gotta get more muddafukka attitude on the ball so I get it into the air and outta the park." Frank Robinson likes to tell the story that in Puerto Rico in January 1969, he and Orioles catcher Elrod Hendricks were discussing the plight of Biafra at the batting cage. "What do you think of Biafra?" Hendricks asked Boomer.

"I've never faced the muddafukka," replied Scott, "but by the third time up, I'll hit a tater off him."

He loved being the star, telling reporters, "The Red Sox traded Babe Ruth, too," when he was sent to Milwaukee in a ten-player deal for Tommy Harper and Marty Pattin in October 1971. He once told teammates in winter ball that "if it hadn't been for muddafukka Luis Aparicio, I'd have had three thousand hits"; that means Aparicio robbed Scott of 1008 hits. In 1974, Brewers manager Del Crandall listed him seventh in the batting order one day at Fenway; Scott refused to play, saying, "Superstars don't bat seventh," and when Crandall fined him $1000, Scott filed a grievance with the Players' Association and won back the money. In September 1977, Zimmer put him seventh in the order for the second game of a twinighter in Toronto because he was slumping. Scott walked into the manager's office and announced, "Skip, I'm not mentally prepared to play," so Zimmer had to scratch his name. The next day, Scott admitted that he wasn't "mentally prepared" because "a player of my stature can't concentrate batting so low in the order." It wasn't until 1979, after a disastrous .233 season in 1978 that made him the target of the harshest boo-words, that he finally lost weight, but it was too late. After a deceiving .420 spring training, he couldn't get his thirty-seven-ounce bat around on fastballs, and when Zimmer benched him in May, Scott first said, "What he should do when a man's struggling is to put him in the cleanup spot so he'll get better pitches to hit," then demanded to be traded. In Texas, he pulled two reporters aside right before the June 15, 1979, trading deadline and finished his tirade against Zimmer by saying, "You see that sign? Well, E-X-I-T me the ——— out." In 1982, after hitting .335 in Mexico, Boomer admitted, "I wish I'd listened to Zimmer in 1979 when he told me to go to a lighter bat."

Scott could go on a June tear, hit nine home runs in ten games, then go into a stretch in which he had three hits and didn't drive in a run in the next eight games, all losses, then break out of it in the eight-homer, 9–6 barrage of the Toronto Blue Jays. After July 10, he hit but eight homers. Those three weeks in June would be the last time George Scott rubbed elbows with stardom, and twenty-five home runs by the All-Star break wasn't enough. Home runs never were enough, as the history of the Red Sox has made perfectly clear.

It wasn't any failure of George Scott that cost the Red Sox the 1977 pennant; it's just that the decision to trade a hitter of Cooper's skills for a home-run hitter symbolized the unimaginative nature of the Red Sox management. They didn't win in 1977 because they didn't have starting pitching. Campbell was reduced to a cortisone shot a week by September; he led the league in saves with thirty-one, led the Boston staff in wins with thirteen, and the next March was encountering so much pain that it wasn't until 1982 with the Cubs that he could work effectively again, much less approach the skills that made him the Fireman of the Year in both 1976 and 1977. Tiant was the winningest starter at 12–8, and his 4.53 ERA was the worst of his career. Rick Wise and Reggie Cleveland each won eleven games with ERAs of 4.77 and 4.26, and Ferguson Jenkins won three games — none against a .500 club — after June 23. In one Fenway series, the lowly Brewers battered Boston pitching for fifty-nine hits and forty runs in four games. If it hadn't been for rookies Mike Paxton and Don Aase coming up from Pawtucket and going a combined 16–7, they might not have ever been in the race. It was Aase, in fact, who gave them the impetus for their second run at the Yankees. With the staff in desperate straits and Zimmer begging the front office to release Lee, Aase came up July 26 with the Red Sox on a three-game losing streak that dropped them to two games behind New York and beat the Brewers 4–3, striking out ten in the process. Five days later, Aase shut out the Angels 1–0 in Anaheim, came back in his next start to beat the A's in Oakland 2–1, and got them rolling on a nine-game sweep of the West Coast in the midst of an eleven-game winning streak that led to a three-and-a-half-game lead on August 16. As happens with inconsistent teams that rely solely on offense, they proceeded to lose ten of their next twelve after the 16th — including seven in a row — and by the first of September were four games behind New York.

There are those who feel that considering the plight of the pitching staff, 1977 was Zimmer's finest hour as a manager. However, there are also those who believe that Zimmer was at least partly responsible for the degeneration of the staff, and that it was in 1977 that he actually lost his job as manager because he lost control of the veteran pitchers. Zimmer had only one pitcher — Tiant — who had not had at least two stints in the bullpen. From Zimmer's standpoint, that was the fault of the pitchers. Even Tiant wasn't in shape at the beginning of the season following his contractual holdout; he was so unlike himself that he begged out of games three different times, once with a 3–1 lead. Tiant turned on the manager, claiming that "going with a five-man rotation early in the season ruined all our control." That, in Zimmer's defense, was probably a lame excuse. But Wise, Jenkins, and Lee all felt that they were jerked in and out of the rotation and never left out there long enough to work out their problems. Wise made four starts at the beginning of the year, allowed twenty-two hits and sixteen runs in ten and two-thirds innings, and was exiled to the bullpen. Jenkins, too, was banished, as was Reggie Cleveland. Wise called Zimmer's handling of the staff "a joke." Lee openly questioned Zimmer, and on July 28, only the direct intervention of John Claiborne kept Lee from being released outright.

It was during this season that the Buffalo Head Gang was formed, a group of pitchers plus Carbo who felt they were in Zimmer's doghouse. Jenkins coined the name, as he said Zimmer reminded him of a buffalo "because buffaloes are the ugliest animals alive." Jenkins, Lee, Wise, Jim Willoughby, and Carbo were the Buffalo Heads, with Dick Pole (whose run-ins with Zimmer at the end of the 1976 season were so bad that he kept giving Zimmer the finger from the mound when he started for Seattle against his former teammates in May) and Rick "Tall Boy" Jones the pledges and Tom House and Tom Murphy honorary members. Lee maintained that "Zimmer's beanings as a player caused a psychopathic dislike for pitchers." After Jenkins was dumped in November 1977 for something called a John Poloni (he was 1–7 in the Boston farm system in 1978 and released), Willoughby, Cleveland, and Carbo were sold between March and June 1978, and Lee was traded for Stan Papi the following year, Zimmer had cleaned the rack. Wise, Jenkins, and Lee all came back, winning fifteen, eighteen, and seventeen games, respectively, after the Red Sox had given up on them.

The final blowup between Zimmer and Jenkins occurred September 18 in Baltimore, which also happened to be Brooks Robinson Day and the four-for-four debut of one Ted Cox. Paxton started, and was in second-inning trouble. Zimmer had pitching coach Alvin Jackson call Walter Hriniak in the bullpen to tell him to get Jenkins warmed up. Three minutes later, Hriniak called back. He couldn't find Jenkins. The story Zimmer told Jackson was that Hriniak finally found Jenkins, asleep, in the TV truck. Jenkins claimed that Hriniak knew he'd gone into the truck to watch the football game that was on. Whatever, Jenkins never pitched again, and when he and Wise openly criticized Zimmer's handling of the staff at the end of the season, Zimmer vowed that neither would ever start for him again. And they didn't.

Wherever the fault, when it came down to the series they had to win in Yankee Stadium September 13, 14, and 15, they simply did not have the pitching to beat the Yankees. The rivalry between the two teams, which had been so keen in the late 1940s, was approaching as manic a state as it could get. By the time they met for their great playoff game in 1978, "Yankees ———— " and "Red Sox ———— " T-shirts were selling on every corner outside Fenway Park and Yankee Stadium, and chants of "Reggie ———— " and "Fisk ————" ran long into the night. In a June 1977 game in Fenway, Mickey Rivers had iron bolts thrown at him from the bleachers; in 1974, Chris Chambliss had a dart thrown by one fan stick in his arm. Red Sox players wore helmets in the field in one Shea Stadium doubleheader in 1974, and in 1976 and 1977, Fisk said he got pelted by at least one dangerous object per game while in his crouch. The rivalry had been rekindled in 1973, when the Red Sox went into Yankee Stadium, won four out of five, and sent the Yankees out of first place. In August of that year, there was the Fisk-Munson fight and the Red Sox sweep in Fenway. In 1975, it was a June series with the Yankees that put the Red Sox in first place for the first time, and in 1976, it was the May brawl in The Stadium that put the Yankees on their way.

The 1977 series had none of the fights or history, but there was no season series between the two teams any better. It

Final American League Standings and Red Sox Statistics, 1977

	W	L	PCT	GB	R	HR	BA
EAST							
NY	100	62	.617		831	184	.281
BAL	97	64	.602	2.5	719	148	.261
BOS	97	64	.602	2.5	859	213	.281
DET	74	88	.457	26	714	166	.264
CLE	71	90	.441	28.5	676	100	.269
MIL	67	95	.414	33	659	125	.258
TOR	54	107	.335	45.5	605	100	.252
WEST							
KC	102	60	.630		822	146	.277
TEX	94	68	.580	8	767	135	.270
CHI	90	72	.556	12	844	192	.278
MIN	84	77	.522	17.5	867	123	.282
CAL	74	88	.457	28	675	131	.255
SEA	64	98	.395	38	624	133	.256
OAK	63	98	.391	38.5	605	117	.240
LEAGUE TOTAL					10247	2013	.266

MANAGER	W	L	PCT
Don Zimmer	97	64	.602

POS	PLAYER	B	G	AB	H	2B	3B	HR	R	RBI	BA
REGULARS											
1B	George Scott	R	157	584	157	26	5	33	103	95	.269
2B	Denny Doyle	L	137	455	109	13	6	2	54	49	.240
SS	Rick Burleson	R	154	663	194	36	7	3	80	52	.293
3B	Butch Hobson	R	159	593	157	33	5	30	77	112	.265
RF	Dwight Evans	R	73	230	66	9	2	14	39	36	.287
CF	Fred Lynn	L	129	497	129	29	5	18	81	76	.260
LF	Carl Yastrzemski	L	150	558	165	27	3	28	99	102	.296
C	Carlton Fisk	R	152	536	169	26	3	26	106	102	.315
DH	Jim Rice	R	160	644	206	29	15	39	104	114	.320
SUBSTITUTES											
2B	Steve Dillard	R	66	141	34	7	0	1	22	13	.241
DH	Tommy Helms	R	21	59	16	2	0	1	5	5	.271
DH	Ted Cox	R	13	58	21	3	1	1	11	6	.362
DO	Bobby Darwin	R	4	9	2	1	0	0	1	1	.222
2B	Doug Griffin	R	5	6	0	0	0	0	0	0	.000
1B	Jack Baker	R	2	3	0	0	0	0	0	0	.000
2B	Ramon Aviles	R	1	0	0	0	0	0	0	0	—
OF	Bernie Carbo	L	86	228	66	6	1	15	36	34	.289
OF	Rick Miller	L	86	189	48	9	3	0	34	24	.254
OF	Dave Coleman	R	11	12	0	0	0	0	1	0	.000
OF	Sam Bowen	R	3	2	0	0	0	0	0	0	.000
C	Bob Montgomery	R	17	40	12	2	0	2	6	7	.300
C	Bo Diaz	R	2	1	0	0	0	0	0	0	.000

Final American League Standings and Red Sox Statistics, 1977, continued

PITCHER	T	W	L	PCT	ERA	SV
Ferguson Jenkins	R	10	10	.500	3.68	0
Reggie Cleveland	R	11	8	.579	4.26	2
Luis Tiant	R	12	8	.600	4.53	0
Bob Stanley	R	8	7	.533	3.99	3
Bill Campbell	R	13	9	.591	2.96	31
Bill Lee	L	9	5	.643	4.42	1
Rick Wise	R	11	5	.688	4.78	0
Mike Paxton	R	10	5	.667	3.83	0
Don Aase	R	6	2	.750	3.12	0
Jim Willoughby	R	6	2	.750	4.94	2
Tom Murphy	R	0	1	.000	6.75	0
Ramon Hernandez	L	0	1	.000	5.68	1
Tom House	L	1	0	1.000	12.91	0
Jim Burton	L	0	0	—	0.00	0
Rick Kreuger	L	0	1	.000	∞	0
TEAM TOTAL		97	64	.602	4.16	40

began on May 23 in New York with a 4–3 Boston victory, won by Lee, saved by Campbell, with a Paul Blair catch off Fred Lynn that outdid Willie Mays's in the 1954 World Series and Fisk throwing out Rivers trying to steal after leading off the ninth with a single. The following week in Fenway, Rivers threw out Hobson at the plate in the ninth to save a Yankee 5–4 victory. Then came the two weekend blowouts. But that eleventh-inning, 6–5 loss June 24, and the 2–0 loss to Figueroa September 14 were the games that reflect generations of might-have-beens for Red Sox fans in the Yankee shadow.

As it turned out, had Boston won that June 24 game and knocked the Yankees to six games back, George Steinbrenner probably would have fired Billy Martin the next day. Steinbrenner had been upset by the Martin-Jackson tussle on national television the previous weekend, the club was losing, and he stated, "If we get swept here, it's over." The might-have-beens read like a Red Sox history: had a fan not pulled Yastrzemski's glove off his hand as he caught Blair's second-inning fly ball off Lee, it would have been an out, not a home run, and it would have been 5–2, not 5–3 in the ninth inning. If Yastrzemski had just not overrun Randolph's ball . . .

Then, in September, came the crucial loss to Figueroa. The Red Sox rocketed a half-dozen balls more than four hundred feet off him, all of which were tracked down by Rivers. On the other hand, Cleveland pitched a masterpiece. The night before, Rivers had three hits on the first pitch, so Reggie opened his start by drilling a fastball into Rivers's ribs. The crowd of more than fifty thousand began showering beer and objects out of the stands, so Fisk went out to see if Cleveland was upset by his beginning. When Fisk got to the mound, Cleveland's first words were "Let's see the little bastard hit *that* first pitch." He had established his tempo.

The Red Sox had the bases loaded, none out in the fifth. Lynn hit a sharp one-hopper right back at Figueroa for an easy 1-2-3 double play, then when Yastrzemski hit a vicious liner through the middle and Figueroa desperately scrambled to get out of the way, the ball struck him flush on the left buttock, dropped to the ground aside the mound, and gave Figueroa time to turn what looked like a two-run single into an inning-ending out. Jackson hit a two-run homer in the ninth, and the rest of the race was academic.

Fisk had hit two of the balls that traveled more than four hundred feet. "That," he said afterward, "was the luckiest shutout I've ever seen. Ever since I can remember, the Yankees always get the luck when they need it. And I remember back a long way. Growing up where I grew up, you learned to hate the Yankees early."

It was especially easy for Red Sox fans to hate the Yankees in the late 1970s, as Boston's "dynasty" failed to materialize and year after year found New York in the World Series. Adding salt to these fans' wounds was the way the Yankees appeared to be the biggest beneficiaries of the first years of the new free-agent era, ready to spend any amount to grab the greatest stars.

When Catfish Hunter slipped a bit in 1976 (after pitching thirty complete games and 328 innings in 1975), the Yankees signed Cincinnati's best starter, Don Gullett, to replace him. The biggest name in that 1976 free-agent pool was Reggie Jackson, and the Yankees had snapped him up for 1977, too. Steinbrenner's stockpiling of talent knew no bounds: super short reliever Sparky Lyle was the American League Cy Young Award winner in 1977, but would turn thirty-four the next season, so New York grabbed free agent Rich "Goose" Gossage, then only twenty-seven.

And so it was Goose — who quickly replaced Lyle as the league's dominant relief ace — who was on the mound at the culmination of that next season, on October 2, 1978, when the Red Sox–Yankees competition reached a peak of intensity rare even in that legendary rivalry.

SIX

1978

SUPERTEAM TO ARMAGEDDON

The Yankees–Red Sox rivalry reaches peak intensity as Boston opens a huge lead by midseason only to fall behind New York in September. A dramatic surge enables them to draw even with the Yankees on the very last day of the season, setting up the momentous playoff game of October 2, 1978.

*T*HE 1978 SEASON represented the fullest flowering of the greatness forecast for the Red Sox after the 1975 World Series. Not coincidentally, it was also the year Jim Rice certified his status as a serious Hall of Fame contender with 213 hits for a .315 average, a majors-leading 46 homers and 139 RBIs, and an astonishing 406 total bases. Of course, as the Red Sox left fielder, Rice might have been expected to produce some pretty fancy numbers . . .

There is no comparable one-team, one-position tradition in sport, not the USC tailback, not the Montreal Canadiens goalkeeper. The Red Sox left fielder has, with asterisks of interruptions caused only by war or injury, been a Hall of Famer since the days of Wendell Willkie's campaign. From 1940 to the present, the Red Sox have had three left fielders — named Williams, Yastrzemski, and Rice — marking the position as one of privilege that, like Eton, seems applied for at birth. After all, Yaz was born months before Williams moved over from right, and Rice had just turned seven when Yastrzemski walked out to the shade of The Wall for the first time. To put such a tradition in perspective, only four of the current American League and five of the National League teams were even located in their present states when Ted Williams first played left field, and only four current National Football League, six National Hockey League, and no National Basketball Association clubs then existed.

9	Williams, LF
8	Yastrzemski, LF
14	Rice, LF

Williams was what John Wayne might have portrayed as the swashbuckling, tempestuous, tunnel-visioned frontier hero who controlled his own destiny and believed in America as America. Williams was a superstar who out-Reggied Jackson, and the mere thought of the millions of dollars that his looks, style, magnetism, and duende would have been worth in today's electronic market is beyond the estimation of even the wiliest agent.

Yastrzemski, on the other hand, always had a plodding aura to him, seemed a kind of dank, WPA figure with a foreboding personality who doggedly went about his job with a hard, competitive drive. He became, like his countryman pope whom he idolized, a symbol of the workingman on the throne of stardom — the average Joe who worked for everything he got. When it came time for him to retire, he reached out to touch the fans, showed them his emotions, and proved that unlike Ted or other unreal stars whose flesh and spirit were above the madding crowd, he was, indeed, only human.

Williams and Yastrzemski were both extraordinary baseball players, and they were traditional heroes, albeit from the extreme wings of the heroic figure. Both of their relationships with the New England fans were turbulent and hilly. They both came in with much anticipation and were always the center of attention. Rice was different. Not that he didn't come in with some fanfare: his minor-league manager, Joe Morgan, predicted he would exceed Jimmie Foxx as the franchise's all-time right-handed hitter, and he had won back-to-back minor-league MVP awards and was the *Sporting News* Minor League Player of the Year. But Rice was black, and Boston never had had a black superstar. Reggie Smith and George Scott were good players, good enough to be all-stars, but Scott was his own worst enemy, while Smith's emotionalism was fanned by both the political/racial climate of the city in the late 1960s and early 1970s and the volatile nature of the fans. Rice would seem to have been a perfect figure for idolatry, for everyone had some sort of Jim Rice tall tale that made him one of those rare athletes who is described in legends: of how he snapped baseball bats and golf clubs in half by checking his swings, of how he hit the longest home run in the history of Fenway Park and outdrives even Jack Nicklaus by forty yards, of how his athletic ability caused the desegregation lines of the Anderson, South Carolina, high schools to be changed, of how in 1978 he had an offensive season that was last equaled by Joe DiMaggio back when the balls were juiced and the league slugging percentage exceeded .400.

Yet except for that one shining season of 1978, Rice never really was the center of attention like Williams or Yastrzemski. When he hit .309 and drove in 102 runs as a rookie, it was good for only a runner-up's mention for Rookie of the Year; Fred Lynn was the MVP. One night that June, when he checked his swing in Detroit, the bat snapped in half and a poll of old-timers revealed no one could remember ever seeing this happen before. But it not only wasn't on television, it rated only a line in the newspapers because the next night Lynn hit three homers and knocked in ten runs. When the Red Sox became America's darlings in the 1975 World Series, Rice watched from the side; he'd had his hand broken September 22 when he was hit by a pitch by Detroit's Vernon Ruhle. When, in 1977 at the age of twenty-four, he exploded into stardom with a .320 average, 206 hits, 39 homers, 114

RBIs and 104 runs scored, he wasn't even the Boston Baseball Writers' club MVP; Carlton Fisk was one of four catchers ever to hit .300 and both score and knock in 100 runs, and, after all, Fisk was a *catcher* and Rice was only a *designated hitter*. Even when he bounced back in 1983 from three years of nagging injuries (and The Strike) to hit .305 and lead the league in both homers and RBIs, he did so in the shadows of Yastrzemski's farewell, Wade Boggs's .361, and the front-office intramural brawl that ended up in Suffolk Superior Court. That off-season, the Red Sox public relations department admitted that Rice ran a distant third in picture, auto-graph, and personal appearance requests behind Boggs and Yastrzemski, and that for every request for Rice they had five for Boggs.

Part of that was Rice's own doing. Williams could be brooding, foreboding, and at odds with the media, but then Joe Cronin didn't even allow the writers in the clubhouse. Rice's suspicions about the public and the media came in an era when athletes mingled with and used the public like con-summate politicians. He felt burned, betrayed, and "mis-quoted" by two of the three major national publication stories on him, and stared like the Old Man of the Mountain at most national reporters. His agent, Tony Pennacchia, lined up a truckload of endorsements for him after the 1978 season, but within two years most were gone. "I send Butch Hobson out to a shopping center and everyone's happy," Colonial Provision president Jack Satter warned Rice one year into his three-year, $225,000 deal with that company, "but I send you and I get nothing but complaints." Finally, after the 1980 season, Satter fired Rice for various abridgments of their agreement, beginning with failure to show up for personal appearances and culminating in Rice's acceptance of $500 cash from a small Connecticut meat company to do a thirty-second spot.

"I don't feel as if what I've done is fully appreciated around here, I admit it," Rice said after the 1983 season. "I don't know what they want from me. I'm not going to kiss writers' butts just to get better hype, and while the good writers have had a very good relationship with me, the lousy ones think a player's performance is somehow linked to the volume of stupid statements one gives out. I don't know what the public wants, either. I go out there and play every day, whether I'm hurt or feeling great."

"What you had was a young black man from rural South Carolina thrust into one of the intellectual capitals of the world," Pennacchia once said. "He wanted to ease into it, but he didn't have a chance." And, as Rice recoiled into his cool façade, so, too, the public, not exactly sure how to interact with a black baseball hero, recoiled into its own standoffish pose. Boston's uneasy view of blacks came from the faces of anguish and hatred, black-and-white lithograph images of James Meredith and Watts and Roxbury and Louise Day Hicks.

Rice is still known as Ed Rice back home in Anderson, South Carolina. Not surprisingly, he was a standout high school athlete in baseball, basketball, football, and track (he ran a 9.9 hundred as a 188-pound senior) who had football scholarship offers from big-time schools including Clemson, North Carolina, and Nebraska. His background was solid and stable. His father, Roger, is a similarly large, strong man, but he didn't have time for athletics growing up; the times were different for southern blacks and sports then, and he worked the cotton fields. Roger Rice eventually worked his way to an upper-middle-class job as supervisor of a company that makes CB antennas, and he and his wife, Julia Mae, raised their nine children in a house long since paid for with traditional American values. "His head isn't ever going to get out of place. I'll never allow it," Mrs. Rice told Leigh Montville of the *Globe* in the midst of Rice's rookie season. "He's going to come home here, and if we're eating pinto beans for supper, he's going to eat pinto beans."

How good an athlete was he? They altered the high school

desegregation line for him. The line was supposed to go right
down the middle of Murray Street, and if you lived to the
right, you went to Westside, which had been the black
school. Rice was going into his senior year when the plan was
to be implemented; he had gone to Westside for three years
and lived to the right of the line. His senior year found him at
Hanna, though. "They moved the line," said then–Westside
coach William Rogers. "They made a little square off Murray
Street, right about his block. The next year the line was
straight down Murray Street again."

Despite his skills, Rice was always reserved, shy. Roger
Rice remembered the time Jim had gone up to Charlotte to
play in the North Carolina–South Carolina high school all-
star Shrine Bowl. Roger and Julia Mae drove past the bus on
the way home, and Jim Ed had the bus driver pull over and
allow him to ride home with his parents. "He was," Roger
Rice told reporters, "a very shy kid."

Jim Ed Rice is the product of the South's integration pro-
grams of the late 1960s and early 1970s. "We didn't have any
problems with integration," Rice always said. "The North
had all the problems. Don't forget that." His American Legion coach, a former minor leaguer named Olin Saylor, says,
"There's a good chance no one would have ever known about
him before integration. The scouts never went to black baseball games. The results weren't in the papers. There wasn't
any black Legion. I'll say for certain that Jim Rice would
never have been a number-one draft choice were it not for
integration."

Rice was a starter for Saylor's Legion team at the age of
thirteen, a varsity starter for Westside as a fourteen-year-old
eighth grader. In no way was he ever pampered in the traditional style of the exceptional athlete. "Some people pamper
the exceptions," remembers Westside baseball coach John
Wesley Morgan. "That's the worst thing you can do, because
it can mess up their values and drive." When Morgan belit-
tled Rice for mistakes as an eighth grader, Rice quit, and

when he came back the next year, Morgan chased him away. "I wanted to make sure he wanted to play, so I told him I didn't want a quitter," Morgan relates, and when Rice came back the third straight day, he was allowed to rejoin the team. Roger and Julia Mae Rice encouraged his athletics, but if he wanted spending money, he had to work for it, either at a store or loading boxes at the Carolina Produce Company. The Rices never asked for anything, and in 1978 when Julia Mae was in a dime store outside Boston and saw a hat with a picture of her son on it, she plunked down the four dollars and bought it like anyone else. It was because of that loading job and Jim Ed's refusal to leave his position unattended when his replacement was late that he arrived minutes before a Legion game and had to lie down for a rest rather than take infield, prompting scouts from the Angels, Pirates, and several other teams to rate him as "lazy." Red Sox scout Mace Brown realized that Jim Ed had a job and was working. "Mace knew the family and the kid," says fellow Boston scout Sam Mele. "He knew that Jim Ed Rice was anything but lazy. We all know who's right now, don't we?" Now we all know that Jim Ed Rice never smokes, never drinks anything but an occasional Kahlua and cream ("heavy on the cream"), and is on record as saying "Eating's overrated."

Jim Ed Rice was blessed with extraordinary skills. He is one of the strongest men ever to play the game, yet he always boasted not only that he never lifted a weight but "anyone who has to doesn't have a chance." That explosive strength— uncorked with only a short stride and a flick of the bat—enabled him to generate bat speed that could propel baseballs five hundred feet. The strength and bat speed were there at the age of thirteen when he asked Saylor for a tryout. Saylor threw him five pitches. Rice blasted four out of the park. When he first reached the stardom plateau in 1977 and 1978, opposing players used to gather around the batting cage to watch and listen to him hit. One night in Fenway, he hit sixteen consecutive pitches out of the park, but as his

friend and golf partner Ken Harrelson observed, "It's the
sound Jim gets when he hits. It sounds like a rifle shot out in
the wilderness, and when he hits a ball squarely, he makes it
hiss as it takes off. I don't think anyone ever made a better
sound hitting than Jim Rice."

Furthermore, Rice always worked at his skills. In the
minor leagues, he picked up Ted Williams's book *The Science
of Hitting* and carried it everywhere with him. Despite his
speed, arm strength, and body balance that allowed him to
dive and cradle the ball without the jar of landing, he had to
work hard on playing left field. For years, when the Red Sox
were playing at home he would go underneath the center-
field stands two or three times a week with Johnny Pesky and
hit against the pitching machine. Five days a week he would
take fungoes from Pesky, first practicing charging grounders,
then taking flies off The Wall. After eight seasons, he finally
got out of the shadow of Yastrzemski, whose unique style of
playing left field like a shortstop had paled anyone else who
went out there. But by his ninth year in Boston, Rice, too,
owned the new Wall, and in 1983 he had as many assists
(twenty-one) as Yaz ever had in one season and probably
should have won a Gold Glove for fielding excellence.
Dwight Evans, who had the worst defensive year of his
career, won one instead, proving clearly the value of a reputation.

When Rice was a rookie, Henry Aaron predicted, "If anyone breaks my [home-run] record, it'll be Jim Rice." The
stories they tell about Rice are about his awesome strength:

• Indeed, he did try to hold up on his swing that June 1975
  night in Detroit and had the bat snap in half. "That's the
  third time it's happened to me in my life," he confided
  rather modestly when Al Kaline, Ralph Houk, Don Zimmer, George Kell, and several other long-timers admitted
  they'd never heard of it. Rice did it again in Minnesota in
  1983. "You see guys in batting practice find that their

wood is cracked, try to snap the bat with a checkswing and claim they did the same thing," said Orioles outfielder Jimmy Dwyer after he was caught by Eddie Murray trying that very stunt during batting practice before a World Series game. "Hitting a home run in the World Series is great, but we'd all like to have someone tell his grandchild that he saw me snap a bat in half checking my swing. As much as we try, Jimmy probably will be the only man who'll ever do that." Harrelson claims he saw Rice snap a triple-X (extra stiff) shaft driver by holding up on his golf swing, too.

- He hit a fastball down over the plate from Kansas City's Steve Busby in 1976 that went out on the rise over the thirty-seven-foot-high fence and screen by the flagpole in left-center and disappeared into the night, a shot Tom Yawkey pronounced "unquestionably the longest ever hit in this park."

- In 1978, exasperated by Rice's hot streak (.522 with sixteen RBIs in one week going into the game), Royals manager Whitey Herzog put on a special Rice shift. He put second baseman Frank White at third and stuck third baseman Jerry Terrell in left field. "What I'd really like to do is put two guys on top of the Citgo sign and two in the net," Herzog explained. "He pulls [pitcher Jim] Colborn well, and he pulls him in the air, as my charts show. Heck, I might put five outfielders out there sometime." Rice hit one ball over the screen, blooped a single into shallow right where White would have roamed, and walked. Unlike Williams, who tried to pull everything despite the shift Lou Boudreau devised for him, Rice was someone they quickly gave up on. "Normally," admitted Herzog, "he hits the ball too hard to too many areas of the field. The fact that he hit fifteen triples two years in a row tells you that."

- Former U.S. Open champion Lou Graham admitted that Rice hits a golf ball farther than anyone on the pro tour.

But unlike Frank Howard or other fabled strongmen of the game, Rice was, despite his penchant for swinging at the first strike he sees and his high strikeout ratio, always a pure hitter as much as a slugger. "I don't ever think about homers" was his response to Aaron's prediction. "I'm not really a home-run hitter. If I hit three hundred, the thirty-five or forty home runs will come because of my strength. If I ever hit three-sixty, I might hit fifty or seventy. But I try to hit the ball where it's pitched and get my hits." In reaction to that, Rice never wanted to bat cleanup; like Williams or Yastrzemski, he always preferred the third position, "the hit-ter's position" as he called it, and proudly pointed to the fact that he is the only player in baseball history to have two hundred hits and thirty-five homers three consecutive years (1977–79).

In the first nine full seasons of his career, Rice batted .300 six times and had a lifetime average (including his fifty-seven-at-bat trial in 1974) of .305. To get some idea of his relative accomplishments in those nine full seasons, only three players — Steve Garvey, Mike Schmidt, Dave Winfield — played in more games than the 1310 Rice appeared in. Only Garvey had more at-bats. Only Schmidt scored more runs (915) than Rice's 877, only Garvey had more hits (1620) than Rice's 1602, only five players compiled better than his .306 average, and only Schmidt had more homers (337) than Rice's 275 or had a higher slugging percentage (.550) than Rice's .532. And, in that time, Rice led the major leagues in total bases, runs batted in, and runs produced, for while Schmidt barely out-slugged him, Rice's average was thirty-nine points higher than the Phillies' third baseman's. While Yastrzemski retired to the song that he was the greatest all-around player in Red Sox history, the average of Rice's first nine full seasons outhit (.306–.295), outhomered (31–27), out RBIed (105–91), out-slugged (.532–.505), and outproduced (165–159) the nine best years of Yastrzemski's career. That despite three consecutive "off" years in 1980, '81, and '82: in '80, he missed six weeks in

Jim Rice's First Nine Full Seasons

Games: 1310 (4th. Garvey, 1343; Schmidt, 1331; Winfield, 1313)
At-Bats: 5239 (2nd. Garvey, 5325)
Runs: 877 (2nd. Schmidt, 915)
Hits: 1602 (2nd. Garvey, 1620)
Average: .306 (6th. Carew, .338)
Home Runs: 275 (2nd. Schmidt, 337)
RBIs: 941 (1st)
Total Bases: 2785 (1st)
Slugging Percentage: .532 (2nd. Schmidt, .550)
Runs Produced: 1483 (1st)

	BA	R	H	HR	RBI	TB	SP	RP[°]
Rice	.306	817	1602	275	941	2795	.532	1483
Schmidt	.267	915	1257	337	903	2580	.550	1481
Brett	.320	801	1542	148	749	2494	.517	1402
Baylor	.267	727	1270	202	752	2129	.447	1277
Lynn	.297	691	1241	170	702	2096	.501	1223
Jackson	.268	690	1172	263	806	2213	.507	1233
Cooper	.312	720	1484	185	789	2385	.502	1324
Winfield	.286	768	1397	224	829	2403	.493	1373
Garvey	.304	725	1620	179	828	2484	.466	1374
Carter	.268	607	1179	187	681	2006	.456	1101
Foster	.284	728	1358	262	909	2422	.507	1375
Parker	.307	684	1377	158	715	2244	.500	1241
Luzinski	.278	649	1251	237	842	2240	.497	1254
McRae	.299	667	1419	120	716	2229	.470	1263

Rice vs. Eddie Murray's Seven Full Seasons, 1977–83

	BA	R	H	HR	RBI	TB	SP	RP
Rice	.309	650	1264	228	751	2237	.546	1176
Murray	.299	615	1175	198	697	2007	.507	1114

Rice vs. Dale Murphy's Six Full Seasons, 1978–83

	BA	R	H	HR	RBI	TB	SP	RP
Rice	.307	546	1060	189	640	1857	.538	997
Murphy	.271	504	823	162	505	1444	.475	847

Rice's Nine Years vs. Carl Yastrzemski's Nine Best ('65, '67, '68, '69, '70, '74, '75, '76, '77): The Average Season

	BA	R	H	HR	RBI	TB	SP	RP
Rice	.306	91	178	31	105	309	.532	165
Yaz	.295	95	162	27	91	277	.505	159

[°] RP = Runs Produced

Players Averaging .300, 30 HR, 100 RBIs per Season over Careers*

	SEAS.	BA	HR	RBI
Henry Aaron	23	.305	33	100
Babe Ruth (as P–OF)	20	.344	35	110
Babe Ruth (as OF only)	17	.345	41	127
Ted Williams	17	.344	30	106
Jimmie Foxx	16	.326	33	118
Lou Gehrig	14	.340	35	141
Jim Rice**	9	.306	31	105

* Full seasons, only
** Through 1983

the prime home-run period of June and July after having his wrist fractured by a pitch by California's Chris Knapp; in '81 he missed the two sluggers' months because of The Strike; and in '82 he was troubled in June and July with a bad back that at one point had him in traction.

Part of the reason Rice hadn't received what he felt was his due was his personality. Not that any manager ever disliked him, for, as Zimmer once said, "He is a manager's player — write his name in the lineup every day, he gives you a hundred percent and never says anything." Once when the fans were booing Zimmer and demanding his firing in 1979, Rice walked into the manager's office after a particularly tough loss and said, "Don't worry, Skip, I won't let them get you. You're a good man, and it's not your fault."

He could be jovial and sometimes even loud on buses. But once Cecil Cooper was traded after the 1975 season, he didn't have any close friends among the players. He and Tommy Harper became close when Harper joined the team as a coach in 1980, but Rice's quiet, sometimes moody nature made him one of the targets of extra players like Frank Duffy, Jack Brohamer, and Steve Renko who pointed out that one of the problems with the Red Sox of that era was that, as Duffy once said, "The team gets off a plane and twenty-five players go off in twenty-five different cabs."

As he reached thirty, Rice relaxed and seemed to have more fun with his teammates. He also had begun to relax with the media, which from Salem to Seattle viewed him as one of the game's most distant, arrogant, and temperamental stars. To some of those writers who traveled with the team, Rice was never particularly difficult. If he made an out or an error that had some effect on the outcome of the game, he would explain what happened, honestly. "What I don't like," he'd say, "is to stand there in the middle of a crowd of reporters and microphones expected to announce how wonderful I am because I hit two home runs. The game comes back to haunt you when you boast, and, anyway, you can say it better than I can. You get paid to say nice things about me better than I can say them. When there's something to explain, I'll explain it." And he usually does.

Rice never talked a lot about racism and the Red Sox; it first cropped up publicly in a *Sport* magazine story in 1978, and he quickly issued a statement denying the quotes attributed to him. But, privately, Rice would talk about the Red Sox and their whiteness, and he talked about it rationally and sensibly. "I don't believe that Haywood Sullivan or Ed Kenney or Eddie Kasko are racists," he said. "No way. They've been too good to me. But they don't go after black athletes. How many scouts do we have in the cities? How many scouts do we have getting black players out of certain areas? I'm not saying it's racism, it's just poor scouting. When you look at some of these scrawny white boys we have around here, you wonder who's scouting." With the reference to "white boys," he laughed.

When he was a senior at Hanna High School in Anderson, Rice hit .500, but the team MVP award went to a white who hit .270. Rice outhit Lynn by fifty-eight points in double-A and fifty-three points in triple-A, but Lynn got the starting job in 1975 first and went on to grab most of the publicity.

ABOVE: With the 1976 season barely a month old, the 1975 pennant winners were mired in a ten-game losing streak from which they never recovered. Here Salem witch Laurie Cabot tries to power up Bernie Carbo's bat with some game-winning hits.
(*UPI/Bettmann Archive*)

RIGHT: A few weeks later, on June 3, 1976, World Series hero Carbo was more serious—he'd just been traded to the Milwaukee Brewers.
(*Boston Globe Photo*)

ABOVE: It started here: Carlton Fisk and the Yankees' Lou Piniella tangle after a close play at the plate in the famous sixth-inning brawl at Yankee Stadium, May 20, 1976.

(UPI/Bettmann Archive)

RIGHT: And it ended in disaster: pitcher Bill Lee is helped from

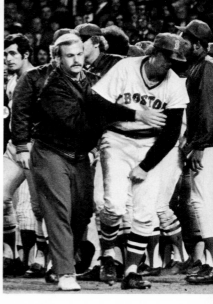

the field after injuring his arm in the fight. The Red Sox won the game, 8–2, on two Yastrzemski homers, but lost Lee, whose next win didn't come until August.

(UPI/Bettmann Archive)

LEFT: Here Lee meets the press after flying back to Boston. Note the Ouspensky book, typical reading fare for The Space Man.

(Boston Globe Photo)

LEFT: Seldom seen without his substantial cigars off the field, on it Luis Tiant, "El Tiante," was Boston's, and perhaps the American League's, best pitcher through the mid-to-late 1970s. His 21–12 mark in 1976 was one of Boston's few bright spots.
(Boston Globe Photo)

RIGHT: Agent Jerry Kapstein and client Fred Lynn are all smiles in August of 1976 after signing an enormous (for that time) contract following prolonged negotiations.
(Boston Globe Photo)

BELOW: The Deal That Never Was. Commissioner Bowie Kuhn voided their sale to the Red Sox for one million dollars apiece before Joe Rudi (left) or Rollie Fingers ever played for Boston. But for a few hours in June of 1976 they were indeed Red Sox.
(UPI/Bettmann Archive)

ABOVE: A 1977 meeting of the Red Sox brain trust. From left: assistant general manager John Claiborne, general manager Dick O'Connell, scouting director Haywood Sullivan, and manager Don Zimmer. *(Boston Globe Photo)*

BELOW: Bill Lee never missed an opportunity to vent his opinions, which often differed from those of manager Don Zimmer—especially when, as here, Zimmer was yanking him from a game. *(Boston Globe Photo)*

ABOVE: Two guys who could really fill out a uniform: George "Boomer" Scott and Don Zimmer during spring training of 1977. The Boomer had just returned to Boston via the famous Cecil Cooper trade with the Milwaukee Brewers, and would slug 33 homers for the Crunch Bunch Red Sox that year. *(Boston Globe Photo)*

BELOW: In 1978 Jim Rice was unstoppable, hitting .315 with 46 homers, 139 RBIs, and 406 total bases. Here Kansas City tries a four-man outfield against him in May, moving third baseman Jerry Terrell to the outfield and second baseman Frank White to third. Rice got a single when White misjudged his pop fly to third. *(Boston Globe Photo)*

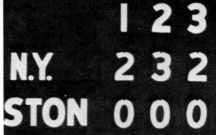

ABOVE: Late in 1978, manager Don Zimmer wonders where his fourteen-game lead over the Yankees went.
(Boston Globe Photo)

RIGHT: Yastrzemski slumps against the left-field scoreboard in Fenway Park as the Red Sox make a pitching change in the fourth inning. September 8, 1978: the Boston Massacre is under way as the Yankees surge past the Red Sox in the pennant race.   *(Boston Globe Photo)*

ABOVE: From his arrival in spring training of 1978 until he hurt his arm in August 1979, Dennis Eckersley was 36–14 for the Red Sox. From August 1979 until May 1984, when he was traded to the Chicago Cubs, his record was 47–52.
(Boston Globe Photo)

RIGHT: The Red Sox have had an unbroken succession of Hall of Fame–quality left fielders, beginning with the arrival of Ted Williams in 1939. Here are the other two men to fill the position since then, Carl Yastrzemski (by the 1980s playing mostly first base, or DH) and Jim Rice.
(Boston Globe Photo)

RIGHT: The Red Sox were in for many strange moments in the early 1980s—and Carlton Fisk playing third base in July of 1980 was surely one of them.
(Boston Globe Photo)

BELOW: Manager Ralph Houk guided the Red Sox through a difficult transition period from 1981 through 1984. Jim Rice, with Houk in this 1981 shot, was, along with Dwight Evans, one of the few consistent performers through the Houk years.
(Boston Globe Photo)

Rice admitted that he felt slighted when Fisk was voted the team MVP in 1977, and he felt slighted when Rick Burleson won it in 1979. At the end of the '75 season, Skip Bayless, then a writer for the *Miami Herald*, did an interview on a golf course with Rice in which Rice revealed that he felt Lynn got more than his due of publicity. Rice denied he had said that, but he later would openly question Lynn's injuries. Rice denied saying "It looks as if we have another Fred Lynn on our hands" when Wade Boggs was sent home from Chicago with a bad back in 1983 (the implication being that Boggs was protecting his average), as he denied saying certain things reported in the *Sport* magazine story. If he said them, he was just blurting out feelings of a lack of appreciation. "I think he may be a little jealous of both Lynn and Boggs," Pennacchia said when Rice left his representation firm and Pennacchia's other client, Boggs, was steaming about Rice's published comment.

"I'm paid and should be judged by my numbers," Rice always said. He never understood stardom, or at least the elements that prompted Jim Palmer to sit in department stores for two hours at a crack autographing beefcake pictures for fifty-year-old women. "For reasons not entirely clear, even to Rice himself, he has an unfortunate penchant for being rude and unpleasant to newspaper reporters and even, heaven forbid, to television interviewers," wrote Ron Fimrite in the April 9, 1979, *Sports Illustrated*. One writer who regularly covered the team refused to speak to Rice after he turned his broad back to him in the middle of an interview in 1977.

Yet, with some reporters whom he categorized as "those I respect and trust" Rice could be both outgoing and incisive. If he made an error or struck out, he would never back down, finishing almost every remarkably honest explanation with "I screwed up — I'm not going to hide from that." He always said, "What I hate is to stand there after I've had a good game and say time after time how great I am. What am I supposed to say? 'I hit a hanging slider'? 'It was a fastball out over the plate'? What does that mean? People in the media make too much of what a player says right after a game. What you write should be held up for more lasting examination, because you get paid for what you write, but I get paid for what I do on the field." The best time to talk to Rice is 4:30 in the afternoon, as he sits in front of his locker, relaxes, and talks the game.

Many of Rice's views of the media make undeniable sense; some of his moods don't. He may have gotten only half the chance that a Williams or Yastrzemski got. But someday he may look back at all he did in 1978 and ask himself just how he did lose the public. Of course, at the same time, he and everyone associated with the Red Sox uniform or heart will forever ask how it came to pass that the Red Sox failed to win the pennant that year.

Like his illustrious left-field predecessors, Rice in 1978 found out that one can't do it alone, particularly no one hitter. Like Williams and Yastrzemski, he still had never finished a season on a victorious note. Williams went six-for-eight to finish at .405 on his final day of the 1941 season, but the Red Sox finished seventeen games out; in 1960 he capped off his brilliant career with a home run in his final bat, a swing so glorious that it was frozen in time by John Updike, but all it did was help the Red Sox finish thirty-two games behind the Yankees. With those great teams of 1946, 1948, and 1949, all the final games brought was frustration. So, too, was it for Yastrzemski, either making the last out of the 1967 and 1975 World Series, finishing half a game behind Detroit in 1972, or experiencing two emotional October 2 farewells: his own in 1983, which only brought the Red Sox to within twenty games of the Orioles, and the momentous, frustrating playoff of 1978. At the time, the Red Sox and the Yankees appeared to the world as the United States and USSR of sport, and it did not cross Yastrzemski's mind that he would never again feel the thrill of a real pennant race.

As for Rice, who missed the divisional clinching, the play-offs, and the World Series in 1975, it was the only teasing taste of his career. "We have the home-field advantage, we have the momentum of eight straight wins, we have Rice," Burleson said on the eve of the playoff that would finish the year in which Jim Ed Rice led the major leagues in hits, triples, home runs, runs batted in, total bases, slugging, and runs produced. "But they have Guidry."

The Yankees had Guidry. They also had the rainout of the July 4 game in Fenway when they were having double-A pitchers drive to Boston from West Haven to try out, their veterans were battered and in psychological disarray, and their manager was turning irrational and was twenty days from losing his job; when the rescheduled game was played on September 7, Mike Torrez didn't even get four outs and they began the historic Boston Massacre with a 15–3 slaughter. They had sixty years of history dating back to the sale of Babe Ruth, which on that fatalistic final afternoon brought out all the Calvinistic torment: *Why did the wind change the inning right before Bucky "Bleeping" Dent hit his home run? Why is it that when Remy's ball came out of the sun it came out on Lou Piniella's glove side?* But, most of all, on October 2, 1978, they had Guidry, finishing (at 25–3) with the best won-lost percentage in history, and a reliever named Rich Gossage who was close to the best of his era. And when Yaz and Rice struck blows against the great Guidry, Gossage would reduce the difference between the two teams over 163 games to ninety feet by retiring Rice and Yastrzemski with Burleson on third for the final two outs of the game, the season, and an era for the Sox.

This was the season that this Red Sox team appeared to have come together in all its power and glory. It appeared ready to dominate the game like the '72–'74 A's or the '75–'76 Reds. In July, the *Boston Herald American* ran a week-long, front-page series entitled "How SuperTeam Was Put Together," and midway through that month, when rookie outfielder Garry Hancock came to the plate for his major-league debut, he received thunderous standing ovations when he stepped into the batter's box and as he headed back to the dugout after striking out. They had apparently buried the Yankees, winners of the last two pennants, putting fourteen games between them as late as July 18. They still had a nine-game lead over both Milwaukee and New York as late as August 13, and upped their lead from five games on August 1 to six and a half games going into September . . .

They'd had a six-and-a-half game lead on September 1 before — in 1974, to be precise — and blown it. They'd lost a pennant on the final day to the Yankees before, too, going into Yankee Stadium with a one-game lead for the last two games of the 1949 season and losing them both. But 1978 was the worst fears, phlegm, and fates all coughed up at once: from fourteen games ahead to Bucky "Bleeping" Dent, a year when what Roger Angell calls New England's "Calvinistic clouds of self-doubt" were ingrained into a won't-get-fooled-again depression that won't be relieved until the Red Sox finally win a world championship for the first time since 1918.

And yet, on balance, in this season of eerie symmetry— the Yankees dottering like the Autumn of the Patriarch in June and early July, the Red Sox unraveling like the stitches of Mussolini's empire in late August and September — Rice and the Red Sox did not *fold* like the 1914 Giants, who led the Braves by fifteen games on July 4, or the 1951 Dodgers, who led the Giants by thirteen games on August 11. The Red Sox in a span of sixty days and fifty-eight games between July 17 and September 16 lost seventeen and a half games to the Yankees — who went from fourteen back to three and a half in front — then turned around and won twelve of their last fourteen, including their final eight to force the playoff game. They led 2–0 in that game, saw Torrez give up the three-run homer to Dent, eventually fell behind 5–2, then battled back in the final two innings . . .

All of which, in this game in which many players are great drag-strippers but few make the five-hundred-mile flag, meant that in clear perspective the 1978 Red Sox were ninety feet — which, in reality, is a fraction of an inch, the difference between Yastrzemski fouling Gossage's last pitch back or striking it well enough to make any kind of a hit — short of the Yankees.

This was a team that on July 19, when Mike Torrez beat the Brewers 8–2 to up his record to 12–5 and Butch Hobson scored the infamous run that nobody saw, was 62–28. Rice was off in pursuit of the Triple Crown, and the Rice-Lynn-Evans "best outfield in baseball" was hitting a combined .310 with fifty-eight homers and 175 RBIs in those ninety games. Most surprisingly, their five starting pitchers (Eckersley, Torrez, Lee, Tiant, and rookie Jim Wright) were a combined 44–13.

On July 19, when Torrez got that twelfth win, he had equaled the victory high of any 1977 starter. And with the SuperTeam series in print, the ballpark filled to more than 85 percent of capacity, and a nine-game lead, this was also the high-water mark of Haywood Sullivan's executive career. Basic logic read: if they were nine games in front, he must be a genius. So, for two months, the Haywood who soon would be perceived as the Dumwood partner in the tragicomic duo of Dumwood and Shoddy was riding popularity he'd never experienced as a .226-hitting bullpen catcher. When it was announced the previous September that the Yawkey Estate would sell the team to the group headed by Sullivan and Buddy Leroux, the firestorms that erupted didn't really burn Sullivan personally. Except for a few doubts about his intelligence and ability to make decisions, Sullivan was generally well liked by the media, and many of them openly cheered him into office. He had nothing to do with the shaky financing revealed by the *Globe*, and when the league overwhelmingly voted down their application at the December winter meetings, Sullivan was perceived as the victim, Leroux the

shyster. "We were following a very successful operation
[headed by his long-time internal rival Dick O'Connell] and
we had to establish credibility with the fans, with the media
and, frankly, with the league," Sullivan later admitted, and
taking that lovable-albeit-flawed Phi Slamma Jamma of a
team that had finished two and a half games behind New
York, he used the leftover Yawkey money to sign four free
agents and make three significant trades.

First, he seemed to have reversed generations of frustration
by stealing playoff and World Series hero Mike Torrez from
the Yankees, not knowing that once the fans watched Torrez
in action in games that counted he would be considered an
even crueler hoax than the sale of Ruth or Hoyt or Ruffing,
because his pennant-drive performances only gave New
Yorkers belly laughs. Ever since Babe Ruth began the parade
of talented players shipped by the Red Sox to the Yankees
and the fortunes of the two franchises were reversed, it had
always been the New Yorkers who took; even in 1972 when
they went to make a trade, the Red Sox handed the Yankees a
dominant relief pitcher in Sparky Lyle for a singles-hitting
first baseman named Danny Cater. George Steinbrenner had
been convinced by his general manager, Gabe Paul, that his
money would be better spent on reliever Rich Gossage than on
Torrez, so the Yankees backed off and Sullivan rushed in with
a $2.7 million, seven-year contract that at the time seemed to
be a stroke of baseball and public relations genius. Torrez sa-
shayed into town with his beautiful French-Canadian wife,
Danielle, and as it was noted that he was 38–11 in the second
halves of the last four seasons and that he'd averaged seventeen wins over those full seasons, he played the star's role.
Broadcaster Dick Stockton used to call Torrez "George Raft"
because of his gold chains, open-to-the-waist shirts, colognes,
and hair spray. One day during spring training, Luis Tiant,
drenched in sweat after doing his wind sprints, watched Torrez go out of the clubhouse in white pants and a black shirt
open to the waist, engulfed in a cloud of perfume. "Hey,

Taco," Tiant yelled at him. "Just remember — you're just another *speeeeek.*"

After signing Torrez, Sullivan signed relief pitchers Dick Drago and Tom Burgmeier, to give Bill Campbell some much-needed help in the bullpen, and infielder Jack Brohamer as a backup. Drago had been dumped in 1976 as the player to be named later for Denny Doyle, despite sixteen saves in the second half of the '75 season. With his deep, resonant bass voice and ability to see the dark cloud around any silver lining, Drago had worn out his welcome with Darrell Johnson, but he had been a tough and versatile pitcher for them in 1974–75 after being acquired from Kansas City for Marty Pattin. Burgmeier was a left-hander, which they desperately needed in the bullpen, and he came with the recommendation of his Minnesota sidekick Campbell. Doyle had fallen into Zimmer's disfavor in 1977, and Brohamer was signed in case they couldn't deal for Jerry Remy. Sullivan's inexperience in these matters showed when he was signing Brohamer, for when John Harrington, the businessman holdover from the O'Connell regime who remained for six months to ease the transition, looked at the terms he pulled Sullivan aside and told him that he'd just given Brohamer and agent Ed Kleven the first fully guaranteed contract in the history of the franchise. Sullivan had forgotten to put in some of the restrictions that would have gotten the club off the pay hook had Brohamer gone and shot Yaz or done something equally preposterous.

Sullivan, with the advice of Zimmer, was trying to deal with the reality that the pitching needed rebuilding. He and Zimmer were also trying to break up what they perceived to be one of the forerunners of the drug culture that burst into notoriety in the early 1980s, believing that the Buffalo Heads were part of that scene. So while they added Torrez, Burgmeier, Drago, et al., they also subtracted: first Jenkins (for John Poloni, who won one game in double-A and was released), then Reggie Cleveland and Jim Willoughby, for whom they got nothing in return. They fell victim to the historic Red Sox versus Yankees flaw: where the New York management has traditionally said, "You can't have enough pitching," Boston's has said, "We should have enough." When Tiant, Lee, Torrez, and Wright all weighed anchor, all that was left was Bobby Sprowl, who never won a major-league game.

At the winter meetings in Hawaii, Sullivan traded pitcher Don Aase and the cash necessary for the Angels to sign free agent Rick Miller for California second baseman Jerry Remy. Like Torrez, the acquisition of Remy seemed to fill a vital need, both at second base and with speed at the top of the lineup. Not only that, but Remy was a local kid who'd grown up in Somerset, a mill town thirty miles from Boston, and had been raised so much a Red Sox fan that his father had taken him to the final, victorious game of the 1967 season. All the unloadings were overlooked when Sullivan pulled off the March 30 deal for a twenty-three-year-old starting pitcher named Dennis Eckersley who Zimmer proclaimed would "do for us what Tom Seaver does for Cincinnati."

Rumors of a multiplayer trade with the Indians had been rife since late February, when Gabe Paul moved to Cleveland and began looking for something in which he could get quantity for quality. Eckersley was only twenty-three, and the year before he'd thrown the second longest consecutive-hitless-innings streak (twenty-two and a third innings) in history, but Indians people claimed to worry about the strain on his arm from his side-wheeling motion, his troubles with left-handed hitters (.283 in '77, as opposed to .180 by right-handers), his inability to hold runners on base (thirty-three of thirty-five had successfully stolen on him in '77), and the possible strain on the team because of his marital problems. It didn't come put publicly until September, but Eckersley was going through a difficult divorce, as his wife had become involved with his best friend, center fielder Rick Manning.

On March 30, as the Red Sox played the Mets in an exhibition game in Winter Haven, Florida, the final scene in the trade drama took place. Scouting director Eddie Kasko came out of Sullivan's office down the left-field line, walked briskly through the stands and around to the Boston dugout on the first-base side, shouted in to get Zimmer's attention, and while Mets pitcher Nino Espinosa stared in amazement, the Red Sox manager chugged out of the dugout, around behind home plate, and down the left-field line to Sullivan's office. Ten minutes later, as Lee watched from the mound, Zimmer walked back around to the dugout, and soon Ted Cox and Bo Diaz stepped up out of the dugout and began walking down the right-field line for the Boston clubhouse. Lee finished off the inning with one pitch, and then took a dashing detour en route to the dugout, racing over to a writer sitting on a bench down the right-field line and breaking into song: "Send lawyers, guns and money, the shit has hit the fan." That week, *Sports Illustrated* writer Curry Kirkpatrick was in Winter Haven working on what would turn out to be the best profile of Lee ever written, a profile woven around the words of another Warren Zevon song, "Excitable Boy."

In return for Eckersley and Fred Kendall, a catcher with absolutely no significance in Red Sox history, Sullivan had given up what he said was "a gamble." Besides Cox, the International League batting champion, and Diaz, the best catching prospect in the organization despite unimpressive minor-league batting statistics, they had given up Wise and Mike Paxton, who'd won ten games as a rookie in 1977. Sullivan and Zimmer were determined to unload all of the Buffalo Heads: Jenkins had gone, Wise was next, Willoughby was moved within days, and by the following Christmas the last two members, Carbo and Lee, had also been sold. Paxton was, as they liked to say, "gutsy," but he was a sinker-slider pitcher of mediocre stuff and, at twenty-six, three years older than Eckersley. Players and fans in both cities wailed that each team had given up too much, but Sullivan had made his point: he could make decisions, which O'Connell had said he couldn't do. He'd signed four free agents, traded for a twenty-three-year-old all-star pitcher, a twenty-five-year-old all-star second baseman, and a utility infielder (Frank Duffy) whom several teams had sought. When Eckersley, who'd pitched only ten spring-training innings while waiting to be traded, got in shape, started off 10–2, and began talking, it appeared that Sullivan had made one of the few great trades for a pitcher in the long-suffering history of the franchise.

The Eck, the brash wise guy from Fremont, California, rolled in to the beat of "Little GTO." He came with his own DialEck that seemed to tilt H. L. Mencken's *The American Language*, one he claimed he began learning from former teammate Pat Dobson. "Here comes Mr. Slickermaster with the oil," he cracked when he saw the dapper Stockton coming into the lobby of the New York Sheraton with a bottle of fine wine under his arm. *Oil* is liquor. "Sorry, gentlemen, I've got to go lick some beef," he told media types around his locker when apologizing that he had to end an interview. *Beef* is a date. When he pitched, he seemed to dance, and he was so outwardly cocky that he was hated by opponents. Remy had been with the Angels when The Eck threw his no-hitter against them in 1977, and Remy remembered that when Eckersley would get two strikes on a California batter he would point to the on-deck circle and shout, "You're next." Hobson remembered swinging hard and missing one time and hearing Eckersley scream "Swing harder, bleeper" from the mound. When Texas outfielder Juan Beniquez protested a called third strike, Eckersley walked off the mound, pointed to the Rangers' dugout, and yelled, "Take a seat."

A brief glossary of DialEck:

Iron:	money
Grease:	food
Oil:	liquor
Beef:	a girl, preferably a date

Tuna:	a fat girl
Cheese:	a fastball
Yakker:	a breaking ball
Gas:	a good fastball, as in "I had the good gas to make the yakker"
Salad:	easy, as in "salad teams"
Bogart:	a big game
Ta-ta:	a home run, as in "He went ta-ta"
Bridge:	out of the park, as in "He took to the bridge"
Master:	the best at anything, as in the oilmaster or bridgemaster (his self-proclaimed title for giving up home runs)
Kudo:	the bow a batter makes as he bails out on a breaking ball, as in "cheese for your kitchen and a yakker for your kudo"

Eckersley was very disappointed not to have signed his new contract before pitching the opener in 1979. "I wore a three-piece for the occasion and they chilled me," he said. "It was bogus, a real turnoff. I wanted the Bogart, but I didn't want it without the iron up front."

But for all the jive, this pitching answer to Chuck Berry became an immensely popular figure with his teammates and the media. By the time he arrived in Boston, it was evident that he was no longer going to be the power pitcher who had more strikeouts than hits allowed in Cleveland. And when, after going 37–14 from his arrival until August 15, 1979, he went through more than four years of struggle totaling but forty-three wins, the fans began turning on him. Still, he settled down, marrying the daughter of a Boston policeman, and remained one of the fairest and most honest players who ever came along. In the aftermath of the total collapse on September 9, 1978, when a pop fly landed amidst five Boston players and opened up a seven-run inning that knocked Eckersley out of a 7–1 loss to Ron Guidry and moved the Yankees within one game of Boston, all the regular Red Sox players were hiding in the trainer's room as the media milled around the clubhouse. The only one who didn't was Duffy, who, as the replacement for the injured Remy, had been closest to the catastrophic pop-up, and nearly seventy-five media people from around the country surrounded the articulate infielder demanding answers. Eckersley came out of the shower, saw the interrogation that Duffy was enduring, and began pushing his way through the notebooks and tape recorders. "Frank Duffy's not the reason we lost this game," Eckersley shouted. "Leave him alone. I pitched ———— and we didn't hit Guidry. Frank Duffy didn't put the three guys on base before that pop-up. I did. Frank Duffy didn't hang the oh-and-two slider that Bucky Dent hit for two more runs. I'm the one who should face the music, not him. The *L* goes next to my name," and for nearly twenty minutes, with all his big-name teammates except Carl Yastrzemski hiding, The Eck described the three and two-thirds innings he pitched and the seven runs he allowed.

The Eck was see-you-later-alligator jive, and color. For half a season, in fact, the Red Sox had a colorful pitching staff complementing a team in which eight of the nine starters at one time or another would be all-stars. Torrez was a name, a vision, and was 11–5 by the All-Star break. Even Allen Ripley, whose father had pitched for the Red Sox in the 1930s, who didn't pitch at North Attleboro High School and made the bigs after a 15–4 season at Pawtucket, became a sort of Buffalo Heads pledge and amused the media ("My mother warned me to be careful with the press and not use any barnyard epitaphs," he explained in spring training) before being sent down. Both Tiant, after breaking his finger in spring training, and Lee, emerging for half a season from Zimmer's doghouse, revived their extraordinary popularity by being a combined 17–5 in July. Lee's return was a sort of vengeance, and when he was going well, he could not resist constantly reminding Zimmer that he'd tried to release the Excitable Boy the previous season. Lee knew that in intellectual and populist terms, Zimmer was no match for him, and flouted the severe clashes between their Cincinnati and San Rafael upbringings. Zimmer would later say, "The only people in baseball that I'd never allow in my house are Bill Lee, Mike Torrez, and Derrel Thomas," and his feelings for Lee — whom he convinced Darrell Johnson to start in the '75 World Series — stemmed from Lee's cruel baiting. Zimmer lashed out in his way, the traditional manner of the baseball man who gets to the park at 1:30, spits tobacco, and longs for "tough sumbitches." Lee ridiculed him, whether by calling Zimmer a "gerbil" or lampooning the steel plate in his head or further belittling his appearance and intellectualism. In 1977, Zimmer told the players in spring training that they'd have to wear a "sports jacket" on the road; the first trip, Lee wore a warm-up suit jacket, and when one of the coaches approached him, he laughed and called it a "sports jacket." The day his sidekick Willoughby was sold to the White Sox, Lee got a candle, lit it, and left it on Zimmer's desk in the manager's office in Winter Haven. On the third morning of the new season, Zimmer awoke in Chicago to a *Sun-Times* column by John Schulian in which Lee vilified the manager ("There's no way I can communicate with that man"), but after they had blown two tough games to the White Sox, Lee went out and threw a shutout for Boston's first win of the new, expectant season. Lee further mocked Zimmer's rules by wearing bowling shirts and going barefoot on charter plane rides.

"A lot of people around here are sick and tired of Bill Lee," Zimmer snapped in late July after Lee gave up his seat on a flight from Kansas City to Minneapolis because a number of people were denied seats due to the Players' Association three-seats-for-two-players rule for anyone forced to ride in steerage, that is, anywhere but first class. Traveling secretary Jack Rogers had asked players to surrender that agreement two months before, but Bernie Carbo had put up such a stink, Rogers dropped the request. Rogers reminded Lee of that fact when The Space Man finally got to Minneapolis.

Now, Carbo by this time had rubbed management the wrong way. Not that he was entirely new at this, for while Bernardo was a wacky, wonderful character, he had very strong feelings about authority. He clashed with Sparky Anderson in Cincinnati and Red Schoendienst in St. Louis. After he missed workouts, Darrell Johnson wanted to get rid of him in '76 in the Bobby Darwin–Tom Murphy deal, and he had nothing but conflicts in Milwaukee. Some, with manager Del Crandall, resulted in fines. By June 1978, Carbo was refusing to go out and make his throws from right field during infield practice; in fact, he was seldom fully dressed a half-hour before the game. So Zimmer and Sullivan rationalized selling him to Cleveland by saying that he was playing out his option. Most teams try to pick up potential free-agent players in the stretch drive because (1) they are playing for their contract; and (2) the cost is usually slight. By the end of the year, Carbo and manager Jeff Torborg nearly came to blows.

Lee knew that he was the only one left from the old Buffalo Heads gang of five, and he realized that these moves represented a statement about his lifestyle. The night Carbo was sold to Cleveland, Lee cleared out his locker and left the ballpark, making all kinds of wild antiestablishment charges against Zimmer and Sullivan. The next day, prompted by a phone call from his father and the strong arm of his wife, Mary Lou, he jogged to Fenway Park from their Belmont house and sat down with Zimmer and Sullivan. "My father told me I should apologize," he told them, and that afternoon he was back in uniform. Zimmer probably never really understood; few did. He certainly never forgave or forgot.

One can viably argue that Carbo could have been kept around for the remainder of the season, for when Lynn began limping and Evans was seriously beaned in late August, all that remained was Garry Hancock. That ensuing off-season, after being "traded" to Montreal for infielder Stan Papi, Lee wore a T-shirt that read "Here Comes Gossage, Here Comes

Bailey . . ." — a reminder that in the playoff Zimmer had had to send up Bob "Beetle" Bailey to take three called strikes against Gossage. Sullivan had calmly unloaded two workable veterans in Jenkins and Cleveland, then the week of the trading deadline in June was asked about Charlie Finley's offer to sell right-handed pitcher Rick Langford for $400,000. "What would we do with him?" Sullivan asked in the Seattle press box. "We've got enough pitching." Ninety-one days later, all that stood between the Yankees and first place was Bobby Sprowl. Any New Englander can tell you that there are certain lessons that the Red Sox never learn, one of them being the worth of pitching depth: hence Mike Garman had to start against the Tigers in the last week of 1972, five days before another rookie named John Curtis had to be thrown out against Mickey Lolich to decide the division; Mike Paxton had to face Ron Guidry in Yankee Stadium in September 1977; and in 1981, half a game behind the Brewers with four games to play, they had to send a nervous Bruce Hurst to the wolves in Milwaukee.

In June and July 1978, that didn't seem to matter. As the Red Sox seemingly buried the tattered Yankees by winning four of six in late June and early July, the victories by scores of 9–5, 10–4, 9–2, and 4–1, George Steinbrenner was in a state of panic. When rookie right-hander Jim Beattie was knocked out in the third inning of an eventual 9–2 loss at Fenway on June 21, Steinbrenner was so incensed that he humiliated the Dartmouth graduate by optioning him to Tacoma in the seventh inning with a statement that called Beattie "gutless." Although sore-shouldered Don Gullett did manage one June win against the Red Sox, he was at the end of the line, as was Andy Messersmith. With Catfish Hunter disabled and Ed Figueroa struggling around or below .500, Billy Martin had to try all sorts of career farmhands, such as those named Kammeyer, Rajsich, Clay, and McCall. When the Yankees came in to Boston for two games July 3 and 4, they had right-handed pitcher Paul Semall drive up from

West Haven to throw batting practice. "If he looks good," Martin admitted, "we may start him." Semall didn't, and they didn't, but in the 9–5 pasting July 3, veteran first baseman Jim Spencer went out to the bullpen to warm up with the possibility of pitching in the eighth inning. Willie Randolph and Dent were injured, so the double-play combination was the then-unknown twenty-one-year-old Damaso Garcia and Fred "Chicken" Stanley, and the outfield was so shorn that Thurman Munson was learning to play right field to open a spot for rookie catcher Mike Heath. "The rain's come at a good time," Martin said about the holiday rainout of the matchup between the 8–3 Lee and Gullett, who his previous start against the Tigers had earned what would turn out to be his last professional victory.

Anyway, as Reggie Jackson said before the rainout, "The way the Red Sox are going, not even Affirmed can catch them." The starting pitching had been so good that the shoulder woes Bill Campbell carried from the 157 appearances, 30 wins, 51 saves, and 308 innings he threw for Gene Mauch and Zimmer in 1976–77 didn't really get noticed. They hit, and even George Scott was at .256 and Yastrzemski .298 with nine homers by the All-Star break. But, most of all, the Red Sox were playing with astounding rolling thunder and self-confidence. Individual players get on these streaks, as do golfers when they run off two or three tournaments in a row. Basketball teams get that feeling where everything *seems* in its place and everyone knows where everyone else is and the touch is perfect.

The Red Sox pitched, they hit, but most of all, they played defense. Evans, Lynn, and Rice played the way Evans, Lynn, and Yastrzemski had in 1975. Fisk, Scott, Burleson, and Remy played with brash confidence, cutoffs and relays were in perfect sync, double plays were executed with vengeance, and if ever there was an *offensive* defensive team, this was it. Then on July 9 in Cleveland (where else?), the last game before the All-Star break, Burleson hurt his ankle sliding into second base. Duffy stepped in at shortstop (in his defense, it must be said that he had played only a handful of innings at the position all season). Duffy was not a lithe, springy athlete; he depended on the rhythm and feel he could get only from playing behind pitchers and with his fellow infielders, and when he was pulled out of the icebox and stuck at shortstop, he never rediscovered the flow that had made him such a fine defensive infielder for the Indians. The sync and rhythm of the defense was never again the same; they lost ten of seventeen in Burleson's absence. Soon other parts began disintegrating.

The Red Sox hardly noticed on July 24 when Steinbrenner canned Martin in Kansas City after Billy had told Murray Chass of the *New York Times* and Henry Hecht of the *New York Post*, "One's a born liar, the other's convicted," concerning Reggie and George. Martin had to be led away from the news conference in tears, which was good for a few laughs, and while the easygoing Bob Lemon stepped in, saying, "The season starts today," few outside the Yankee clubhouse imagined what Lemon's restoration of the enjoyment principle to such a talented team would do. Steinbrenner disguised that when he took the Barnum & Bailey approach of announcing on Oldtimers' Day that Martin would be brought back, himself not realizing that Martin's second and third stints as manager would only turn into scenes from a Scorcese movie.

Lemon got the Yankees back into gear, and the Yankees in gear were an awfully good team. "The Red Sox had better talent, but we knew how to win," Lou Piniella would say in retrospect. "Somehow, we always knew that we could beat them when we had to." They could beat the Red Sox because they were good, as evidenced by the fact that they were 53–21 after July 18. They were good enough to beat any good team, not just the Red Sox, as not only were they 37–12 from August 24 through the World Series, but in that time they were 17–5 against Boston, Kansas City, Los Angeles, Baltimore, and Milwaukee, arguably five of the six best teams in baseball — after the Bronx Bombers. On July 17, Hunter, a month earlier consigned to the Gullet-Messersmith Memorial Scrap Heap, returned from an arm manipulation by Dr. Stanley Cowan, won six in a row in August, and was 10–3 the rest of the season. Figueroa won thirteen of his last fifteen decisions, including his last eight in a row. Randolph, Dent, Jackson, and Rivers got healthy. Munson went back behind the plate.

When, during the Yankees' September Boston Massacre, Zimmer had to stand and listen to a Brahmin businessman yell, "This time you've done it, Zimmer, this time you've really broken my Red Sox heart," the Boston manager realized that he would have to take some of the blame for the collapse. What was his fault?

First, Zimmer probably did worry too much about winning each game, and his Buddy Baker pedal-to-the-metal managing may have not only caused some of the physical breakdowns but rendered his reserves incapable of oiling the rust once they got to play. The most serious breakdown was Fisk, who played more games in the field than any other Boston player. He caught 156 games, more even than Texas's Jim Sundberg in his most active year and fewer only than former Cub Randy Hundley, who broke down after that season and was never the same again. Fisk cracked a rib diving for a foul pop the first week of August, yet remained in the lineup, and when writers asked Zimmer about it, he got so defensive that he had Red Sox publicist and statistician Dick Bresciani produce a report that from the start of spring training Fisk, between rainouts and other off-days, had had twenty-nine days off. The pain ("I feel as if I've got a knife stuck in my side") from the cracked rib forced Fisk to alter his throwing motion, and that in turn rearranged the scar tissue from old elbow injuries and left Fisk in constant pain the last two months. "He kept taking drugs to kill the pain," Fisk's wife, Linda, said, "and all it did was change his personality and get him all screwed up."

Zimmer steadfastly refused to take out Butch Hobson, despite the fact that the chips in his elbow were so bad that at least once a day the elbow would lock, forcing Hobson to rearrange the chips with his other hand while teammates blanched at his toughness. Lynn wore down, and soon Yastrzemski's back and shoulder bogged him down and Scott injured his finger. Ken Harrelson's theory was that part of the reason the team got so many injuries down the stretch was that they were so tired from pushing so hard to blow it out in the first four months. But Zimmer and the Red Sox also had an extraordinary amount of bad luck: Remy cracked a bone in his wrist on August 26 and missed sixteen games, including the Massacre. Evans was beaned by Seattle right-hander Mike Parrott on August 29 and wasn't the same player again; he tried to play and discount his problems at first, but he went nine for fifty-four the rest of the season and after dropping four fly balls in a week admitted that "every time I look up I get dizzy."

Then, too, the starting pitching that was 43–14 broke down. Tiant won one game between June 24 and September 6. Lee lost seven straight after July 15, was banished to the bullpen, clashed with Zimmer, and would never win another game for the Red Sox. Jim Wright was 7–2 on August 12 and didn't win again. Torrez won one of his last ten starts.

Duffy and Brohamer always felt that the Red Sox "twenty-five guys/twenty-five cabs" caste system had something to do with their inability to cope with adversity. For most of the regular players — Rice, Lynn, Burleson, Evans, Fisk — sellout crowds, adoration, paternal ownership, and pennant races were the facts of their major-league lives. When Bobby Darwin came to the Red Sox in June 1976, Evans one night said to him, "How are you going to enjoy the Fall Classic?"

Darwin scrunched up his face. "Ummm . . . ," he replied, "what classic is that?"

"The World Series, of course."

Rookie outfielder Sam Bowen so hated the dichotomy between regulars and nonregulars that when he was sent back to the minor leagues in July, he told his Pawtucket teammates that he preferred the minors. "Yastrzemski one time spit on my raincoat as I got on the bus, another spilled his beer on my sportcoat, and neither time did he so much as apologize," said Bowen. "And I'm supposed to have respect for them?"

On a spring-training day trip to Sarasota, Brohamer had finished batting practice, was in the clubhouse, and went to make a sandwich with the cold cuts, bread, and garnishes laid out by the clubhouse attendant. "Hey, you can't eat the spread until the regulars have had it," he was brusquely told by Evans. Brohamer, an excellent golfer who'd arranged for several teammates to play the prestigious Firestone course when they were in Cleveland, was waiting to play on an off-day with trainer Charlie Moss, Dick Drago, and others. When the car pulled up and Brohamer started to get in, Rice said, "Who invited you? We're only going to have room for four." Brohamer was left behind. Players who came in from other teams said that the Red Sox were the only team where in batting practice they used good, new balls for the regulars and stained, hacked balls for the nonregulars. "Maybe," Duffy suggested, "the Red Sox were founded on traditions brought to the Western World from India. They even put us off in a corner together."

The effect, in the mind of the cum laude psychology major from Stanford, "was that when things suddenly got very tough, instead of pulling together, the team pulled apart. Players started pointing fingers." Duffy should know. The highlight film from that season could have been titled "For What Happened in '78, We'd Like to Blame Frank Duffy."

One thing that seriously affected the team came after the

first month of the season when Burleson declared he couldn't hit second. Burleson was at the time hitting .180, and he blamed it on having to give himself up trying to utilize Remy's speed. So, on May 1, Zimmer moved Burleson back to the lead-off spot and dropped Remy to the second position, which wasted Remy's talent for stealing an occasional run.

The Yankees charge and the Red Sox slide weren't really noticed until September. One reason was that the last time the two teams had seen one another was the two long nights of August 2 and 3, when the Red Sox rallied from a 5–0 deficit to tie the first game, sent it fourteen innings to a 5–5 rain-drenched tie until 1:15 A.M., then came back the next night to win the first game 7–5 in the seventeenth inning before Torrez won a six-inning, rain-shortened, 8–1 finale, the only win he ever had over the Yankees in a Boston uniform. No one noticed that when Zimmer used Campbell for five and two-thirds innings on the first night, it was by far his longest as well as his best outing of the season, and the resulting stiffness rendered him virtually ineffective the rest of the way. Despite the pieces chipping off the statues erected for the SuperTeam, they finished August with a bigger lead (six and a half games) than they started (five games). The problem was that the closest team on August 1 had been Milwaukee. On September 1, it was New York.

For all the physical bad luck the Red Sox had encountered, they had also had their share of good fortune. There was a ten-inning 6–5 win over the Indians on August 10 when (1) Ted Cox loafed from first on a Bo Diaz drive he thought would be a home run and got thrown out at the plate, and (2) Andre Thornton dropped Hobson's tenth-inning pop fly to start a multiplayer comedy skit that provided Hobson with a game-winning, two-run, inside-the-park boo-boo. In one week on the West Coast, Nolan Ryan messed up three consecutive bunts to turn a sure 2–0 Angels victory into a 4–2 Boston win, Ken Brett balked in the winning run for an 8–6

Red Sox gift, and that Sunday in Oakland, home-plate umpire Durwood Merrill made one of the biggest gaffes of the
season.

The A's Matt Keough had a 2–1 lead with two outs in the
eighth and an 0–2 count on Remy. He then threw him a spitter that broke so much that it dipped down on Remy, ticked
the bottom of catcher Bruce Robinson's glove, and hit the
ground. As Robinson scooped up the ball and tagged Remy
for what should have been the final out, Merrill signaled a
foul ball. Remy, who had already started back to the dugout
knowing he'd swung and missed the pitch "by nearly a foot
and a half," turned around in disbelief. Keough charged from
the mound and was tackled by Robinson, and when the argument and melee ended fifteen minutes later, Merrill's decision stood. Foul ball. The rattled Keough missed with the
next two pitches, then threw a fastball that Remy hit out over
the right-field fence for a three-run homer and Eckersley's
4–2 victory. "We've had Bunt Night, Ball Night, and Foul
Tip Day for five aways in one week," laughed Remy. Oh, yes.
It was the seventh — and *last* — home run Jerry Remy hit
in the big leagues.

In the next week, however, the cracks began to show. Two
nights after Foul Tip Day, in Seattle, Torrez was to pull a
stunt that Zimmer — and his teammates — would never
forget. He was cruising along with a 3–0 lead over the Mariners, warming up for the bottom of the sixth, when he spotted Haywood Sullivan sitting with then–Mariners owner
Danny Kaye in the glassed-in box directly behind home plate.
Fooling around, instead of throwing a pitch, Torrez fired the
ball as hard as he could at the Plexiglas in front of Sullivan,
then giggled. Zimmer did not giggle. Neither did Fisk. When
Torrez couldn't get an out that inning and left down 4–3 before Zimmer could get a reliever ready, Zimmer fumed. And,
afterward, when Torrez told reporters, "We're not doing the
little things," and implied that Zimmer should have had Rice
and Fisk bunt in separate situations, Rice roared back that

Torrez was "an excuse-maker." One week later, at home, Zimmer had to start Andy Hassler in the second game of a doubleheader against Toronto, which seemed to work out fine with a 5–2 lead into the sixth, but Duffy and Hobson so collapsed in the infield that when Zimmer took Stanley out of the 6–5 loss, he said, "It was pathetic — both the fact that they didn't hit the ball hard enough to make plays and the way Duffy played at second." Within the next forty-eight hours, they lost two games to the lowly A's, and on Saturday night Zimmer put the blame on Brohamer's play at second when he failed to get to a pop fly in short right field. Brohamer long after resented the fact that Rice, in right because of the Evans beaning, had broken back and felt that it was his, Rice's, play all the way. "The thing that galls me," said Brohamer, "is the idea that you can't criticize what's supposed to be the greatest everyday lineup ever put together. Heck, Rice is always the first to admit he's made a mistake when he makes it, but no one wants to ruffle any of the stars."

Starting with that Toronto loss, the Red Sox would lose fourteen of seventeen. "But what seemed so unbelievable," said Fisk, "was that a good team could play so badly. Little Leaguers could play better than we did in that stretch." Indeed, in the seventeen games through the Massacre, the Red Sox made an astounding thirty-three errors, and it was more than just Hobson, for whom every ball was a potential act of terrorism.

The Yankees had won twelve of fourteen and the Red Sox had lost five of seven when they met for the four-game series in Fenway beginning on September 7. By then, Zimmer had ditched Lee from the rotation and replaced him with rookie Bobby Sprowl, who'd spent half the season in double-A and who'd been shaky in his first start September 5 in Baltimore, a start he lost 4–1. By the Yankees' vaunted arrival, the lead was down to four games, and it stood at four on the Wednesday, September 6, return of El Tiante. After winning one game after June 24, Tiant went to the mound following two quiet losses to the Orioles and a five-of-six slide and shut them out, so that when his ageless partner Yastrzemski homered off Dennis Martinez, the Red Sox took a 2–0 victory's worth of momentum back to Boston for the most important series of the season.

That Saturday night, Yankee fan (and rock entrepreneur) Dick Waterman walked into a Cambridge bar, held up a sign that read "NY 35–49–4, BOS 5–16–11," and announced, "Today was the first time in history that a first-place team was mathematically eliminated." That afternoon, as Guidry fired a two-hitter and the Red Sox defense unzipped in a seven-run fourth inning for a 7–0 loss that cut the lead to seven games, NBC's Tony Kubek had said, "This is the first time I've ever seen a first-place team trying to chase a second-place team."

As the four-game series — which was to be followed by a three-game series the next weekend in New York — started, Bob Lemon announced, "We'll be happy with a split." By 9:05 Friday night, in the third inning of the second game, Lemon turned to pitching coach Clyde King and said, "Now we can settle for nothing less than three out of four."

It all started Thursday night with one of Hobson's forty-four errors, a Munson single, and a Jackson single. 2–0. Torrez got but three Yankees out, the game became a 15–3 rout, and it was so boring that in the bottom of the seventh inning someone in the press box noted the Yankees' score-by-innings and tried dialing the 2-3-2-5-0-1-0 number. It was disconnected. That night, Munson was beaned by Drago; he was back in the lineup Friday, which was a Xerox copy of game one.

Boston started the rookie Wright Friday night, and in two pitches — a single and a stolen base with an accompanying Fisk throwing error — Rivers stood on third. Evans had to leave the game dizzy after missing a fly ball. Scott fielded a routine Rivers grounder and was beaten to the bag. 13–2.

The Yankees had at least one player with three hits before Hobson even got one plate appearance in each of the first two drubbings.

Then, Saturday afternoon, with two on and two out in the fourth inning and with the game scoreless thanks to a crashing, twisting catch by Yastrzemski against The Wall, Piniella — that tormentor of New England's hallowed souls — lofted a pop fly into shallow right center. Lynn took off after it, but as Eckersley pointed out, "It must have blown a hundred feet across, like a Frisbee." The ball landed nearest second baseman Duffy with both the shortstop, Burleson, and first baseman, Scott, also in pursuit. 1–0. Eckersley walked Nettles intentionally, but Dent dunked a hanging 0–2 pitch into left for two runs, and by the time the inning was over, a walk, an error, a wild pitch, and a passed ball gave Guidry the 7–0 lead. The lead was down to one game, and all that stood between the Yankees and first place was a nervous twenty-three-year-old pitcher named Bobby Sprowl.

All weekend, Tiant had begged pitching coach Al Jackson and Zimmer to let him come back with three days' rest against the Yankees. Zimmer wouldn't listen. "The Baltimore game Monday night is as important as the one with the Yankees," Zimmer insisted.

"Bool cheat," Tiant replied. "Sunday, we're either tied for first or have a two-game lead on the Jahnkees. We gotta beat the Jahnkees." Tiant knew Jim Palmer was scheduled for the Orioles on Monday. Palmer doesn't like to pitch in Fenway Park. Tiant knew that was a better spot for Sprowl because he knew he'd get runs.

Other players pleaded with Zimmer to put Lee back in the rotation, but Zimmer was seething at Lee. Earlier in the week in Baltimore, Zimmer had called to the bullpen to get Lee up when Eckersley got into trouble in the second inning. Lee wasn't there. "He screams about not pitching, then when I try to pitch him, he's in the clubhouse," Zimmer fumed.

Lee said that he was in the trainer's room getting work on his back and that no one had told him he might be used early.

Whatever, Sunday came along and Zimmer steadfastly refused to reconsider despite the career records of his two available veterans against the Yankees. Lee finished his career with the third best record (12–5) of any opposing pitcher in Yankee history. Tiant (22–15) was the winningest active Yankee opponent. And the Sox had sold Reggie Cleveland, who was 8–2 against New York in a Boston uniform.

Broadcaster Ken Harrelson walked through the Red Sox dugout at 11:05 A.M., figuring that Zimmer would change his mind and go with one of the two veterans instead of the rookie, who after being 9–3 in double-A in the first half had been a mediocre 7–4 with a high 4.15 ERA at Pawtucket in July and August. "The kid's got icewater in his veins," Zimmer assured Harrelson and other members of the media. Then, for emphasis, he repeated his statement. "——ing Icewater. Everyone tells me."

Zimmer never did say who "everyone" was. It most certainly wasn't Pawtucket manager Joe Morgan, who when the Red Sox were in Pawtucket for an exhibition game two weeks earlier had said that he didn't think Sprowl was ready. "He's kind of a jittery kid," Morgan said.

Sprowl walked Rivers and Randolph to open the game, then when he tried to get out of the jam, Jackson muscled a single through the middle. A third walk later, Sprowl was gone: to the showers, to the minors, to a timeless niche in the Red Sox pantheon of heroic flops. Stanley came in, surrendered a two-run single to Nettles, and the Yankees were off to a 6–0 lead and a 7–4 victory. "——ing Icewater" stuck in many people's minds the next spring when the nervous, self-conscious Sprowl tried to pitch in spring training. The first time he went to throw batting practice, he threw half a dozen pitches outside the cage. One teammate threw his bat away and hollered at him, another refused to get in, and his mental block continued to build. Zimmer tried him in an exhibition game in Daytona Beach against Montreal; he hit the backstop five times and allowed five runs in one inning. He tried pitching him in an 8:30 A.M. exhibition game against Pawtucket, but in two innings he allowed ten runs and twelve walks, and threw five wild pitches, three of which hit batsmen; as he went to warm up that morning, he heard one veteran player kiddingly yell to other teammates, "Everyone stay in the trainer's room for fifteen minutes. Sprowl is warming up." Sprowl heard the crack, gave a humiliated stare at the clubhouse, then bounced his first pitch off the corner of the warm-up plate into the stands. Sprowl was sent to a Houston farm club in June in a trade for Bob Watson, eventually hurt his arm, and never won a game in the majors. "That experience shattered a fine person and a tremendous talent," lamented Sprowl's close friend Bruce Hurst. "It's amazing how miscalculations like that can ruin a person's career."

When the Boston Massacre mercifully had ended, the Yankees had outscored the Red Sox 41–9 and outhit them 84–29. The four Boston starters — Torrez, Wright, Eckersley, and Sprowl — had retired a total of twenty New York batters. "I don't feel sorry for them," said ex–Red Sox reliever Sparky Lyle. "I pity them."

It got worse. After splitting with Baltimore and holding onto their first-place tie, the Red Sox went into Cleveland and lost two straight to David Clyde and (of course) Mike Paxton. They arrived at the New York Sheraton at 3:30 A.M. Friday for the final Yankee series one and a half games out. Fisk turned to a writer and, looking as befuddled as Jack Lemmon in *The Out of Towners*, asked, "What *is* wrong with us?"

Guidry shut out Tiant 4–0 on Friday night with yet another two-hitter, but on Saturday Torrez battled Hunter right down to the ninth inning. In the bottom of the ninth, with Yastrzemski playing shallow in left presuming that Torrez would keep the ball down to Rivers, the Yankee lead-off man got a high pitch. Rivers lined it over Yastrzemski's head for a triple, scored on Munson's fly ball, and New York had its sixth straight win, 3–2, and a seemingly insurmountable three-and-a-half game lead with fourteen remaining games. "The abuse we have taken and the abuse we must be prepared to take for the entire winter," said Burleson in a monastically stark clubhouse, "we richly deserve."

"There are no words to describe this," said Yastrzemski, staring straight down at the floor. "I can't ever remember feeling so humiliated. It just doesn't make sense. When has this good a team ever been so badly whipped?"

Eckersley went into the next afternoon's start with a three-game losing streak, a period of frustration started in Baltimore September 4 when he and his wife attempted one last try at reconciliation. She flew in to meet him in Baltimore with their daughter, Mandy. The brash Eck was visibly nervous on the flight to Baltimore, then broke down when he saw his daughter. "You like to say that outside things don't weigh on your mind," said Fisk, "but family things do. If they didn't you wouldn't be worth knowing. Eck is a great competitor and a very tough person. But he is twenty-three. That's his daughter he's been separated from. That's a lot to deal with at that age." Eckersley had lost that game in Baltimore, lost the 7–0 game to Guidry in Boston, then lost 2–1 in Cleveland when — yes — Rick Manning nicked him for the game-winning single.

"I was loose and life was always easy, no complications," Eckersley later admitted. "If my daughter weren't involved, it wouldn't be complicated. But she is. Then I made up my mind to go out and pitch *for* her to prove something to myself and everyone around me." He did not lose one of his last four starts. That Sunday, with the help of two Rice homers, Eckersley stopped the Yankee humiliation 7–3 for his seventeenth win to bring the Yankee lead back to two and a half games, but even after taking three out of four in Detroit, it seemed as if the clock had ticked down. Friday night in Toronto, they blew a horrid 5–4 game to the last-place Blue Jays — one of only four wins in twenty-six games the Jays had in September — that, coupled with a Yankee comeback in Cleveland, left Boston two games back with eight to play. "Let's face it," Burleson said afterward, "tonight finished us." As Burleson was so telling the writers, Hobson was in Zimmer's office telling the manager that after his forty-fourth error he should get out of the field. "I'm no quitter," Hobson said to Zimmer, tears welling in his eyes. "But I can't get the ——ing ball across the diamond. I'm killing this team. Get Brohamer in there."

Later that night, Zimmer told the writers about Hobson's request. As he recounted Hobson's words, Zimmer wiped a tear from his own eye. "He's one of the greatest sonavabitches I've ever known," said the manager.

Burleson was not the only player who felt a pang of resignation, but he was one of the few who said it. One who did not was Luis Clemente Tiant. At breakfast, he said, "Bleep these guys who want to throw in the towel. Win today, win tomorrow, win the next day . . . The easy thing in life is to give up. Too many players on this team don't know what it's like to be treated like cheat most of their lives."

Tiant was so anxious that he didn't want to wait for the bus. "If we lose today," he said in the cab ride to Exhibition Stadium, "it will be over my dead body. They'll have to leave me face down on the mound." El Tiante treated the fans to a gutsy replay of the fourth game of the '75 series, when he had thrown 172 pitches. Thirteen Toronto batters reached base, nine got into scoring position, only one scored, and when Rice hit his forty-third homer in the fifth off Jesse Jefferson, the difference was back down to a game. The Yankees had lost to the Indians 10–1 in Cleveland, and in one week, the lead had been chiseled back down from three and a half games to one.

The next day, the Red Sox encapsulated their struggle back into the race with a fourteen-inning, 7–6 victory in which

Yastrzemski tied it in the eighth with a two-run double off
left-hander Balor Moore and Drago won it by twice intentionally walking nemesis Roy Howell with runners on first
and second to strike out Otto Velez. The Yankees also won
that day, and for a week the two teams seemed on parallel
tracks to the end. Eckersley, Tiant, and Torrez (his only win
in his last ten starts, a seven-walk shutout) beat Detroit in
Fenway, while Figueroa, Hunter, and Guidry beat Toronto
in The Stadium. Stanley and Eckersley overpowered the Blue
Jays 11–0, 5–1 on the last Friday and Saturday, Beattie and
Figueroa beat Cleveland 3–1, 3–1. Some fans tried to maintain enthusiasm ("Pope dead, Sox alive, details at 11,"
boomed WBCN's theatrical Charles Laquidara at 7:10 A.M.
one day), but there was a grim sense of fighting U.S. Steel.
"With a pennant on the line, I don't feel too good," George
Scott said the morning of October 1, the day of the last regular scheduled game. "Oh, Tiant will win for us. He's the best
money pitcher in the last ten years. But Catfish Hunter's the
second best, and he's going for the Yankees against the Indians."

Before the game, old friend Tom Murphy sneaked into the
left-field scoreboard and clanked an "8" down next to CLE.
The fans roared. Then, as Tiant pitched the top of the first
inning, a roar broke out in the bleachers. "I was trying to
figure out where to play Howell," said Jack Brohamer, "and
all of a sudden I heard all the cheering in the bleachers. All of
a sudden it dawned on me that someone must have taken
Catfish deep." Andre Thornton had, and fans who brought
transistor radios to the game to listen to the other half of this
tale of two cities on a Fall River radio station began chanting
as the Indians battered Hunter in the second inning. A girl
handed Stanley a radio in the bullpen, and he used hand signals to orchestrate the fans.

As Tiant whirled and rhumba'd and toyed with the Blue
Jays with the 5–0 two-hitter that was his third straight win
and brought his September–October record in a Boston uni-

form to 31–12, the Indians' rout increased: 2–0, 6–2, 7–2. The megaboard flashed: "Next game — Tomorrow, 1:30, Guidry (24–3) vs. Torrez (16–12)." Then, when that flashed off, the Red Sox management added a note: "Thank you, Rick Waits." For all of that winter and most of the next season, Waits, the Indians' left-hander who beat the Yankees to bring the season to a playoff, got a steady barrage of mail from Red Sox fans across the country. "I'll always feel as if I were a part of that team, at least a part of its fans," Waits has often said.

So it was as if some divine force had decreed that this pennant should be decided face to face, that the Red Sox return — winning twelve of their last fourteen and making up three and a half games in that time — earned them a chance for ultimate redemption in a confrontation unlike those in June, July, and September when the two teams were on different sides of the Expressway. Now both were hot. On October 2, 1978, the Yankees had fallen into a playoff because they lost one of their last seven games, one more than the Red Sox. The two best teams in baseball would meet to give one its hundredth win. To quote Dickens, "It was the best of times, it was the worst of times, it was the age of wisdom, it was the age of foolishness, it was the epoch of belief, it was the epoch of incredulity, it was the season of Light, it was the season of Darkness, it was the spring of hope, it was the winter of despair, we had everything before us, we had nothing before us, we were all going direct to heaven, we were all going direct the other way."

There were seventy-five years of preparation that went into the twenty-one hours between games. Athens versus Sparta, Ruth, Frazee, DiMaggio, Williams, 1949, Lyle, Cater, Munson, Fisk, Rivers, Lee, 1976, 1977, and, now, Guidry and Torrez. "A playoff like that is totally different from the divisional playoffs or the World Series," Gossage said later. "If you make those, you've already been a winner because you've won something. You lose a playoff, and you've won nothing. Nothing. Then make it the Red Sox and the Yankees after all we went through and I was more nervous pitching in that game than I was at any other time in my career."

Burleson remembered driving in to Boston from his suburban Acton home, "being so excited I kept wanting to scream." Remy said that "the anticipation was so tremendous that few people said much of anything," and as one walked down Boylston Street from Copley Square the bright, crisp fall morning seemed perfectly clear, as if everything were focused on that game. The Giants and the Dodgers were like this in 1951, only the Dodgers had never had the opportunity to regather their self-respect as had the Red Sox. On this rarest of fall days, with a press contingent so large that it sprawled out across Fenway's roof, both teams had the feeling that they had been climbing for months to reach this final all-or-nothing fight for the mountain.

Few so ballyhooed sporting events ever match the anticipation; this one did. In the second inning, Yastrzemski — one of the greatest dead fastball hitters who ever played — "turned up the dials," jumped on a high, inside Guidry fastball, and lined it inside the right-field foul pole for a home run and a 1–0 Boston lead. "I watched him down the stretch in '67," said Ken Harrelson, "but that might have amazed me more than anything he's ever done. At that age [thirty-nine] against that pitcher in that situation. That's leadership."

So it seemed as if this were to be the afternoon of redemption for sixty years of torment for New Englanders. Torrez threw a sumptuous, meaty 0–2 gift to Jackson in the top of the first inning and Reggie hit what on most summer days would have been what Fenway loyalists call a net job. Instead, the wind was blowing down from the north (the true believers' gift?), Jackson's fly ball was knocked down, and Yastrzemski caught it against The Wall. Torrez from there settled down, and in the sixth — when Burleson doubled past third and was singled in with Rice's four hundred sixth total base — Boston seemed in control of the game.

Now if the Yankees had then been run from above, for the stars' and the owners' egos' sake, as they would be three and four years later, Jackson would have been playing right field. But the low-keyed, practical Lemon was managing and had made out the lineup with the crusty, crafty Piniella in what is Fenway's most treacherous position, particularly on fall afternoons with a high sky and a falling sun that at that time of year comes directly from behind the roof to the position. "We weren't as talented, but we were better — one run, ninety feet or however better," was the way Piniella always described the difference between the Yankees and Red Sox, and on this day he was the key player in the game. "The man just wins," Zimmer later said admiringly. "Don't ask me how he does it, because he's one of the worst-looking players around. But he beats you."

Bucky Dent never would have been anything but a nice journeyman shortstop with little to distinguish him from Eddie Kasko or Eddie Bressoud or Gene Michael were it not for the two Piniella plays. The first came in that bottom of the sixth, with two on, two out, and Lynn up against Guidry. "He wasn't throwing the way he had the two times we faced him in September," said Lynn. "He was working on three days' rest, he didn't have that overpowering fastball — Yaz proved that — and was throwing an extraordinary number of sliders. Not only that, but his slider wasn't that sharp, unhittable kind. This slider could be pulled." Which is precisely what Lynn did with two out and two on, belting a line drive to the right-field corner. "As soon as I hit it, I took off, figuring it was either a three-run homer or a two-run double," said Lynn. "As I was rounding first, I looked up and saw Piniella catching it.

"I couldn't believe it. How ——ing lucky can the Yankees be? That was a completely ridiculous place for him. He was twenty yards out of position toward the corner, a hundred-to-one shot. There wasn't any reason to that, just a hunch. The man's just a gambler."

When told of Lynn's comments afterward, Piniella laughed. Sure, Sweet Lou loves the tracks. Sure, he has horses. Sure, he used to use hand signals from the Yankees dugout to Zimmer in the middle of games to apprise him of the results of races they'd both bet on. That's Sweet Lou. "Sure, I'm a gambler." He smiled. "I've guessed on every pitch that's ever been thrown to me, and I don't do too badly, do I?

"Actually, I did have a good reason for being out of position," Piniella continued, explaining why he was deep toward the corner instead of in straightaway right field where he'd normally play Lynn against a left-hander he usually tried to take to The Wall. "Munson and I talked about it between innings, and we agreed that Guidry's slider was more the speed of a curveball, far slower, and that Lynn was apt to pull him. Remember, Lynn doesn't bail against most lefties. So before the pitch, I yelled to Mickey [Rivers], 'Let's move six steps to the left.' "

Besides the little thing that turned out to be huge executed by Piniella, the Red Sox *should* at that point have had a 3–0 lead. Scott led off the third with a double and was bunted up by Brohamer, but Burleson failed to get Scott home from third with less than two out. Burleson tapped back to the mound, the twenty-fourth time in the final month that a Boston batter had failed to execute that vital fundamental of scoring the runner in that situation. Five of those twenty-four failures in the final thirty-four days were the margin of difference because they came in one-run defeats. So instead of coming down to a playoff . . .

Instead — ah, how many times New Englanders have heard that: in '49, and when Roy White took Campbell deep in '77, or when the 1978 July 4 game was rained out! Now, instead of Guidry possibly being knocked out with a 4–0 or

5–0 Boston lead, he had survived and it was 2–0 in the seventh. White and Chris Chambliss singled, and with two out, Dent came to the plate. A number of Yankee players have said that if Billy Martin had been there, they wouldn't have been, because if Martin had been there that afternoon, Dent probably wouldn't have batted in that position, for one of the complaints Dent had with Martin (who later said that Dent was a below-average player covered for by the great Nettles at third) was that the manager constantly pinch-hit for him and put Chicken Stanley in at short in the late innings. But even with Lemon managing, if Randolph hadn't been hurt the day before, Dent would still have been hit for by Jim Spencer, but Lemon had used Spencer to bat for Brian Doyle and didn't choose to juggle his infield too much, preferring only to substitute Stanley for Doyle. Martin had watched Dent's average go from .274 in 1974 to .264, .246, .247 and, that '78 season, .243. At that at-bat, his three hundred seventy-eighth of the season, he had four homers, thirty-seven runs batted in, and a .242 average, and when Torrez got two quick strikes on him and he fouled a ball so violently off his instep that he collapsed on the ground in pain, a number of New York writers questioned why a Jim Spencer or a Gary Thomasson wasn't being used as a pinch hitter. As Dent called him to recover from the stinging pain of the foul ball, the Yankees' greatest weapon against the Red Sox in this era, Rivers, picked up Dent's bat. He noticed a crack, took the bat back to the dugout, and replaced it.

At that point, few had noticed what eventually would lead one Red Sox fan, an Episcopal minister, to say, "This may prove that being a Red Sox fan is God's way of making New Englanders learn the meaning of suffering." Between the sixth and seventh innings, the wind had shifted, and instead of blowing straight in, it had begun blowing out to left. Fisk, for one, hadn't noticed. So when Torrez threw a bad 0–2 pitch and Dent got it up in the air to left field, Fisk breathed a sigh of relief. Two innings to go.

"Then I looked up, saw Yaz looking up . . ."

Right below where Fisk's histrionic home run had crashed in 1975, Dent's fly ball nestled into the screen inches above the top of the fence. As in the seventh World Series game in 1946 (1–0, 3–2) and the seventh series game in 1975 (3–0 in the sixth), a Red Sox lead on the final day of summer had dissipated.

New York, 3; Boston, 2.

Torrez was then unglued. He walked Rivers, who, naturally, stole second. Even though Torrez had struck Munson out thrice earlier, Zimmer had seen his big right-hander go up in flames too many times before and rushed in Stanley. Munson hit The Wall, it was 4–2, and in the top of the eighth Jackson hit a Stanley fastball into the center-field bleachers to make it 5–2. It was made to seem even worse in the bottom of the seventh when with one on and two out, Zimmer sent Bob "Beetle" Bailey to bat for Brohamer. That prompted Lemon to bring on Gossage, and as he warmed up, the Boston fans had time to ponder all of poor Bailey's symbolism: a Zimmer protégé, an ex–National Leaguer who was the first player the manager announced had made the club in spring training ("He'll win us six games off the bench") and another in a long line of end-of-the-road players who supposedly would have been terrors in Fenway. He was all Zimmer had on the bench for the situation; Carbo was driving from Cleveland to Detroit at that moment, and Boston's depth was so pitiful that in one game in Yankee Stadium Scott had to be used as a pinch runner, which was a little like making John Madden a wide receiver.

To know what it is to be a Red Sox fan is to be, years later, at a Beacon Hill party filled with Massachusetts political figures and out of a dry Chablis have someone say, "Bucky Bleeping Dent," and instinctively blurt back, "Bob Bleeping Bailey." It wasn't only that Bailey struck out, it was that he took three Gossage fastballs as if he were at a Quaker meeting.

The Playoff Game, October 2, 1978

New York	AB	R	H	RBI	Boston	AB	R	H	RBI
Rivers, cf	2	1	1	0	Burleson, ss	4	1	1	0
Blair, cf	1	0	1	0	Remy, 2b	4	1	2	0
Munson, c	5	0	1	1	Rice, rf	5	0	1	1
Piniella, rf	4	0	1	0	Yastrzemski, lf	5	2	2	2
Jackson, dh	4	1	1	1	Fisk, c	3	0	1	0
Nettles, 3b	4	0	0	0	Lynn, cf	4	0	1	1
Chambliss, 1b	4	1	1	1	Hobson, dh	4	0	1	0
White, lf	3	1	1	0	Scott, 1b	4	0	2	0
Thomasson, lf	0	0	0	0	Brohamer, 3b	1	0	0	0
Doyle, 2b	2	0	0	0	Bailey, ph	1	0	0	0
Spencer, ph	1	0	0	0	Duffy, 3b	0	0	0	0
Stanley, 2b	1	0	0	0	Evans, ph	1	0	0	0
Dent, ss	4	1	1	3					
TOTALS	35	5	8	5		36	4	11	4

New York	000	000	410–5
Boston	010	001	020–4

LOB–New York 6, Boston, 9. 2B–Rivers, Scott, Burleson, Munson, Remy. HR–Yastrzemski (17), Dent (5), Jackson (27) SB–Rivers, 2. S–Brohamer, Remy.

	IP	H	R	ER	BB	SO
Guidry (W, 25–3)	6⅓	6	2	2	1	5
Gossage (Save, 27)	2⅔	5	2	2	1	2
Torrez (L, 16–13)	6⅔	5	4	4	3	4
Stanley	⅓	2	1	1	0	0
Hassler	1⅔	1	0	0	0	2
Drago	⅓	0	0	0	0	0

Stanley pitched to one batter in the eighth. PB–Munson. T–2:52. A–32,925.

But the season was not yet over. Remy, battling to the end, doubled and scored on a Yastrzemski single in the eighth, and when Fisk and Lynn singled, Gossage's lead was down to 5–4 with runners on first and second and one out. Gossage promptly reared back and pumped high, rising fastballs to

Final American League Standings and Red Sox Statistics, 1978

	W	L	PCT	GB	R	HR	BA
EAST							
NY	100	63	.613		735	125	.267
BOS	99	64	.607	1	796	172	.267
MIL	93	69	.574	6.5	804	173	.276
BAL	90	71	.559	9	659	154	.258
DET	86	76	.531	13.5	714	129	.271
CLE	69	90	.434	29	639	106	.261
TOR	59	102	.366	40	590	98	.250
WEST							
KC	92	70	.568		743	98	.268
CAL	87	75	.537	5	691	108	.259
TEX	87	75	.537	5	692	132	.253
MIN	73	89	.451	19	666	82	.267
CHI	71	90	.441	20.5	634	106	.264
OAK	69	93	.426	23	532	100	.245
SEA	56	104	.350	35	614	97	.248
LEAGUE TOTAL					9509	1680	.261

MANAGER	W	L	PCT
Don Zimmer	99	64	.607

POS	PLAYER	B	G	AB	H	2B	3B	HR	R	RBI	BA
REGULARS											
1B	George Scott	R	120	412	96	16	4	12	51	54	.233
2B	Jerry Remy	L	148	583	162	24	6	2	87	44	.278
SS	Rick Burleson	R	145	626	155	32	5	5	75	49	.248
3B	Butch Hobson	R	147	512	128	26	2	17	65	80	.250
RF	Dwight Evans	R	147	497	123	24	2	24	75	63	.247
CF	Fred Lynn	L	150	541	161	33	3	22	75	82	.298
LF	Jim Rice	R	163	677	213	25	15	46	121	139	.315
C	Carlton Fisk	R	157	571	162	39	5	20	94	88	.284
DH	Carl Yastrzemski	L	144	523	145	21	2	17	70	81	.277
SUBSTITUTES											
UT	Jack Brohamer	L	81	244	57	14	1	1	34	25	.234
UT	Frank Duffy	R	64	104	27	5	0	0	12	4	.260
DH	Bob Bailey	R	43	94	18	3	0	4	12	9	.191
1C	Fred Kendall	R	20	41	8	1	0	0	3	4	.195
OD	Garry Hancock	L	38	80	18	3	0	0	10	4	.225
OD	Bernie Carbo	L	17	46	12	3	0	1	7	6	.261
OF	Sam Bowen	R	6	7	1	0	0	1	3	1	.143
C	Bob Montgomery	R	10	29	7	1	1	0	2	5	.241

Final American League Standings and Red Sox Statistics, 1978, continued

PITCHER	T	W	L	PCT	ERA	SV
Dennis Eckersley	R	20	8	.714	2.99	0
Mike Torrez	R	16	13	.552	3.96	0
Luis Tiant	R	13	8	.619	3.31	0
Bill Lee	L	10	10	.500	3.46	0
Bob Stanley	R	15	2	.882	2.60	10
Jim Wright	R	8	4	.667	3.57	0
Dick Drago	R	4	4	.500	3.03	7
Allen Ripley	R	2	5	.286	5.55	0
Tom Burgmeier	L	2	1	.667	4.40	4
Bill Campbell	R	7	5	.583	3.91	4
Andy Hassler	L	2	1	.667	3.00	1
Bobby Sprowl	L	0	2	.000	6.39	0
John LaRose	L	0	0	—	22.50	0
Reggie Cleveland	R	0	1	.000	0.00	0
TEAM TOTAL		99	64	.607	3.54	26

the long, looping swings of Hobson and Scott, getting the necessary pop-up and strikeout.

The Red Sox still hadn't given up. Burleson worked Gossage for a one-out walk in the ninth, and the 155-pound Remy again jumped on the mammoth Yankee fireballer. Remy pulled Gossage's fastball hard into right field, and as the ball screamed out, it was obvious that in the late afternoon sun Piniella had no idea where it was. Burleson had started for second, then stopped to see if the ball would be caught. "He is so smart, I couldn't help but think that he might be decoying me," Burleson later explained. "I couldn't be doubled off first base to end the game."

The ball landed a few feet in front of and to the left of Piniella. Had Jackson been there, the glove would have been on his right hand, and there would have been no way to stop it from scooting all the way to the bullpen for a pennant-winning inside-the-park homer. But Piniella's glove was, of course, on his left hand, and when the ball came out of the sun and hit the ground, he reacted like a hockey goalie picking a slapshot out of a screen at the last moment. "It was pure luck," Piniella admitted. "Pure luck that I was in the right place and that I could get my gloove out there in time."

Piniella reacted, flashed the glove out, snatched Remy's single on the quick hop, and fired a quick throw back in the infield. Burleson, because he'd hesitated, had to stop at second, which meant that when Rice followed with a fly to deep center, Burleson was only on third. Second-guessing is tempting, but he'd felt the choice was to be on second base with one out and Rice and Yastrzemski coming to the plate or to end the season being doubled off first.

So the 1978 season came down to Gossage, the premier power reliever of his generation, and Yastrzemski, perhaps his generation's premier fastball hitter. By the time Gossage delivered ball one, all 32,925 in attendance were on their feet, and that second pitch was Goose's power at its overpowering best. "It looked as if it were going to be on the inside corner, so I started to swing," said Yastrzemski. "At the last instant, it took off and ran inside on me. I tried to hold up . . ."

The ball went high in the air toward the third-base coach's box. Burleson broke for the plate, turned, then jogged across the plate, watching Nettles. "I was thinking, 'pop him up,' " Nettles later recounted. "Yaz did, and I said, 'Jeez, not to me.' " But Nettles caught the pop-up and threw his fist in the air triumphantly.

Gossage waved his arms as Munson ran out to him. "My God, it's over, we've done it," Gossage said to himself. The Yankees had done it, by ninety feet, by a twist of the wind, by Piniella's "pure luck." They had done it over 163 games and 173 days and a life of emotion. Gossage, a future Hall of Famer, had beaten Yastrzemski, a certain Hall of Famer. The Yankees almost always beat the Red Sox. Great pitching almost always beats great hitting. Baseball's mightiest clichés seemed vindicated.

Yastrzemski would break down into tears afterward, and when Jackson came over to the Boston clubhouse, the two stars exchanged embraces. "Yaz, you are the greatest," Reggie told Yastrzemski.

"Please," Yaz replied, "win it all. For us. We are the two best teams in baseball." Catfish Hunter asked Hawk Harrelson for his black cowboy hat to wear through the playoffs and World Series as a good luck charm, "to remind us what we did to get here."

Because of the game in Boston, the Yankees were without Guidry to pitch the first two games of either the playoffs or the World Series. Hence, it took four games to beat Kansas City and, after losing the first two games in Los Angeles, they beat the Dodgers four straight.

The Sixth Game was the ringing proclamation of what was to be the coming Boston dynasty. The playoff game was the peak of their era as challengers. But when Nettles caught Yaz's pop-up that October afternoon, the tide had begun its long, inexorable retreat on the way out to mediocrity.

SEVEN

1979-80

DECLINE AND FALL

The post–Tom Yawkey owners, baffled by the winds of change that have turned the game's power structure inside out since 1975, let Luis Tiant leave, exile Bill Lee, fumble away Carlton Fisk, and trade Fred Lynn, Butch Hobson, and Rick Burleson.

*F*OUR AND A HALF YEARS LATER, all they talked about was Luis.

They had played the Orioles in Fenway Park in a Monday night game in mid-August 1982 and had to charter a flight to California to play the Angels the next night. "Ell-Tee," coach Tommy Harper boomed out, contrabasso, as the bus pulled out of the parking lot onto Yawkey Way. "Next opponent, Ell-Tee. He won't look up when he walks out to the bullpen to warm up before the game, and he'll try not to look into our dugout as he walks in. But someone'll yell something about his being ugly, he'll start laughing and scream, 'You gotta lotta nerve,' then start getting on me and Yaz. I'll never forget the time Gorman Thomas started getting on him in Milwaukee, and Tiant turned to him and hollered back, 'You gotta lotta nerve. Women cover their kids' faces when you come up. You could be anything in the jungle but the hunter.' "

On the bus to Logan Airport, on the five-hour flight to Ontario (California) Airport, and on the forty-five-minute bus ride to the Anaheim Marriott, the subject was Luis. Ell-Tee. El Tiante. Players came up and circled around Harper, Dwight Evans, pitching coach Lee Stange, and Yastrzemski up near the front of the plane, listening to stories about that round, high-voiced man who for anyone born after Pearl Harbor was the best starting pitcher ever seen in a Red Sox uniform. "How could they not have understood?" Evans asked on the plane that night. "How could Buddy and Sully and Zim and the people who run this team not understand what Luis Tiant meant to us? Heck, we're desperate for pitching right now: Why couldn't they have bought him from Mexico instead of the Angels? He might win us a pennant, even if he didn't pitch an inning. What was it Yaz said the day they let him go to New York at the end of the '78 season?"

To be precise, Yastrzemski said, "When they let Luis Tiant go to New York, they tore out our heart and soul."

"Unless you've played with him," Evans continued, "you can't understand what Luis means to a team. What it is to play behind him. Off the field, he keeps a team loose. It is as if he knows exactly when to clown and when to be serious. If you play this game long enough, you know that the bus rides and plane rides along the road are vitally important, and Luis knew exactly when to turn a bus ride into something out of *Saturday Night Live.* And there's no way of describing it [George Kimball came the closest in the *Boston Phoenix*, comparing him to comedian Robin Williams]. Then when it comes to going to the mound, well, as great as Catfish Hunter and Jim Palmer were, if I'd had one game I had to win, I'd have wanted Luis Tiant pitching for me. Anyone who played with him would agree. Ask Carl."

Carl Yastrzemski agreed. So did Luis Aparicio. Ken Harrelson. Carlton Fisk. Rick Burleson.

At the end of the 1972 season, in which Tiant came back from two and a half years of injuries and nearly pitched Boston to the pennant with a 1.91 earned run average, rookie pitcher John Curtis, who had also been an integral part of the late-season surge, tried to explain to his wife what he meant when he said, "I love Luis Tiant." He could not. "I guess it's something that comes only between people who are in some-thing together, be it war or a pennant race," Curtis said. Ten years later, Curtis reiterated the same feelings for Tiant. "He is special. He was the magic element that brought that '72 team from last place to first in the final month. I will never forget him."

After Eddie Kasko refused to listen to writers and fans who demanded Tiant's release in April 1972 following a dreadful spring training and a 1–7 record in 1971, Tiant gave the Red Sox seven full years. In that time, he won 121 games and lost 74, won 20 or more games thrice, led the league in earned run average once, won half of their six postseason victories in 1975, and, including the playoff and World Series triumphs against Oakland and Cincinnati, was 32–10 in September and October games. In that time, they finished first once, third once, and second five times. The last game he started in a Red Sox uniform was on October 1, 1978, and he two-hit the Blue Jays to put the Red Sox into the playoff game with the Yankees. The morning of that game, George Scott said, "I don't care if Luis Tiant is a hundred years old. With him out there in this situation, this is one game we *know* we're going to win."

It was not only the last big game the Red Sox *knew* they were going to win for a long time, it was close to their last big game, period. Only the 1981 strike gave them a semblance of a serious run at a half-pennant (decided in a seven-week sea-son), and in the five years after Tiant's departure they didn't finish higher than third; in the four-year period 1980–83, they finished in the second division thrice, finally tumbling to a 78–84, sixth-place debacle in 1983. For when El Tiante left to become a Yankee — or, as he called it, a "Jahnkee" — on

November 13, 1978, the first-year ownership of Haywood Sullivan and Buddy Leroux had allowed George Steinbrenner to tear what Yastrzemski called "the heart and soul" out of their club. Three weeks later, they traded Bill Lee to Montreal for a utility infielder named Stan Papi. Thirteen months after that, Rick Burleson, Fred Lynn, Carlton Fisk, Butch Hobson, and Don Zimmer were gone.

Luis Tiant won his two hundred twenty-ninth and final major-league game on August 17, 1982, by the score of 10–2. "Tell Mister Buddy Leroux and Haywood Sullivan that maybe I'm not the only thing that isn't as good as I used to be," El Tiante said afterward. His final big-league win had been against the Red Sox.

Luis Tiant and Bill Lee were more than the third and ninth winningest pitchers in Red Sox history. They were El Tiante and The Space Man. Fans admired and revered Yaz, Rice, and Lynn for their skills. They adopted The Rooster because he channeled downright feistiness into an all-star prominence. Fisk was "one of us," emotional, jagged. But Tiant and Lee were what being a fan was all about, and before Lynn and Rice and Burleson came along in 1974 and 1975, El Tiante and The Space Man were already folk heroes. They were at the heart of the tremendous Red Sox boom that engulfed New England in the mid and late 1970s. They were striking individuals performing for an audience of strident individualism, and when within a month in 1978 they were exiled by men who grew up in Alabama and Cincinnati and perceived baseball in a far, far different light from the Boston fan, much of the personality that made the Red Sox more than just a good, powerful second-place team was gone. And, personality aside, between them Tiant and Lee won thirty games in 1979. Until rookie John Tudor started in late August of that year, Boston didn't have a game started by a left-hander, and they began an oft-repeated mistake of rushing young pitchers and ruining them, as in the wake of the banishment of the veteran pitchers the promising careers of not only Bobby Sprowl but Joel Finch and Steve Crawford were set back.

Lee brought an entire culture into the ballpark, for in a city with fifty-odd colleges and universities and a historic taste for antiestablishmentarianism he was baseball's irreverent forerunner to *Saturday Night Live*. He punted bubble gum from the bullpen into the bleachers, put his career in Vonnegut terms ("In nonsense is strength"), and challenged authority with an adolescent spirit irresistible to all the children of the 1960s and 1970s. Along with winning seventeen games in 1973, 1974, and 1975, this spirit made him the hero of the *Phoenix* and WBCN and brought their readers and listeners into Fenway as if he were some rock star. Boston is not Cincinnati or Houston, where The Space Cowboy and his irreverence would have been denounced by social and sporting establishments that could not have stood for a man who said he put marijuana on his pancakes. Bill Lee was a star in Boston, an attraction, the way WBCN's Charles Laquidara and local rocker George Thorogood were mass heroes, and through the 1970s the odd bond between baseball and music — and all the beer and dope that goes with that — seemed personified by a locksmith from the University of Southern California named William Francis Lee III. "The fans liked me," Lee said when he left. "I got exiled by members of the media who resented me telling the truth more than they did and a manager and a general manager who couldn't understand the New England fans. They thought if they got rid of me, the mentality of New England would change. In a couple of years, the fans changed, all right. They changed their entertainment habits and stopped going to Fenway."

While Lee packed the bleachers, Tiant's appeal was more universal. Yastrzemski used to say, "Fenway Park is Tiant's palace." When he pitched, it was El Tiante that people watched. Fans pay to see great pitchers: Nolan Ryan,

Steve Carlton, Ron Guidry, Jim Palmer. But some athletes have something beyond the rational and statistical. The causes must be unique to the individual and the situation, as with Fernandomania in Los Angeles. Tiant took the stage and turned batters into Rosencrantz and Guildenstern, and he did musically. He was the original, rounded street dancer, pitching to a samba beat. Lee once described watching Tiant as being "like going to a concert or listening to an opera — the orchestra comes out and starts banging and the place shakes, then in the middle it gets quiet and sweet and then, all of a sudden, the whole gang lets go with all the instruments."

When Tiant walked out to the bullpen to warm up before the second game of a crucial twinight doubleheader in 1972 against the Orioles, he received a raucous standing ovation from the near-sellout crowd, a tradition that continued in the next five years to virtually every pregame walk out to and in from the bullpen. That night, and most times he strutted to the mound, the result was the same: he won.

On September 16, 1975, when he was matched up against Jim Palmer to stop the Orioles' annual persistent final-month push and (pre–fire laws) Fenway Park had what officials later estimated as nearly 45,000 crammed up and down the aisles, El Tiante strolled in to a standing ovation, whirled, twirled, and shut out Palmer and Baltimore 2–0. As was his style, not only did he beat them, he did it with show. No American League pitcher of the last twenty years pitched better with a lead than Tiant; if he was behind 1–0 after the seventh inning, he could become frustrated and angry and give up more runs, and he could become frustrated in a tie. But when he had a lead, he defended it as if it were his family, and it seemed that with each out he got closer to victory, the longer look he took at the center-field bleachers in his hitch/lurch/spin/swirling motion. It was that night against Palmer that the late-inning chant of "LOO-EEE, LOO-EEE" began, a chant that became the symbol of Red Sox

victory. It would be echoed across the mountains of New
England that October as he took them to within a game of
their first world championship since 1918, as he shut out the
A's to begin the playoff sweep, shut out the Reds to begin the
World Series, and threw the game that personified Tiant
more than any other in that series's fourth game. He had a
5–4 lead after the top of the fifth inning in Cincinnati, had
two runners on base in every one of the first five innings, and
through 172 pitches clung to that 5–4 lead. "Some guys can't
pick up the pot," Indians president Gabe Paul once said, "but
Luis's nostrils dilate when the money's on the table."

Tiant wasn't some Boston phenomenon that sprouted up
out of the snow one spring. He came out of the Cleveland
farm system with Sam McDowell, who got all the publicity.
But once Tiant got his feet on American soil — after leaving
Cuba in 1959 he pitched three years in Mexico, then went
through a transitional year in 1962 — he quickly established
himself as one of the best young pitchers in the game. In 1963
and 1964, which included a full year in Burlington, North
Carolina (the then–Class B Carolina League) and half a year
in both Portland of the Pacific Coast League and Cleveland,
he was 39–14 and struck out 466 in 468 innings. He and
McDowell were called up the summer of 1964, and in the excitement over Sudden Sam's fastball, few noticed that Tiant
was 10–4 with a 2.83 earned run average. In 1968, he was the
best pitcher in the American League; problem was, Denny
McLain won thirty-one games and no one noticed Tiant.
That year Tiant was 21–9 for a typically mediocre Indians
team, allowed 152 hits in 258 innings, struck out 264 while
walking 73, and had the lowest earned run average (1.60)
since Walter Johnson's 1.49 in 1919. That winter, he didn't
go to winter ball for the first time, and in 1969 struggled
through a terrible 9–20 season more in tune with the capaci-
ties of his teammates. After being traded the next year to the
contending Twins (for, among others, a young third baseman
named Graig Nettles), he tore a rib cage muscle after getting

off to a good start. The rib cage in turn affected his shoulder, but penurious Calvin Griffith wouldn't listen to Tiant's explanations. The next spring Griffith saw only that Tiant wasn't throwing right and released him. He signed on for a one-month deal with the Braves' Richmond farm club, but still wasn't throwing well, and when the Red Sox offered him a job with Louisville as the Braves' deal finished, he grabbed it on May 17, 1971. The Red Sox recalled him the next month, and while he showed flashes of his old form — a ten-inning shutout against the Twins — he was 1–7 and the *Globe*'s Clif Keane one morning led his story about a losing Tiant start with "Enough is enough." To Kasko's credit, despite the panning he got from much of the media (which never gave him a chance, since he was the man who replaced Dick Williams), he never wavered on Tiant.

Then came El Tiante's great streak in 1972, when he won thirteen of fifteen, finished 15–6, and again led the league in earned run average at 1.91. He won twenty in '73, twenty-two in '74, and twenty-one in '76; the only other Red Sox pitchers to have won twenty games more than twice were Cy Young (six times) and Jesse Tannehill (thrice), and Theodore Roosevelt was president when each of them did it for the last time.

He never really understood why he made people laugh. "Half of the time they don't even know what I said, but they start laughing," he'd say, shrugging.

"I'd just be sitting there in front of my locker, turn around and just *look* at Luis and I'd start laughing," Bill Campbell once said. "Then he gets in the whirlpool . . ." Tiant's physical presence is striking to begin with. He was balding when he arrived in 1971, and had a round face with the folds of a golden retriever, a Fu Manchu mustache, and long sideburns. He is a barrel-chested man with huge thighs and a wiggling walk and a derrière that would have him look fat even if he had fasted for months. Players new to the club would do double takes at the first sight of Tiant smoking his dollar cigar in the whirlpool or sometimes even the shower. Then when he opened his mouth, out came a high-pitched alto voice that sounded as if he were trying to breathe in while speaking out. "Bill Dana made millions with José Jiminez," Campbell observed. "Hell, Luis is three times as funny."

Tiant and Tommy Harper were friends together in Cleveland. In spring training, 1972, Yastrzemski came into the clubhouse with a huge bass he'd just caught out on one of the Winter Haven lakes. Tiant took it, dressed it in Harper's uniform, put a cap over it, and laid it in front of Harper's locker. He used to call Harper "Liver Lips," and had a nickname for everyone: "Polacko" (Yastrzemski), "Pinocchio" (Rico Petrocelli), "Frankenstein" (Carlton Fisk), "No Color" (reliever Ken Tatum), "Mandingo" (Rice). Every time he'd walk by a mirror in the clubhouse, he'd stop and say, "Seex-two, blond hair, blue eyes . . . Looking gooood!" Once in spring training when he and Harper were test-driving a new car, he got stopped on Route I-4 for speeding. When the policeman reached his window and asked him what he was doing, Tiant looked out, grinned, and said, "I'm a pitcher and I was bringing some heat."

Ballpark humor isn't meant to be Euripides or Thurber, and Tiant screaming "Get your black ass out of here" or issuing blood-curdling yells every time a plane took off or landed or his getting on teammates for their clothes ("Hey, Polacko, did you clean the bus in that raincoat?" or, to a Reggie Smith jumpsuit, "Are you an airplane mechanic on the side?") somehow always had the right effect. The emotional highs and lows seemed far more exaggerated after Tiant left.

Tiant is a passionate man. The reunion with his parents in 1975 exhausted him; he had left Cuba and couldn't go back, and when they arrived in Boston in August 1975, it was the first time he'd seen either one since 1967. Then when they died within three days of each other that winter, it affected him for months. He is also a very proud man, for whom contract problems became personal issues. After the 1976 season, he claimed that he had had a promise from Tom Yawkey before he died that he would have his contract, which had one year remaining, adjusted. Dick O'Connell, John Claiborne, and John Harrington didn't agree. Tiant felt that he had carried the team for five years, and that if Lynn could walk in and get $1.65 million after one good season, he should get his share. Part of the problem came in the conflict between his agent, Bob Woolf, and the front office. While Woolf was writing a piece in the *New York Times* saying that he'd never ask for any form of renegotiation, he was trying to renegotiate Tiant's contract, and in March, Woolf convinced Tiant to stay in a Tampa motel but out of spring training until they did renegotiate, advice that hurt Tiant publicly, left him unprepared for the start of the season, and cost him his worst year in a Boston uniform. In 1978, he broke his right thumb in spring training, which kept him out the first three weeks of the season.

But he did come back and did pitch them to the playoff game. Except the new Red Sox ownership had decided to hardball him on his contract. Tiant was no victimized saint; Yawkey had bailed him out of severe tax problems in Mexico in 1973, they had adjusted his contract once, and Luis was known to like to spend money at the dog track. But, as the Red Sox misread the need for experienced pitching, so, too, they really didn't understand Tiant as a man. "I've been screwed all my life," he'd often say. "Everyone always give me bool cheat. Bool cheat all the time, you know what I mean? What can I do?" That was part of his motivation, and he knew what it was to leave his family and his country, struggle to learn English ("When I came to this country, the only word for food I knew was *chicken*, so I ate nothing but chicken for two and a half months"), get released by Calvin Griffith, and survive.

In August 1978, the Red Sox were in Oakland when the *Globe* ran a list of potential free agents. Tiant, of course, was

one of them. In the accompanying story, Haywood Sullivan
was quoted as saying, "We'll sit down with Luis in September." Tiant waited, but the only discussion he had was with
Buddy Leroux in the clubhouse, and Tiant claims that Leroux
said to him, "Before you think about becoming a free agent,
think about your age, Luis. I hope you have a lot of money in
the bank."

That challenged Tiant's machismo, as Kimball pointed out
in the *Phoenix* the next spring. "They never took me seriously
in those negotiations, they treated me like some old fool, but
I was wise to their bool cheat," Tiant later said. They would
offer him only a one-year deal until it was too late. By the
time Sullivan began changing, Tiant's pride had been pricked
so badly that it would have cost the Red Sox far more than
the $840,000 for two years that George Steinbrenner gave
him. They just didn't measure Tiant, and as would become
increasingly obvious in the next two years, it wasn't purely
Sullivan's fault at all. One of Leroux's selling points was to
trim the front office dramatically, which left Sullivan trying
to act as owner, league statesman, general manager, assistant
general manager, contract negotiator, and personnel director. No one in the organization had any experience dealing
with agents, who had really only sprouted in the mid 1970s.
Sullivan, a tough Alabaman whose fiery temper rivals Tiant's
machismo, had no buffer between their two personalities.

Steinbrenner, who was moving in on the border Red Sox
markets of Connecticut, western Massachusetts, Vermont,
and the Lake Champlain area of upper New York state, understood the relationship between Tiant and the New
England fans. Gabe Paul, who had Tiant in Cleveland, had
convinced him of Tiant's value in the Boston clubhouse.
Steinbrenner swooped in and smartly stole Tiant not so much
for what he'd do for the Yankees but for what his departure
would do to the Red Sox.

Lee's appeal was very different from Tiant's. Other than

the fact that he's one of three left-handed pitchers to win seventeen or more games thrice since The Wall was erected, nowhere else could Lee have been the cult hero he was in Boston. In an era when iconoclastic humor began sweeping the seventeen-to-thirty-five-year-old audience, Lee was John Belushi, Monty Python, George Carlin, and Dan Aykroyd. And in a city filled with students, Lee was what those fans wanted to be. But then, one of the elements of living in New England is trendism, and Lee fit a segment of the area perfectly: he backed Greenpeace and Zero Population Growth, embraced the Red Chinese, called Judge W. Arthur Garrity "the only man with any guts in Boston," refused an agent, said the Yankees were "robotized" by Billy Martin's "Brown Shirt mentality" and decried Steinbrenner's win-at-all-material-and-personal-costs philosophy, kept ginseng in his locker, and left Yankee Stadium after the fight in 1976 carrying a copy of P. D. Ouspensky's *The Psychology of Man's Possible Evolution*. "I'm a southpaw in a northpaw world," he used to say, along with "The object of life is to defy gravity."

Lee came from a conservative background. His father worked for the telephone company and was an avowed Goldwater Republican, and he went to the University of Southern California, a traditionally conservative school. But he earned a reputation for eccentricity at USC, going down the baggage shoots in airports and once taking off his uniform and shagging batting practice in his jockstrap to collect a twenty-five-dollar bet. When he left USC, he was the winningest pitcher in the school's history, and he was good enough to be in Boston less than a year after he was drafted. He was, however, in the bushes long enough to rub traditional, lifer minor-league managers the wrong way, as he got into a fight with his own manager in Winston-Salem, Rac Slider, then had Salem (Virginia) skipper Don Hoak chase him into the parking lot after a game because Lee started two double plays by catching balls behind his back. Long before he ever met Don Zimmer, he could open his mouth and get himself in trouble: he had to leave Puerto Rico one winter when he got into a fight with catcher Elly Rodriguez; he had to leave Venezuela another winter when he, Jim Rooker, and Joe Keough got into a huge barroom brawl; he twice fought Reggie Smith and once was even charged in the dugout by Rico Petrocelli. The nickname came from a pregame radio show he was doing with Ned Martin that day in 1969 when Neil Armstrong and Buzz Aldrin set foot on the moon, as a couple of teammates heard him talk more about the space landing than baseball. The day Bill Lee got the name Space Man (or Moon Man), Jim Bouton was compiling his notes for *Ball Four* in a Seattle Pilots uniform.

There was *always* some media person at Lee's locker, which in turn always had books and herb bottles and signs around it. He was outrageous, but for the first few years, he meant nothing by it:

- When American League President Joe Cronin fined Texas's Jim Merritt for admitting he'd thrown a spitter in 1973, Lee stomped out to the pool in Oakland, grabbed a writer, and announced, "Tell Cronin I threw a spitter in Detroit a while back. Tiny Taylor hit it into the upper deck. Yes, I have a tube of K-Y jelly in my locker. So do a lot of other pitchers who throw it a lot more than I do. Hell, if K-Y jelly went off the market, the Angels' whole staff would be out of baseball. So you'd better tell Cronin to fine me, too." Cronin did, but not before saying "Lee is the kind of color this game needs" and reminding Red Sox fans that he brought a previous number 37 — Jim Piersall — to the big leagues.
- "Rod Dedeaux teaches more in one season at USC than the Red Sox organization does in ten years," proclaimed Lee.
- When the Red Sox traded Sparky Lyle to the Yankees for Danny Cater in spring training, 1972, Lee screamed, "It's stupid." It was, of course.

- On Henry Aaron's finishing his career with the Brewers, he said, "Someone has to clean the pigeon shit off his shoulder every day."
- When he was flown home to Boston from spring training in 1973 to have his foot examined, he looked at the x-rays and exclaimed, "That loose thing's just an old Dewar's cap floating around."
- He was quoted in the *Globe* as saying that his wife, Mary Lou, "went to singles bars with male models" when he was on the road, which came as quite a shock to her.
- He said, "The Angels could take batting practice in the lobby of the [Anaheim] Grand Hotel and not chip a chandelier." California manager Dick Williams had his team take batting practice the following Saturday with a Nerf ball in the lobby of the Sheraton-Boston and vowed revenge, but Lee went out and shut them out.
- When the Red Sox installed their electronic megaboard before the 1976 season, he said, "That's like having a Mercedes and hanging little dice from the rearview mirror."
- He was quoted as describing his life on the road thusly: "When we go to California, we go to my uncle's beach house in Malibu, and my uncle rounds up five or six girls for volleyball, drinking, swimming, and playing around in the surf all night." His teammates loved that.

He didn't have to simply be outrageous. When Cater got a hit to beat Wilbur Wood, he quipped, "Even a pessimist can hit a knuckleball." Watching the Watergate hearings on a clubhouse television, he commented, "John Dean has the answers even before they ask the questions." During a rain delay in the second game of the '75 series, even though he was pitching, he asked if he could go meet Henry Kissinger. Darrell Johnson asked him why he wanted to see Kissinger at that particular time, and Lee replied, "I want to ask him where our wheat is going." After the game, when asked how he felt the World Series stood, he answered, "Tied." Also that year, when Rogelio Moret totaled his car in Stonington, Connecticut, at 4:30 on the same morning he was supposed to pitch against Palmer and the Orioles, Lee observed that Moret, Lee ("A palm tree jumped out into the middle of a street in Winter Haven and dented my BMW"), Reggie Cleveland, and Rick Wise had all been involved in accidents, so "in the Basic Agreement next year management is going to provide all pitchers with drivers' ed."

He even managed to lampoon his January 1976 trip to Japan sponsored by the leftist *Guardian* newspaper. He marveled at the statistic that 2700 tons of human waste were taken from Peking to the fields every day, then observed, "Everywhere I'd go, someone would be saying, 'As Chairman Mao says, women hold up half the world'; they may hold up half the world, but in Peking they carry three-quarters of the shit." He described a Chinese breakfast as "four-year-old eggs with green and blue yolks." He noted the Chinese people's lack of sensuality, then added, "With eight hundred million of them, they must have something I didn't see." He summed up their commitment to true socialism with a story about a man who asked him how much he got paid for playing "bong-chou" (baseball). "When I told him it came to at least a hundred fifty thousand yuan, he asked me, 'How you play this bong-chou?' " He said he came home because he was tired of listening to Professor Harry Edwards's rhetoric. At dinner one night, Edwards exclaimed, "As Chairman Mao says, 'Only the wise can close their eyes.' Wow." Lee looked up at him and snapped, "As Chairman Bob Bolin says, 'You don't have to go to Chattanooga to see Rock City.'"

Lee got away with saying whatever he wanted to say with Johnson managing. He could call Johnson a "dumb manager," as he did at a New Hampshire banquet in 1974. He could say, "Darrell's been falling out of trees and landing on his feet all year," and Johnson didn't care. First, Lee had won fifty-one games in three years. Second, Johnson was able to close the managerial door to personalities.

There were those who always felt that Lee was, as Clif Keane used to say, "a showoff." White Sox manager Chuck Tanner called him "a bush-league showoff" on August 24, 1975, when Lee clowned around in the rain, caught balls between his legs, threw lob pitches through the raindrops, and laughed in an 8–1 win against a hapless, bankrupt team. Keane, for instance, blamed the loss of the '75 series on his Leephus pitch that Tony Perez hit halfway to Hanover to tie it at 3–3 in the sixth inning of the seventh game, saying, "He didn't know when to stop showing off." It may have been so, and he was probably egged on by his ever-growing entourage who encouraged him to be a comedian playing baseball, not a good pitcher who happened to be funny. But Lee was capable of tremendously constructive energy. He is highly intelligent and clever, he gave himself to kids and groups far more than any other player, and as public relations men Bill Crowley and Dick Bresciani privately recounted, no player in the last twenty-five years did more voluntary tours of hospitals and schools than Lee.

But by the time Zimmer took over in July 1976, Lee was getting to the point where he was trying to be The Space Man all the time, and he had begun to become a caricature of himself. Colleges began inviting him to speak, and not only did they take him seriously, he began to take their immaturity seriously. Lee came from California, listened to Warren Zevon, and admitted he smoked dope and read *Rolling Stone* and *High Times*. Zimmer came from staid Cincinnati, lis-

Top Career Won-Lost Statistics vs. Yankees (Min. 10 Victories)	
1. Dickie Kerr, Chi.	14–4
2. Babe Ruth, Bos.	17–5
3. Bill Lee, Bos.	12–5
4. Bernie Boland, Det., St. L.	16–7
5. Frank Lary, Det.	28–13
(18. Luis Tiant, Bos.	22–15)

tened to talk shows or football games, seldom drank anything stronger than Tab, and read the *Racing Form* and *Sporting News.*

When Zimmer took over, he felt that Johnson had allowed the club to get out of hand. Once Lee stopped winning, as he did after the Yankee Stadium fight, the Keanes and Larry Claflins — with whom he had had personal clashes dating years back — and other traditional, more conservative fans viewed him as a Mass-going, tax-paying, fifty-year-old in West Roxbury viewed Belushi dressed up as the pope. There were a lot of people who supported the Red Sox who never forgave Lee for his statements about Judge Garrity and busing; they had kids being bused across town, he didn't, and they didn't care if City Councilor Albert "Dapper" O'Neil did make the situation humorous to Lee's legions by writing him an angry letter with a dozen spelling mistakes, the use of the word *bullshit,* and reference to Lee's being in "every beachhead from North Africa to Berlin." Zimmer and Lee not only were a clash of two worlds, they became the focus of a clash between two large groups of fans, and their differences became a public rumpus that was referred to on talk shows, in newspapers, and in barrooms.

Zimmer may have finally run Lee out of town at the end of the 1978 season, but Lee effectively ran Zimmer out, too. Don Zimmer grew up respecting authority, played in an area where management told players where to go, and worshiped a man named Gil Hodges who demanded — and got — complete subordination from players. But by July 1976, players could see that the schoolbell had rung and they were running down the hall and into the street. Against a backdrop of what the 1960s, Vietnam, and Watergate had done to traditional authority, the Messersmith decision had taken away the hammer that owners held over the players' heads.

The bleacherites laughed when Lee called Zimmer a gerbil. Zimmer at first didn't know what a gerbil was, then when he found out was hurt by the physical ridicule, and, worst of

all, didn't know how to strike back. He was completely befuddled by Lee's tirade ("Zimmer is an SOB") when Bernie
Carbo was released, not to mention the "Friendship First,
Competition Second" T-shirt he wore when he came into the
manager's office to ask to come back to the team. The manager seethed when Lee went barefoot and wore a bowling
shirt on a plane.

As people he understood kept telling him to "get rid of the
punk" — Keane said on WITS that Lee was "on angel
dust" — Zimmer could only strike back by sitting Lee down
and keeping him there. Lee was naturally a media favorite,
and Zimmy could fight no battle of words. All managers get
blamed when their teams lose; Gene Mauch has had to live
with the collapse of the 1964 Phillies all his life and felt it so
strongly that when his Angels won the first two games of the
1982 playoffs, then lost the final three to Milwaukee, he
talked to only two trusted media allies. But not only had
Zimmer lost and been blamed; he was ridiculed. "The Gerbil" was implanted in the public's mind forever by cartoonists, columnists, fans, television commentators.

Lee was traded for Stan Papi on December 7, 1978. The
game won by John Tudor the next September was the only
victory by a left-handed starter all that season. Lee, of course,
was 16–10 for Montreal. He left threatening class action suits
against the club, giving speeches ("Jack Rogers and Dick
Bresciani do good jobs; Haywood Sullivan has a good job"),
wearing outrageous T-shirts ("Here comes Gossage, here
comes Bailey . . . Where's Bernie?"). Lee never got over Boston, and longed for the attention he received there. He never
found it, however, and he ended up leaving his wife, Mary
Lou, for a nineteen-year-old French girl, then got released by
the Expos when in reaction to the release of teammate Rod-
ney "Cool Breeze" Scott, he broke into Expos President John
McHale's office and assumed a position standing on his head
eating a peanut butter sandwich when McHale came to work
at 8:00 A.M.

By 1979, both Tiant and Lee were gone. Sullivan did not have his finger on the pulse of his clubhouse and did not appreciate Tiant's real worth. He and Zimmer let Lee get to them, even if the players couldn't have cared less. When Lee referred to the "plastic" players in his one-day June retirement, Evans showed up Sunday with a plastic bag over his head. The next year Yastrzemski said, "No matter how bad we were, Lee would be there in front of his locker, twenty-five writers around him. I'd peer around the corner and laugh. So would a lot of other guys. When we'd start to go bad, he'd get on some tirade or do something crazy, and it took a lot of attention away from and pressure off a lot of players. He could also pitch. How many lefties have the Red Sox ever had that won more games?" Two, Mel Parnell and Lefty Grove.

The era of El Tiante and The Space Man was over, but so, too, was the era of thunder, power, and challenges for the 1975 dynasty that never was. The team, the fans, and Zimmer would never be the same again.

Of course, when the 1979 season began, neither the players nor the media nor the fans realized that — like the final two days of bitter disappointment in 1949 that were the end to another purported dynasty — the Red Sox were on the downhill side of the curve. When this writer picked the Red Sox third and the Yankees fourth at the end of spring training, players passed the newspaper around the clubhouse and took turns making derisive comments. (As it turned out, picking Baltimore — Milwaukee — Boston — New York — Detroit — Cleveland — Toronto turned out to be the only time in this writer's career in which he picked the division in its exact order.) Fans bought tickets in record numbers, and the *Globe* was so excited about Opening Day that it had John Updike cover it for page one.

At the All-Star break, it appeared they did have a chance, with a 56–32 record that kept them within two games of Baltimore. But by then the erosion had begun taking place. The pain from the buildup of scar tissue in Fisk's elbow was so bad that he started only thirty-five games behind the plate, most of them in June, and the fact that they were 25–10 with him is evidence of his importance. On May 31 in Yankee Stadium, the two "geezers" (as Rice called them) — Tiant and Yastrzemski — met in New York in the ninth inning of a 2–2 game, and when Yastrzemski waited out eleven head bobs, five bows, two cha-chas, and an olé that produced a 55 mph changeup as if it were the 3:10 to Yuma, he smashed it into the second deck for a dramatic and emotional conquest of his sidekick that gave him .306–16–53 numbers for the first three months. The previous at-bat, Yaz felt a pull in his Achilles tendon, and the rest of the season batted only .233 with five home runs as he counted down to becoming the first American Leaguer to amass four hundred career runs and three thousand hits. The next day, Jerry Remy led off the game with a triple that upped his average to .304, then when he tried to score on Burleson's foul pop down the right-field line, injured his knee in a collision with Thurman Munson and was out for virtually the remainder of the season. Steve Renko, who was signed to replace Tiant, was 8–3 at the break, 3–6 the rest of the way. Mike Torrez pulled his usual Boston late-season fold, winning three games after August 7, and even Dennis Eckersley fell apart. On August 14, he was tied with eventual Cy Young Award winner Mike Flanagan of the Orioles with sixteen wins and only five losses; he began to feel twinges in his shoulder and was 1–5 the rest of the way. And, as for those who were going to replace Lee, Jim Wright (who made only two starts after hurting his elbow in Venezuela), John Tudor, Win Remmerswaal, Joel Finch, and Allen Ripley were a combined 5–6 on the year with one complete game, the rain-shortened seven-inning win by Tudor in September that was the first victory for a Red Sox left-handed starter in more than a year. There simply was not enough pitching.

Sure, they scored runs. Sure, they ran up all kinds of offensive banners. Lynn came to spring training looking like a

fullback after a winter on the Nautilus machines, and proceeded to team up with Rice for the season that outdid '75.
Lynn led the league at .333, Rice was fourth at .325. Each hit
thirty-nine homers. They ran one and two in slugging, Lynn
at .637, Rice at .596. Rice knocked in 130 runs, Lynn 122.
Rice scored 117 runs, Lynn 116. Butch Hobson hit twenty-
eight homers and knocked in ninety-three runs. Dwight
Evans hit twenty-one homers. At the June trading deadline,
they were able to acquire Bob Watson from Houston for two
minor-league pitchers (Bobby Sprowl and Peter Ladd) and
dump George Scott for Tom Poquette. They then watched
Watson hit .337 with thirteen homers and fifty-three RBIs in
eighty-four games and Poquette become an invaluable outfield reserve while hitting .331. Unfortunately, the fact of life
was that they had mediocre pitching, and while Watson was
everything he was advertised to be, you don't win pennants
complementing mediocre pitching with more offense. You do
it with more defense, and with Watson at first, Jack Brohamer at second, Hobson at third, and Gary Allenson catching most of the time with Fisk out, the defense simply wasn't
strong enough.

Yaz, as he would do so many times in his career, covered
up for some of the inadequacies by his pursuit of history. On
July 16, he hit home run number 400 off Oakland youngster
Mike Morgan. Then, in September, he counted down toward
three thousand hits. Number 3000 finally came, simply, with
a hopping ground ball past the outstretched glove of Yankee
second baseman Willie Randolph in the eighth inning of a
9–2 game, after a stretch of thirteen hitless at-bats that was so
excruciating that *Baltimore News-American* writer Peter
Pascarelli at one point exclaimed, "This is like waiting for
Franco to die." But it kept New England's eyes riveted on
Yaz, and off the fall to third place.

For when it became mid-August and time for pitching to
take over, the Red Sox quietly retired. Their four-game winning streak that got them to within four games of Baltimore

was snapped on August 17 in Chicago; the next time they won two in a row was September 18 and 19 in Toronto, and by then they were fifteen out. When they lost 10–6 and 3–2 (to Tiant) in Yankee Stadium September 3 and 4, even Zimmer was resigned to the close of an era. "We've got an off-day tomorrow," he said in the visiting manager's office before the Yankee Stadium finale September 5, "and I'll bet anything I'll get a phone call from Haywood. Tomorrow's the day I get fired. I can feel it."

But the next day's call from Sullivan never came. Inexplicably, the Red Sox management at this crucial juncture made the decision to ignore their team's disintegration in hopes that the problems would disappear by themselves. Status quo was the watchword for the 1980 season. Zimmer remained as manager. Sullivan stayed out of the free-agent pitching market, declaring, "We've got to give our kids a chance." The bench was weak, so when Rice broke his wrist and missed thirty-one games, Remy had to have a knee operation in mid-July, and the staff's top winner, Chuck Rainey, popped his elbow on July 3, thus taking his 8–3 record out of the rotation, there was nothing to pick them up. The only moves made were the signing of Tony Perez to replace departed free agent Bob Watson, the signing of free-agent reliever Claude "Skip" Lockwood, the purchase of a third-string catcher, Dave Rader, from Philadelphia, and the May acquisition of veteran right-hander Jack Billingham.

On the second day of the 1980 season, Lockwood quickly established his legend in the American League. In the midst of an 18–1 loss in Milwaukee, Zimmer called down to the bullpen and asked that Lockwood get up and pitch the eighth inning just so he could get some work; bullpen coach Walter Hriniak called back and said that Lockwood couldn't because "he says he didn't stretch because he never imagined pitching so far behind." Later, right before the strike deadline, Lockwood would claim his arm was "broken," in an attempt to be placed on the disabled list so he could get paid should the players walk out. Later, he pulled a muscle tripping over a garden hose, causing teammates like Rice to mock him openly. He also had a 5.32 earned run average and only two saves. Billingham allowed fifty-seven base runners and six homers in twenty-four innings, and on a plane ride home from the West Coast declared, "I shouldn't be in the big leagues anymore." The good and honest man was soon gone.

The sickness that was apparent by August 1979 was never addressed, and 1980 was just a dreary sequel to those six weeks. Eckersley and Torrez were 21–30, and those kids Sullivan's people told him were ready — Bruce Hurst, Remmerswaal, Keith MacWhorter, and Bobby Ojeda — combined with Billingham for a record of 6–10, 7.01. Despite the heroic attempts of Bob Stanley, Dick Drago, and Tom Burgmeier — who had his personal high of twenty-four saves in 1980 — to hold together the bullpen, the team was in decay and afraid to lose, so afraid that they were 36–45 in Fenway Park. With seven games to go, the fans got the sacrifice they wanted.

Don Zimmer was fired.

Fans always like to believe that their teams' failures are the fault of a manager or a coach, perhaps most of all in baseball because of the game's obvious strategic situations and choices. But few managers have ever taken the public flogging that New England gave Zimmer. "The Sports Huddle," a call-in show on WHDH, cut off its callers if they mentioned Zimmer's name; if they wanted to refer to the manager, they had to use the pseudonym "Chiang Kai-shek." He ran away with the *Herald*'s "Pick-a-Goat" contest, and after releasing Rico Petrocelli in spring training of 1977 received letters so threatening that the club handed them over to the FBI. Every time he stuck his head out of the dugout after mid '78, he was booed unmercifully. Zimmer always said he was worth "an extra twenty thousand listeners a night to the talk shows," and in the late stages of the 1979 season his public image sank even lower when the immensely popular Ken Harrelson began second-guessing him during his telecasts of the games.

One of Zimmer's main problems was handling pitching, on any manager's list of most difficult tasks. Many players felt that his downfall began when he yanked veteran pitchers Ferguson Jenkins, Rick Wise, and Bill Lee out of the rotation in 1977, or that he forfeited the '78 pennant by refusing to start Lee against the Yankees. He was forever trying to catch lightning in a bottle with kid pitchers, despite the difficulties young pitchers have trying to be weaned in Fenway Park. In 1977, he got lucky with Mike Paxton, Don Aase, and Bob Stanley. But after that, the Sprowls, MacWhorters, Finches, Hursts, Ojedas, et al. were rushed to the front too soon, and Sprowl and Finch never regained their confidence. But to blame Zimmer alone isn't fair, for the front office after 1978 kept ignoring free agents such as Tommy John ("We know something about him," Haywood Sullivan explained in not drafting him) and Jim Slaton and kept promising that "the kids" would come through.

Zimmer, unfortunately, listened. He was a man who slept, ate, lived, and breathed baseball, the first man to the park at 1:30 for a night game and, usually, the last to leave. It wasn't that he didn't care about Iran or the Pine Street Inn; he didn't pretend to have any frame of reference to them. His frame of reference was baseball, and he is proud that he has never earned a paycheck outside baseball. But because he had no other frame of reference, Zimmer listened to what others said about baseball. Especially talk shows. He couldn't take his mind off the game and listen to Muzak or the Rolling Stones; no, he had to listen to the talk shows driving home, and, worse, he had friends listen to talk shows when he couldn't and tell him what was discussed. Every night as he drove home, he flipped on Glenn Ordway's postgame show on WITS, and every night he fumed when anyone called to criticize the manager. In Boston and with Zimmer, that was often.

Part of Zimmer's problem with the public was his image. He was heavy, had his hair so short he used to say he toweled it dry, and was not well spoken. "The Sports Huddle" used to ridicule him by playing a tape in which Zimmer said, "I don't know nothin' about it" every time someone called to discuss him. Zimmer's personality couldn't come across because there are certain aspects of the clubhouse, the dugout, and the playing field whose language simply doesn't translate into polite-society English, but inside the walls of the game, Zimmer was a character of no small proportion.

He probably was as popular with the traveling media as any manager in recent Red Sox history. He rarely drank (he'd have a Tab or an iced tea with Sweet'n Low after downing a sundae), but he was sociable and accessible. He believed in the manager's image, and always discreetly picked up all checks around him. He treated his coaches well, and when it was time to go to the mound to get a pitcher — the time when managers really take the heat from the fans — he never sent his pitching coach; he faced the music. He was a master raconteur, partly because of his stories, partly because of the way he told them (at the park, they were punctuated by the splat of his tobacco juice), partly because of the color of his opinions. Zimmer could hold court in hotel lobbies at 1:30 A.M or at the ballpark at 2:30 P.M., usually surrounded by baseball friends like Gene Mauch, Dave Garcia, Pat Corrales, and Walter Hriniak. He'd tell stories of managing in Key West, with twelve-hour bus rides during which he'd get the driver to stop at a 7-Eleven, where he'd buy a few pounds of bologna and cheese, a jar of mustard, and a couple of loaves of bread, then make sandwiches in the front row and pass them back to his players. He had Lardneresque stories about forty-year-old men who tried out in Key West or about being ejected from a game and trying to manage from a telephone pole behind the left-field fence. And there was never any question where Zimmy stood; his opinions were definite. He used to say Rick Miller "couldn't hit a home run if he were standing on second base," and in recounting a knock he took from Ted Cox, snapped, "He got hits in his first six times in the big leagues, thought he was a star, and ain't hit a hundred since." Once during a season when Jack Brohamer got heavy he referred to him as "Santy Claus." There was never any doubt where he stood on a player, be he "out——ingstand-ing" or "can't ——ing play" or "good man — wouldn't say shit if he had a mouthful." He even had lists of his pet dislikes. He always said he enjoyed the media in Boston "except for four people," who were "Sports Huddle" host Eddie Andelman, Ordway, Bob Gamere (for making a joke about his daughter's wedding in Winter Haven), and Mike Andrews.

There were a lot of things about Zimmer that made him a good manager. He was devoted to his job, and freely admitted that "the only thing I want to do in life is be a big-league manager." He knew talent, especially infield talent. He was creative; one of his favorite plays was to send the runners with the bases loaded and one out, which worked every time but once, when Fred Lynn missed the sign and was so surprised he meekly swung and missed at a pitch a foot outside and Rick Burleson was easily tagged out coming down the line. Zimmer also had a strong understanding of right and wrong in the game. In June 1979, in Kansas City, Rice and Lynn got mixed up converging on what should have been a game-ending fly ball by Willie Wilson but became a triple. Steve Braun then homered off Drago to win the game. Drago was a tempestuous sort whose booming deep voice could be heard over any competing noise. As he was coming up the runway, he mumbled, "Some of our fielders must be allergic to the ball," a comment that Zimmer and several players heard. Zimmer charged Drago in the clubhouse, telling him off in a ten-minute tirade before silenced teammates, supporting Rice and Lynn, taunting Drago to "call your ——ing

owner friend," a reference to Drago's relationship with
Buddy Leroux, and reminding him in no uncertain terms that
he and he alone gave up the home run to the slap-hitting
Braun. "It was," Jerry Remy said the next week, "one of the
best things a manager could do," an opinion echoed by Drago
himself after he had apologized to Rice for the remark made
in the heat of defeat.

Zimmer was an old-school, blue-collar man who thought
all players should be do-or-die, gutsy types like Hobson. Lynn
frustrated him, so much so that at the end of his .333–39–116
year in 1979 Zimmer suggested in his coaching staff evalua-
tion report that they try to trade him to San Diego for Dave
Winfield, a suggestion that Haywood Sullivan never accepted. Zimmer never understood Lynn's reactions to injury.
Players, particularly Fisk, were intimidated by Zimmer's
habit of making out the lineup card at 1:30, so that if Fisk, for
example, felt that he couldn't play, he'd have to go into the
manager's office to beg out of the lineup. "He might have
been right to do it then, and there shouldn't be anything
wrong with saying 'Look, I'm hurt,' " Fisk said, "but somehow the whole thing made you feel like a puss. I wish
I'd gone in there a few times in August and September in
1978."

Again and again, the problems Zimmer had as manager
traced back to the fact that he listened to what other people
said. He reacted to what Lee, Jenkins, and Wise said about
him in 1977. He kept playing the starting lineup every day in
1978 with a big lead because he was worried about people
saying he was blowing it; ask Zimmer-haters what they most
remember him for, and it would be playing Hobson every
day until he had set an error record and finally had to ask out
of the lineup himself. After games, he'd often say, "I knew
what you [media] guys would ask." By August 1979, when it
was obvious to those close to the team that it was decaying,
Ken Harrelson began coming down hard on Zimmer.

Harrelson was as much of a figure in New England at that

time as any player but Yastrzemski. He'd been a member of
the '67 Impossible Dream team, he'd been the American
League Player of the Year in 1968, all the while living a colorful lifestyle of Nehru suits and plush apartments that en-
deared him to fans as the lovable "Hawk." In 1975 Dick
O'Connell ingeniously brought him back as a television announcer with the polished Dick Stockton, a move that was a
public relations coup. With his southern accent, cowboy
hats, and often brilliantly incisive commentary, Harrelson
was as much the center of attention as he was as a player.
The Hawk had learned baseball with Alvin Dark, and not
only did he know the game, he loved to talk it and had a way
of making definitive, logical judgments that sounded as au-
thoritative as if they were from the *Encyclopaedia Britan-
nica.* Harrelson also has an uncanny feel for situations, and he
realized that the Red Sox were in trouble before the September collapse. There is a point of no return with a coach or a
manager with almost every team, and it is reached particularly when there is a distance between the coach or manager
and the front office. Not that Sullivan didn't like Zimmer; he
simply had little contact with him.

Zimmer liked Sullivan immensely. But Zimmer had been
hired by O'Connell and had been extremely close to John
Claiborne, and he privately questioned the lack of front office help around Haywood. When the Sullivan-Leroux group
raised the money to take over the club, one of their first
moves was to strip down the front office. "We've got to trim
the fat. There's no need for all the people O'Connell has,"
Leroux said at the time, but like so many other things, he
badly misjudged the era. The Messersmith decision and free
agency had radically changed the game in the front office.
The reserve system had guaranteed management equality,
which in turn had fostered a club of good old boys protected
by the rules of the game. The new system made every judgment and decision important: big-money signings had to be
well conceived, scouting and development became increas-

ingly vital, and the ability to judge and find talent without
trying to spend with George Steinbrenner became what separated Baltimore and Los Angeles from the rest of the teams.
"Free agency," said Dodgers Vice-President Al Campanis,
"forced everyone to be more competitive and make tougher
decisions."

But Sullivan was owner, general manager, contract negotiator, and personnel director. He sat on several important
owners' committees and was proud of the fact that he was the
first former player ever to be elected to the prestigious Executive Council, but when Zimmer asked him about a particular pitcher in their farm system, Sullivan told him he was
left-handed when he was right-handed. On road trips, Zimmer complained that he couldn't reach his boss, that he was
always in meetings. In spring training, 1979, for instance,
Zimmer begged Sullivan to find another veteran catcher because of Fisk's elbow injury. Sullivan did nothing. Zimmer
didn't get along with the club's two major-league scouts,
Eddie Kasko and Frank Malzone, and was riled by what he
considered their inertia. Zimmy wanted to pick up left-
handed pitcher Mike Caldwell in spring training, 1977, was
turned down, and Caldwell ended up winning twenty games
for the Brewers in 1978. He was rejected on Tommy John,
turned down on Mets veteran Bud Harrelson as a backup
shortstop, and, in 1980, was offered Charlie Hough for nothing by Dodgers manager Tommy Lasorda and was told he
couldn't have him. Hough went to Texas and became their
best starter. Kasko, Malzone, and farm director Ed Kenney
made the judgments they thought best. They all believed
Zimmer was too prone to ex–National Leaguers (Bob Bailey,
Tommy Helms, Ramon Hernandez) who flopped. They also
believed in their young players like Finch, Glenn Hoffman,
Remmerswaal, Gary Allenson, et al. Some made it, some
didn't.

Sullivan's distance from Zimmer accentuated his manager's emotions and left Zimmer far more insecure than he

should have been, which in turn affected his managing. Players tired of hearing Zimmy talk about getting fired as the '79 season wore on, and while Harrelson beat on him over the air — The Hawk had thoughts of managing the team that were fanned by Leroux — Zimmer himself was sure he was fired. That first week of September 1979 in New York, Sullivan said he wasn't bringing Hoffman up for a September look despite the fact that they felt he was their best prospect. "They feel I've been too harsh in the judgment of some of their young players," Zimmer reasoned, and guessed further that he was gone. Leroux wanted Zimmer fired at that point. Jean Yawkey, who had considerable affection for Zimmy and his wife, Soot, was strongly against firing him. Sullivan was right that what was wrong with that team at that juncture wasn't entirely Zimmer's fault, but he wasn't about to make the changes — trading Lynn or Dwight Evans, for instance — that Zimmer insisted were necessary to turning the club around. What he did instead was to fire pitching coach Alvin Jackson with four days left in the season and replace him with Zimmer's long-time Brooklyn Dodger sidekick Johnny Podres. He rationalized it later by pointing to a story Joe Giulotti did in the *Herald* quoting Rick Burleson as saying what happened to them wasn't the manager's fault. But in terms of the clubhouse and the nature of the team there was more sense to firing Zimmer at the end of the 1979 season without a personnel shake-up than there was to firing him in 1980 with the ensuing shake-up.

The firing of Jackson badly hurt Zimmer. It hurt him immediately, because several players felt that the manager saved his skin by not standing up for a coach who was respected and extremely hard-working. With two weeks to go in the season, Allen Ripley was shelled in relief in a game in Baltimore and afterward told reporters that his arm was hurting him, that he'd told Jackson before the game and Jackson thought he was kidding. When Clif 'n' Claf jumped on that, Sullivan was handed a scapegoat. Worse, the next spring, Podres quickly lost control of the pitching staff. Pod, as he was known, was a likable nightowl who loved the tracks. He had already raised the eyebrows of rookie pitcher Bruce Hurst when he learned that Podres had told Zimmer, "He's ready for the big leagues — he's finally started chasing girls and drinking." Hurst, who was coming to the big leagues after a half-season in double-A, is a strict Mormon who not only did not drink but was engaged, and when that appeared in a story, Hurst was upset. That fall, in the instructional league, minor leaguers sent up the story of Pod's three pieces of advice for young pitchers: "There are three things you gotta do — throw hard, drink hard, and love hard." The major leaguers already had some questions, such as how Podres could have told Zimmer that the jittery Sprowl "had icewater in his veins." Three weeks into spring training Burgmeier and Lockwood took over the pitching chart and began setting up the times when pitchers would throw on the side or work batting practice. "Pod just couldn't function in the morning," said Lockwood in disgust.

The lack of an assistant hurt Sullivan not only in his support and understanding of his manager but in his ability to make deals. As Zimmer and later Ralph Houk pointed out, the Red Sox never had anyone coming up with ideas and in constant contact with other clubs. From 1978 through 1983, the only players Sullivan acquired in midseason were Andy Hassler ('78), Ted Sizemore ('79), Bob Watson ('79), Tom Poquette ('79), and Jack Billingham ('80). In the cases of Hassler and Poquette, both deals were conceived in bull sessions between Royals manager Whitey Herzog and a writer and then taken to Zimmer, who in turn called Sullivan. Worse, his lack of an assistant and his inexperience in negotiations — John Harrington helped him in the Torrez negotiations — left him on his own in dealing with Jerry Kapstein. If Mrs. Yawkey had brought Harrington back a year earlier or Sullivan had hired Lou Gorman or John Claiborne in the winter of 1979–80, Burleson and Fisk would never have left. But Sullivan was basically alone, and in the eye of an ownership firestorm.

The honeymoon of the Sullivan-Leroux group and the media had lasted approximately one week. Joe LaCour, administrator of the Yawkey Estate, and Mrs. Yawkey announced that the former catcher and trainer had been selected to purchase the Red Sox the last week of September 1977. For a few days, the American dream, as Leroux called it, was the story: former bullpen catcher works his way to ownership with former trainer (actually, former Bruins stickboy, as Leroux had no formal background to be a certified trainer). Soon, however, American League owners began raising questions. So did the *Globe*. It took nineteen months and a complete restructuring, including the intervention of Mrs. Yawkey, to get them approved as owners.

When Tom Yawkey died in July 1976, Sullivan and Leroux were the last ones people thought would get the club. It had been oft-speculated that O'Connell would put together a syndicate; but once Tom Yawkey had died, Jean Yawkey was not going to hand the team over to O'Connell. She later stated that it was her husband's wish, that he had wanted O'Connell fired because of the Rudi-Fingers-Burleson-Lynn business that June. Whatever, by the end of 1976, feelings between Mrs. Yawkey and O'Connell were strained, and the two seldom communicated except by notes, most of them cryptic. By April 1977, the Yawkey Estate did not want Mrs. Yawkey, who was in her midsixties, dying with the future unresolved, thus leaving the ball club tied up in litigation for years. So they put it up for sale, and got three local bidders: Jack Satter of Colonial Provision Company ("Fenway Franks"), Dominic DiMaggio, and Weston businessman Martin Stone of Monogram Industries, who also had been throwing batting practice for three years. Also in the bidding was the A-T-O Corporation of Ohio, which made, among other things, Rawlings sporting equipment. All of them with the exception of Stone planned to retain O'Connell, an issue each was asked to address in the interviews; Stone had planned to retain Claiborne and Harrington as dual general managers.

Mrs. Yawkey was extremely fond of Sullivan, as had been her husband. O'Connell's loyalists — and there were many — claimed that Yawkey liked Sullivan but recognized his shortcomings, which is why he allowed O'Connell to demote him and in fact suggested that Claiborne be hired above him. "He's a very nice man who can't make a tough decision," O'Connell said of the first man he brought in when he took over from Mike Higgins in September 1965. Sullivan claimed that Yawkey had at one moment offered him the number-one job, but he felt at the time that it would cause too many problems to fire O'Connell, and Sullivan's friends felt that O'Connell's treatment of Haywood stemmed from jealousy over his relationship with both Yawkeys.

When Sullivan told Mrs. Yawkey that he and Leroux were putting together a group to buy the club, she wanted him to have it but doubted they could come up with the money. Leroux had quit as trainer after the 1974 season, partly because of his constant clashes with manager Darrell Johnson, partly because of his real estate deals. Leroux is a hustler. No one could put a definite number on his worth because so much was paper, but the man had worked his way up to put together the deal for the New England Rehabilitation Hospital in Woburn and various real estate partnerships. Leroux is also smart, knew the relationship between Mrs. Yawkey, Sullivan, and O'Connell, and went right to Haywood with this deal: I'll get the money, you get inside. What did Sullivan have to lose? He had a house, a car, and three teenage kids, and here he was being offered the option of a piece of the Red Sox or looking for a job elsewhere. It wasn't that the sale was completely a closed shop, because Mrs. Yawkey and La-Cour didn't believe Leroux and Sullivan could come up with the money. But when A-T-O bid $18.75 million, Stone put up $16 million, and Leroux and Sullivan walked off with it with a paper $15 million bid in which each was to put up $200,000 and get 52 percent of the franchise, the other bidders were furious. As was the American League, not to mention the fans, once Leroux's deal became public knowledge.

First, Mrs. Yawkey and LaCour sent for O'Connell, Claiborne, and the highly respected Gene Kirby and dismissed them. Then they turned it over to Buddy and Haywood, who within a couple of years were tagged "Shoddy Leroux and Dumwood Sullivan" by the *Globe*'s Ray Fitzgerald. By the time they were supposed to go before the American League for approval in mid-November, they were in court fighting a suit by the A-T-O Corporation, buried by *Globe* Spotlight Team investigations ridiculing them, and faced with the word of a prominent owner that if their proposed sale came to a vote, it would be rejected unanimously, 13–0. Behind the scenes, O'Connell worked feverishly to destroy the Haywood-Buddy combine, and after thirty years with the Red Sox, O'Connell had a lot of friends on whom to call.

"This isn't Cleveland, it's Boston, the flagship of the American League," said Milwaukee owner Bud Selig, chairman of the league finance committee that reviewed prospective owners. "This is the most important franchise in the American League, and we can't afford to let it be underfinanced or second-rate. The situation is a mess. It seems inconceivable that what Tom Yawkey built has come to *this.*" Neither Selig nor anyone else could ever comprehend how Yawkey could have left the club so unsettled upon his death.

When Selig made the statement on November 10, A-T-O was trying to grab control by claiming that the Yawkey Estate trust had not acted in the best interests of the estate by ignoring the high bid. By then, the newspapers were having a field day with the Leroux package, with Mike Barnicle calling it a "48-month car loan." There were "Save Our Sox" bumper stickers; political, financial, and sports columnists and cartoonists at war; and a daily radio soap spoof called "Boston Red Sox, Boston Red Sox" that detailed what went

on with Buddy, Jean, and Haywood that day. The State
Street Bank, which had agreed to the loan that would finance
the Leroux package, was attacked until the officer who
granted the loan resigned and disappeared to upstate Maine.
The *Globe* revealed that one partner had been subpoenaed to
testify before a grand jury regarding the alleged murder of a
partner in a bankrupt furniture company and claimed that
another had acted in a conflict of interest regarding the ap-
propriation of state funds for handicapped children. A third
partner was accused of conflict of interest in a Woburn kick-
back scandal.

Amidst all this, Speaker of the House Thomas P. "Tip"
O'Neill jumped in, trying to get Bowie Kuhn to block the sale
on behalf of his old friend O'Connell. Players' Association
director Marvin Miller jumped on language in the agreement
specifying an $8 million payroll cap and a 10 percent limit
for raises. The bank had a right of approval on all major
transactions. "If nuclear war were to break out, it would be
page-two stuff," said then–public relations director Bill
Crowley. And Leroux recounted, "Before O'Connell walked
out of the building, he turned to me and said, 'Are you prepared for all this?' I didn't understand what he meant. I soon
did. We weren't."

Globe financial experts estimated that this ownership
could not survive two bad seasons, dredged up unsavory parts
of Leroux's past, and cast serious doubts on the validity of his
net worth claim of $4.7 million. Soon Red Smith dubbed
them "The State Street Sox" in the *New York Times*.

Because of the A-T-O suit, they avoided the 13–0 putdown
in November, but when they went before the American
League at the December winter meetings, they were voted
down 11–3. At that point, Mrs. Yawkey and LaCour advised
Sullivan that perhaps he should go back and talk to Stone or
Satter and be prepared to rid himself of Leroux, and he
talked extensively with Stone. But, in the end, he decided to

stick with Leroux. Six years later, when the ownership was in a state of civil war, he wished he hadn't.

Mrs. Yawkey finally came into the group, donating her name, Fenway Park, enough money for a limited partnership, a loan to Sullivan, and her thrust as president to get it approved. Leroux still had to round up backers, and before going in front of the league in May had to scramble for the last fourteen limited partnerships. He talked Kentucky coal baron Rogers Badgett into increasing his purchase from one partnership for $500,000 to ten for $5 million. Leroux convinced the American Finance Corporation of Cincinnati to float him a loan four points above prime; problem is, Leroux had to pledge both his and Sullivan's general partnerships as collateral to AFC, whose president, Robert Lindner, was part owner of the Cincinnati Reds and eager to get a major-league franchise. Eventually, when AFC gave the *Globe* copies of that loan agreement and they were published, Badgett helped get Leroux out of the loans that, had he missed payment, would have given Lindner control of the Red Sox.

Leroux did come up with the money, however, and the Buddy, Jean, and Haywood troika took official control in May 1978. By then, the team was in the process of running away to the huge lead that turned out to be written in disappearing ink, and ownership approval was a sidebar to the runaway story. That November, when they ignored Tommy John while cutting loose Luis Tiant and Bill Lee, a few fans screamed, but the team had been the second-winningest in the majors. The next year they made a charade of going after pitchers Jim Slaton (while Sullivan insisted he was offering close to the package that Slaton signed with Milwaukee, he failed to mention that less than half was guaranteed) and Dave Goltz, and that increased the complaints. But it was the disastrous off-season of 1980–81 that did Sullivan and the ownership damage it would take years to overcome.

While Sullivan did indeed get Rice and Eckersley signed to

lucrative contracts the previous off-season, that was mostly because their agents had aggressively pursued him. During the 1980 World Series, Sullivan admitted that he was shopping Burleson and Lynn in case he couldn't sign either, and because those two and Fisk could be free agents come November 1981, he had to find their market value. Sullivan's negotiations with Burleson's agent Jack Sands, whom the shortstop had hired because he felt Jerry Kapstein had too many other interests in Lynn and Fisk, were going nowhere. Worse, Sullivan could not communicate with Kapstein. Now, to say the least, Kapstein is different. When the world was changing in 1976, Harrington and Claiborne used to hear Sullivan, Ed Kenney, and Frank Malzone sit in the back of the downstairs offices predicting that agents would never last. Haywood was a traditionalist matched against one of the most brilliant — and often confusing — negotiators in Kapstein. Had Harrington or Claiborne been there, it might have been different, but the Lynn talks went nowhere and Sullivan tried to deal him to Los Angeles for pitchers Steve Howe and Joe Beckwith and third baseman Mickey Hatcher (history will someday guffaw at the Red Sox preference of Hatcher over Pedro Guerrero). The Dodgers put the deal on hold while they signed their potential free agent Dusty Baker. Sullivan made an offer to Kapstein on Lynn, but it amounted to only $3.5 million for five years, far below what Kapstein knew the market price was. Sullivan became frustrated by Kapstein's style of negotiating, a communications rift developed out of misunderstanding, and the situation — which wasn't good after Fisk, Burleson, and Kapstein felt that Rice's signing in 1979 came under their 1976 verbal agreement that they would reopen the contracts if anyone else were renegotiated (to which Sullivan responded, "Where is it in writing?") — worsened. It was as if they were trying to talk across the Berlin Wall.

By the winter meetings the first week of December in Dallas, Sullivan had made up his mind to deal both Burleson and

Lynn. The Burleson trade was easy: Angels owner Gene Autry heard he and Lynn were available, was told "You don't have enough to get both" and gave a bundle in third baseman Carney Lansford, relief pitcher Mark Clear, and outfielder Rick Miller for Burleson and Hobson on a Tuesday. Later that night, the Dodgers agreed to the Lynn deal for Rookie of the Year Howe, Beckwith, and a minor-league phenom named Mike Marshall. When Dodgers general manager Al Campanis phoned Kapstein from Dallas, he would agree to no more than a one-year contract. The reasoning was obvious: San Diego free-agent superstar Dave Winfield had yet to sign, and Kapstein realized that Winfield would establish the market price for Lynn. But the Red Sox didn't understand it, neither did the Dodgers, and at 5:00 A.M. CST the Dodgers called off the deal. They tried to work out deals with the Mets (asking for Jeff Reardon, Mookie Wilson, and Tim Leary) and Reds, to no avail. Then, the last day of the meetings, Leroux made a verbal agreement with George Steinbrenner to send Lynn to the Yankees for Ron Guidry and Ruppert Jones, but Steinbrenner asked for a few hours while he flew back to New York. He never got back to them that night, and when he finally did two days later, wanted to expand the deal to include Bob Stanley. It never worked out.

While they were in Dallas, Sullivan, club counsel Al Curran, Player Relations Committee counsel Barry Rona, and American League President Lee MacPhail had met to discuss the renewals of the contracts of Lynn, Fisk, and Burleson. The three five-year contracts had expired, but since they were signed under the old system (before August 9, 1976) they had option years. Now, under normal procedure laid out in paragraph 10(a) of the standard player contract, the team had to renew them on or before December 20, a date established by Miller to allow a player to know a club's plan for him before the new year. However, these three contracts were unique. According to Harrington and Claiborne, who negotiated them with Kapstein, once they got to monetary figures, they wanted to find a way that, in Harrington's words, "we could make Lynn, Fisk and Burleson Red Sox for life." So they had in the contracts a three-paragraph right of first refusal, which meant that Boston had the right to match any offer the three players might receive on the open market as free agents in 1981. At the time the contracts were signed, the game was in a state of near-suspended animation. Salary arbitration had been suspended for two years. The new Basic Agreement had been drafted but not ratified. All Claiborne, Harrington, and Kapstein were trying to do was rush to get the contracts done before August 9 (Fisk and Burleson signed on the 4th, Lynn on the 8th). Even Kapstein didn't really know at that time what the market would bear, for while Catfish Hunter and Andy Messersmith had been free agents, the first re-entry draft with Reggie Jackson, Don Baylor, Bill Campbell, Rollie Fingers, et al. was still three months away.

"The *intent* involved keeping them in Boston their entire careers," Harrington maintains. The confusion was understandable. Section II ("Option Year Salary and Right of First Refusal") of the addendum to the contract, read, "If, at the expiration of the 1980 Championship Season, club and player are unable to agree upon a new Major League Baseball Contract for the 1981 Championship Season, and if Club elects to renew Player's contract no later than March 11, 1981 for the year 1981, under paragraph 10(a) of this contract, then club guarantees that if this contract is renewed, that compensation shall be fixed by the club at a sum not less than the salary received by the player for the 1980 Championship Season as set forth under the section of this addendum titled 'payment schedule,' and that Player shall be paid the said sum, even though the player may be 'unsigned' and may be playing out his option during the 1981 Championship Season." After that long and winding clause, they set forth the conditions for exercising the right of first refusal.

Sometime after the contracts were signed and agreed to by the league, Marvin Miller and the Players' Association challenged the right-of-refusal clause. Miller claimed that the clause took away rights earned in collective bargaining, which neither club nor player may do. O'Connell, Claiborne, Harrington, club counsel Jack Hayes, and attorney Justin Morreale of Bingham, Dana & Gould wanted to fight for the right to retain the clause, but MacPhail suggested that if they lost, the players would be free agents. O'Connell finally acceded to the ameliorative posture of the league and removed the clause, so the eventual three contracts had the complex "Option Year Salary" clause without what logically followed in the context.

In Dallas, Sullivan, Curran, Rona, and MacPhail met to discuss whether or not the language concerning the guarantee that the 1981 salary would be no less than the 1980 salary and the vagaries of the intent of those clauses required the usual tendering of a contract by December 20. The general legal opinion was that they didn't. Sullivan preferred that, because he knew that if he tendered Lynn and Fisk contracts, he would have to go to salary arbitration, end up paying them a combined $1.5 to $1.8 million, and lose them at the end of the year. They agreed that they would not send out the contracts, and so told Angels assistant general manager Mike Port per the similar Burleson contract.

But on the 17th, Rona suggested to Port that he had nothing to lose by sending Burleson a contract, then filing a grievance to prevent arbitration. Neither Rona nor Port so told the Red Sox, and on December 22, Rona called Sullivan and told him that the Angels had sent Burleson a contract. Understandably, Sullivan was in a dither, and, upon Rona's advice, mailed Lynn and Fisk contracts at their 1980 salaries, "figuring we had nothing to lose."

Except Fred Lynn and Carlton Fisk. Sullivan could have changed the date on the postage machine, but did not. Had the contract not been mailed out by either Port on the 17th or Sullivan on the 22nd, Leroux, Curran, and Sullivan insist that they would have won their case. Miller insists that their

Final American League Standings and Red Sox Statistics, 1979

	W	L	PCT	GB	R	HR	BA
EAST							
BAL	102	57	.642		757	181	.261
MIL	95	66	.590	8	807	185	.280
BOS	91	69	.569	11.5	841	194	.283
NY	89	71	.556	13.5	734	150	.266
DET	85	76	.528	18	770	164	.269
CLE	81	80	.503	22	760	138	.258
TOR	53	109	.327	50.5	613	95	.251
WEST							
CAL	88	74	.543		866	164	.282
KC	85	77	.525	3	851	116	.282
TEX	83	79	.512	5	750	140	.278
MIN	82	80	.506	6	764	112	.278
CHI	73	87	.456	14	730	127	.275
SEA	67	95	.414	21	711	132	.269
OAK	54	108	.333	34	573	108	.239
LEAGUE TOTAL					10527	2006	.270

MANAGER	W	L	PCT
Don Zimmer	91	69	.569

POS	PLAYER	B	G	AB	H	2B	3B	HR	R	RBI	BA
REGULARS											
1B	Bob Watson	R	84	312	105	19	4	13	48	53	.337
2B	Jerry Remy	L	80	306	91	11	2	0	49	29	.297
SS	Rick Burleson	R	153	627	174	32	5	5	93	60	.278
3B	Butch Hobson	R	146	528	138	26	7	28	74	93	.261
RF	Dwight Evans	R	152	489	134	24	1	21	69	58	.274
CF	Fred Lynn	L	147	531	177	42	1	39	116	122	.333
LF	Jim Rice	R	158	619	201	39	6	39	117	130	.325
C	Gary Allenson	R	108	241	49	10	2	3	27	22	.203
DH	Carl Yastrzemski	L	147	518	140	28	1	21	69	87	.270
SUBSTITUTES											
DC	Carlton Fisk	R	91	320	87	23	2	10	49	42	.272
2B	Jack Brohamer	L	64	192	51	7	1	1	25	11	.266
1B	George Scott	R	45	156	35	9	1	4	18	23	.224
2S	Stan Papi	R	50	117	22	8	0	1	9	6	.188
1O	Jim Dwyer	L	76	113	30	7	0	2	19	14	.265
2B	Ted Sizemore	R	26	88	23	7	0	1	12	6	.261
UT	Larry Wolfe	R	47	78	19	4	0	3	12	15	.244
21	Frank Duffy	R	6	3	0	0	0	0	0	0	.000
OF	Tom Poquette	L	63	154	51	9	0	2	14	23	.331
C	Bob Montgomery	R	32	86	30	4	1	0	13	7	.349
C	Mike O'Berry	R	43	59	10	1	0	1	8	4	.169

Final American League Standings and Red Sox Statistics, 1979, continued

PITCHER	T	W	L	PCT	ERA	SV
Mike Torrez	R	16	13	.552	4.50	0
Dennis Eckersley	R	17	10	.630	2.99	0
Bob Stanley	R	16	12	.571	3.98	1
Steve Renko	R	11	9	.550	4.11	0
Chuck Rainey	R	8	5	.615	3.81	1
Tom Burgmeier	L	3	2	.600	2.73	4
Dick Drago	R	10	6	.625	3.03	13
Allen Ripley	R	3	1	.750	5.12	1
Joel Finch	R	0	3	.000	4.89	0
Bill Campbell	R	3	4	.429	4.25	9
John Tudor	L	1	2	.333	6.43	0
Jim Wright	R	1	0	1.000	5.09	0
Win Remmerswaal	R	1	0	1.000	7.20	0
Andy Hassler	L	1	2	.333	9.00	0
TEAM TOTAL		91	69	.569	4.03	29

contention is "absurd," citing the reference to paragraph 10(a), which calls for the December 20 tendering process. Kapstein naturally had anticipated all this, and the players were waiting for the postmark. The grievances were filed, Miller insisted they would be made free agents, and Sullivan was left standing, insisting that it made no sense to pay those two players all that money to allow them to leave. That logic, of course, ran counter to his announced espousal of the "rent-a-star" theory. It also made little sense in terms of player talent inventory or public relations. It did not begin to deal with the failure to competently address the Kapstein negotiations in the first place. It also never answered a logical question: Why not let Fisk and Lynn go to arbitration, then trade them for at least seventy-five cents on the dollar in February or March? That question has still never been answered.

By the time Lynn, Fisk, Kapstein, and the Red Sox party gathered in New York for the arbitration hearing to decide whether the three were in fact free agents, the bitterness between Sullivan and Fisk had erected an insurmountable fence between the two. It had begun in spring training, when they

Final American League Standings and Red Sox Statistics, 1980

	W	L	PCT	GB	R	HR	BA
EAST							
NY	103	59	.636		820	189	.267
BAL	100	62	.617	3	805	156	.273
MIL	86	76	.531	17	811	203	.275
BOS	83	77	.519	19	757	162	.283
DET	84	78	.519	19	830	143	.273
CLE	79	81	.494	23	738	89	.277
TOR	67	95	.414	36	624	126	.251
WEST							
KC	97	65	.599		809	115	.286
OAK	83	79	.512	14	686	137	.259
MIN	77	84	.478	19.5	670	99	.265
TEX	76	85	.472	20.5	756	124	.284
CHI	70	90	.438	26	587	91	.259
CAL	65	95	.406	31	698	106	.265
SEA	59	103	.364	38	610	104	.248
LEAGUE TOTAL					10201	1844	.269

MANAGER	W	L	PCT
Don Zimmer	82	74	.526
Johnny Pesky	1	3	.250

POS	PLAYER	B	G	AB	H	2B	3B	HR	R	RBI	BA
REGULARS											
1B	Tony Perez	R	151	585	161	31	3	25	73	105	.275
2B	Dave Stapleton	R	106	449	144	33	5	7	61	45	.321
SS	Rick Burleson	R	155	644	179	29	2	8	89	51	.278
3B	Glenn Hoffman	R	114	312	89	15	4	4	37	42	.285
RF	Dwight Evans	R	148	463	123	37	5	18	72	60	.266
CF	Fred Lynn	L	110	415	125	32	3	12	67	61	.301
LF	Jim Rice	R	124	504	148	22	6	24	81	86	.294
C	Carlton Fisk	R	131	478	138	25	3	18	73	62	.289
DH	Carl Yastrzemski	L	105	364	100	21	1	15	49	50	.275
SUBSTITUTES											
3D	Butch Hobson	R	93	324	74	6	0	11	35	39	.228
2B	Jerry Remy	L	63	230	72	7	2	0	24	9	.313
2D	Chico Walker	B	19	57	12	0	0	1	3	5	.211
UT	Jack Brohamer	L	21	57	18	2	0	1	5	6	.316
DC	Rich Gedman	L	9	24	5	0	0	0	2	1	.208
2B	Ted Sizemore	R	9	23	5	1	0	0	1	0	.217
3D	Larry Wolfe	R	18	23	3	1	0	1	3	4	.130
SS	Julio Valdez	B	8	19	5	1	0	1	4	4	.263
3B	Stan Papi	R	1	0	0	0	0	0	0	0	—
UT	Jim Dwyer	L	93	260	74	11	1	9	41	38	.285
OD	Garry Hancock	L	46	115	33	6	0	4	9	19	.287
OF	Reid Nichols	R	12	36	8	0	1	0	5	3	.222
OF	Sam Bowen	R	7	13	2	0	0	0	0	0	.154
OD	Dave Rader	L	50	137	45	11	0	3	14	17	.328
UT	Gary Allenson	R	36	70	25	6	0	0	9	10	.357

Final American League Standings and Red Sox Statistics, 1980, continued

PITCHER	T	W	L	PCT	ERA	SV
Mike Torrez	R	9	16	.360	5.09	0
Dennis Eckersley	R	12	14	.462	4.27	0
Bob Stanley	R	10	8	.556	3.39	14
Steve Renko	R	9	9	.500	4.20	0
Dick Drago	R	7	7	.500	4.13	3
Tom Burgmeier	L	5	4	.556	2.00	24
John Tudor	L	8	5	.615	3.03	0
Chuck Rainey	R	8	3	.727	4.86	0
Skip Lockwood	R	3	1	.750	5.28	2
Keith MacWhorter	R	0	3	.000	5.57	0
Bill Campbell	R	4	0	1.000	4.83	0
Win Remmerswaal	R	2	1	.667	4.63	0
Steve Crawford	R	2	0	1.000	3.66	0
Bruce Hurst	L	2	2	.500	9.00	0
Bob Ojeda	L	1	1	.500	6.92	0
Jack Billingham	R	1	3	.250	11.25	0
Luis Aponte	R	0	0	—	1.29	0
TEAM TOTAL		83	77	.519	4.39	43

clashed over reopening the contract, grew when Sullivan cracked, "I think his contract is bothering him more than his arm," and continually got worse. Carlton and Linda claimed that at a pre–All-Star Game party, Sullivan twice avoided them, and Fisk was bitter that there was virtually no attempt by Sullivan to try to get the contract worked out between October and December 1980. By then, Mrs. Yawkey had brought Harrington back to the Yawkey Foundation, as La-Cour was gravely ill. So Harrington tried to sit down with both Lynn and Fisk and work on a new contract; under the $700,000 salary cap set by Rice's standard, he had no chance, so Leroux and Sullivan scrambled to make the best deal they could, which without waivers on Lynn meant that since the interleague trading period was six weeks away they had to deal within their own league.

The Angels badly wanted Lynn, and he was happy to go home to California and live ten minutes from his home park. First, the Red Sox tried to extract first baseman Jason

Thompson and a couple of pitchers. Angels President Buzzy
Bavasi laughed. Then they tried minor-league phenom Tom
Brunansky and a couple of pitchers. Bavasi laughed. Then
Bobby Clark and pitchers. No. The Red Sox had to take what
Bavasi was willing to give them, which was a worn and injured Joe Rudi, Frank Tanana coming off two years of arm
problems, and a minor-league pitcher named Jim Dorsey; the
latter started a game in Fenway in September, and when
asked before the game if he were any good, Angels manager
Jim Fregosi snapped, "If he were, don't you think we'd have
had him up here in June or July?"

In the Fisk arbitration hearing, Miller and Players' Association counsel Don Fehr centered their attacks on Curran,
who in his testimony concerning his opinion that no tender
was necessary admitted that he didn't know what the reference to paragraph 10(a) meant. Miller and Fehr ripped Curran apart on the stand. Harrington couldn't remember the
contract model for these agreements, and when Kapstein remembered that it was that of Ken Holtzman and that he had
drawn it up, another key club argument was blurred. Arbitrator Raymond Goetz — while acknowledging that this was
a cloudy case because of the intent of the 1976 contract and
that losing Fisk was an extreme hardship to the ball club —
ruled that he was a free agent. The decision came the morning that the Red Sox were having a press luncheon. Channel 4
caught all of the announcement, from Bill Crowley shouting
"Shut up" to quiet the boisterous room to a disheveled Sullivan reading the announcement, throwing up his arms, and
saying, "Reopen the bar." If Sullivan and Leroux didn't look
bad enough already in the whole affair, they looked like
complete buffoons now. Dumwood and Shoddy they would
be.

Harrington tried to re-sign Fisk, but the chasm between
the catcher and the ball club was too great. In March, when
Kapstein asked Harrington to come to the West Coast because he was approaching a decision, Sullivan told Harring-

ton not to go. While Harrington tried to talk Fisk and Kapstein into coming to Florida, the White Sox party flew out to San Diego, and twenty-four hours later a press conference was called in Chicago. "Losing Fisk like that," Harrington said on reflection, "probably hurt this franchise more than anything."

All the worst fears about the Leroux-Sullivan ownership — their apparent concern for profits over players, their inexperience in the new system, and their lack of aggressiveness accentuated by the shadows of both O'Connell and Steinbrenner — were realized in the Fisk fiasco. They'd given the best catcher in the history of the franchise away for nothing; the fans didn't know if it was because Sullivan couldn't read a calendar or because the club was too cheap or what. The flagship of the American League had lost dignity and respect, the Sixth Game had been allowed to move west, SuperTeam was in the dim, dark past, and the only remnants of the impending dynasty of the '75 World Series were Dwight Evans, Jim Rice, Rick Miller, and forty-one-year-old Carl Yastrzemski.

EIGHT

1981-83

THE ILLUSION OF
RESPECTABILITY

*Dwight Evans establishes himself as a superstar in
midcareer and new manager Ralph Houk brilliantly
juggles his troops through a transitional period. But by
1983, watching Yaz add to his lifetime stat totals en
route to retirement is all that's left to interest fans.*

WALTER HRINIAK stood on the mound throwing one pitch
after another like a Gatling gun, and he'd been doing so for
nearly an hour and a half. It had been 3:00 P.M., July 3, 1980,
when he started, 101 degrees with Baltimore humidity. All
the time, one player — Dwight Evans — stood in the batting
cage swinging at the Red Sox coach's pitches, with only the
occasional break of Hriniak jumping out from behind the
protective pitching screen to demonstrate a point with his
hands. In the ninety minutes that had elapsed, Evans had
looked like a father stepping into the cage at Paragon Park to
show his kid that he could still hit; some he missed, some he
fouled back into the cage, many he bounced off the pitching
screen, and a few he drove into the outfield. When neither of
them could stand the sun and heat anymore, Hriniak turned
to one of the writers who'd been standing in the outfield
shagging and said, "I think he's got it. I think today's the day
Dwight Evans's career turned around."

At that point in his career, Evans was twenty-eight years old and an above-average player. He was established as the American League's premier defensive right fielder, and his numbers for eight seasons averaged out to a .262 batting average, sixteen home runs, and fifty-five RBIs — fair, although below his expectations. Evans was victimized by his own physical potential, realizing what former Red Sox pitching phenom Ken Brett expressed in a sign displayed in the bathroom of his apartment: THE WORST CURSE IN LIFE IS UNLIMITED POTENTIAL. In 1972, coming all the way out of the Carolina League at the age of twenty to spring training with the Red Sox, "Evans," Eddie Kasko said, "is the best prospect *anyone* has." He went down to Louisville, batted .301 and was named the International League's Most Valuable Player, and came up to Boston that September a colt with ballyhooed potential. Physically, he was ready for it; mentally, he was not. He struggled to hit .223 with thirty-two RBIs on a platoon basis in 1973, and while he had some good years — .281 with seventy RBIs in 1974, twenty-four homers in 1978 — he wasn't able to put together anything like what had been forecast for him, either in 1972 by Kasko or in the 1975 World Series, when Sparky Anderson told writers that he thought Evans might be better than Fred Lynn or Jim Rice.

By July 3, 1980, Evans's potential had apparently finally ground to a median level. He was an offensive defensive outfielder who would miss winning a Gold Glove only twice (1977 when he was injured in June, and 1980, inexplicably) from 1976 through 1984, cutting balls off in the alley, charging singles with abandon, and uncorking his powerful arm with distinctive quickness and accuracy. "The only player I've seen go to the line and come up throwing back to second better than Evans was Roberto Clemente," remarked third-base coach Eddie Yost, and third-base coaches are the ones who must know these things. "The Gold Gloves mean more to me than anything," Evans said before the 1980 season, resigned to forever being a defensive offensive player. Management didn't really mind, at least up until 1980. Rice, Lynn, Fisk, et al. supplied enough runs, and right field in Fenway Park is not only the most difficult to play in the league, it is the most important of the three outfield positions in that park.

Evans's career to that point had been filled with complexities enlarged by his own insecurities. He was twenty-one when he came out of spring training in 1973 as the right fielder, and too young for the pressure that went with that responsibility on a team that was expected to make a run at the pennant. Lacking genuine self-confidence, both socially and physically, he always latched on to veteran players. From 1973 through 1975, it was Rico Petrocelli who, though emotional, was open to helping any younger player. From 1977 on, Evans was Yastrzemski's alter ego; Yaz always had one disciple — Joe Lahoud for a while, then Doug Griffin — whom he took everywhere, and when Griffin was released at the start of the 1977 season, Evans became Yaz's sidekick. Teammates derided Evans for it; Lynn used to pretend he was a puppet being dangled by a string, asking teammates "Who am I?" while Dwight looked on. But Evans simply had a need for direction, a need that manifested itself on the field by his listening to anyone who offered him advice. He changed stances so often a teammate suggested that he was the first player ever to change stances while the pitch was on its way to the plate. He changed agents so much in 1977 that in one day John Claiborne had calls from three different people claiming they represented Evans. "The best thing with Dwight would be to give him a new contract every day," Claiborne once remarked, laughing.

His insecurities drove Zimmer batty. Where Darrell Johnson, who'd managed him in Louisville, coddled Evans, Zimmer treated him as he would anyone else. "Next to Rice, he's the strongest guy on the team and one of the strongest players in baseball," Zimmer once said, "and he's got all the balls of a female cow." Zimmer had suggested trading him several times — once to Milwaukee for Sixto Lezcano, another time to California for right-handed pitcher Chris Knapp, who soon thereafter came down with a career-ending back injury — but Sullivan resisted the temptation. Evans's insecurity was in fact worsened by the constant trade rumors, for he was always the player talked about when it was suggested the Red Sox deal for pitching. Next to Lynn and Rice and with positional players like Fisk and Burleson, he was the expendable player, and it wore on him.

Evans was also dogged with other problems, on and off the field. Just when he started hitting, in August 1973, he was seriously beaned in Texas by left-handed pitcher Mike Paul. He lay unconscious for minutes, was rushed to the hospital, and missed a week. In his first at-bat of his first game back, Nolan Ryan threw a pitch directly at his head; it soon got around the league that if a pitcher brushed him back early, he could get him out with breaking balls the rest of the game. In the 1975 World Series he appeared to be ready to blossom after batting .292 with a ninth-inning, tying homer in game three and his magnificent catch in the Sixth Game, but during most of 1976 he was dogged by hamstring pulls and hit only .242. Then in 1977 he was off to the best start of his career, leading the team in home runs in mid-June, when he hurt his right knee. He tried to come back in August, but soon required surgery, so he was set back again. In September 1978, he was again seriously beaned, this time by Seattle's Mike Parrott, and he played the next two weeks with an inner ear problem that affected his equilibrium. When he looked up, he got dizzy and woozy, and for the first time in his career, in a crucial game in Baltimore, he dropped two fly balls. Within six days, he did it again and had to be yanked out of the lineup.

Off the field, he was trying to deal with his son Timmy's rare illness. Timmy was born in 1973 with what is commonly called Elephant Man's disease, and Dwight and his wife, Susan, spent days, weeks, and months in and out of hospitals with him, an unfathomable burden for a couple in their twenties, made more difficult by Dwight's stature as a public figure and worsened when his youngest son, Justin, became ill. Once Evans came to terms with baseball and began experiencing success at the end of 1980, particularly with the coming of Ralph Houk in 1981, the ballpark became an escape in the early afternoons. He'd get to the clubhouse by 2:30, sit in front of his locker and read, go out underneath the center-field stands and take hitting, or, on the road, take thirty to forty minutes of extra hitting with Hriniak. "It is," he once said, "the only place where I can focus all my attention."

Until July 1980, however, Evans often played the game as if it were being played in the dark, and since the game wasn't fun, the interrelationship of the personal and professional made the game very hard. To make things worse, he had a habit of staring out at pitchers when they struck him out, a stare that pitchers read to mean "How could you get *me* out?" Evans always claimed he wasn't even aware of this quirk, but added to another habit of constantly stepping out of the box as pitchers started into their wind-ups, it gave him the reputation around the league of being a hot dog, which came to his attention in a *Boston* magazine story that called him "the most disliked player in the American League."

In July 1980, he was hitting .186 and being platooned with Jimmy "Pig Pen" Dwyer. But during those first few days of that July, he'd turned himself over to Hriniak, the batting coach and disciple of Charlie Lau. "All I did was give him certain basics to take to the plate every at-bat," explained Hriniak. "Keep his head down. Drive the ball through the middle. Shift the weight to the front foot at the point of impact. It's all very simple."

"When I came up, I drove the ball to center and right-center," Evans claimed. "That was always where my power was. Somewhere I guess I tried to think too much about The Wall and tried to pull too much. I also had no idea what I was doing at the plate, so I was always thinking instead of hitting. I had no idea why I did or didn't hit. If I hit a home run, I'd go back and start thinking, 'I may not ever be able to do that again.' Walter brought me back to my basics and gave me a simple checklist I could go by. All of a sudden, I knew what I was doing at the plate and why I did or didn't hit." Hriniak gave him one consistent voice to listen to, and Evans did it so religiously that one night after hitting a home run he called Hriniak in the bullpen and asked him what he thought of the swing.

From July 10, 1980, through the 1982 season, Evans hit .299 with 67 home runs and 297 RBIs in 350 games. He led the league in homers (22), total bases (215), and walks (85) in the 108-game 1981 season, then came back in 1982 to hit 32 homers, 37 doubles and 7 triples, and walk 112 times. Over those two seasons, Evans led the league in what the *Washington Post*'s Tom Boswell calls "total average," a statistical device that measures offensive performance by dividing bases (total bases, walks, hit by pitches, stolen bases) by outs (caught stealings, outs made, grounds into double plays).

There were two important elements in the blossoming of Dwight Evans. One was Haywood Sullivan's understanding of his insecurities, so after the 1979 season he signed Evans to a five-year contract. Sullivan gambled that Evans would be a better player after signing the contract because he wouldn't be worried about becoming a free agent or being traded. Then there was Sullivan's judgment in hiring Houk.

The populist choice for Zimmer's successor had been Ken Harrelson. The fans wanted it, as The Hawk had become a sort of cult figure. Harrelson was colorful, with his cowboy hats and drawl; he was also an excellent announcer who talked baseball candidly and incisively. Buddy Leroux wanted Harrelson because he knew Harrelson would put people in the park. Sullivan wanted no part of Harrelson; Haywood's idea of the perfect announcer would be the electronic drone on airport shuttles. He resented Harrelson's

open criticism first of Zimmer in 1979, then of Sullivan himself in 1980 when Zimmer felt he was left with twenty-one
players and could never reach the owner–general manager
on the phone. Harrelson was all baseball; he talked it in the
booth, on buses, and half the night over vodka and tonics. He
was also a man of boundless gall who was never afraid of taking a chance. He and Sullivan were as much alike as mar-
garitas and milk. Leroux leaked three other names — Frank
Robinson, then coaching with the Orioles; Frank Howard, a
coach with the Brewers; and Joe Morgan, the manager at
Pawtucket.

None had a chance. Robinson was too controversial,
Howard was going to San Diego, and Sullivan privately admitted the day of the Zimmer firing that there wasn't anyone
in the organization who could or would be a candidate. Sullivan first went to Cincinnati President Dick Wagner and
asked for permission to talk to John McNamara, with whom
Sullivan had worked in the Kansas City organization in the
early 1960s. Wagner denied him permission (Sullivan eventually did hire McNamara, in October 1984). So, near the end
of the World Series, Sullivan called Houk in Florida. Houk
had retired from the Tigers two years before, but he wanted
to get back into the game. He'd always been interested in
Boston, as Tom Yawkey had always wanted him to manage
the Red Sox. In fact, when the Red Sox were struggling in
early June 1975 and Darrell Johnson was close to being fired,
Dick O'Connell talked to the Tigers — then in a state of total
decline — about the possibility of hiring Houk. Before anything was resolved, the Sox won nine out of thirteen on a road
trip, came home and took three out of four from the Yankees,
and were never out of first place after July 5.

Houk probably saved Sullivan's neck. By this time, Leroux
had his sights set on taking over. His largest investor, Kentucky coal man Rogers Badgett, was at odds with Jean Yawkey. At that point, Leroux had nearly two-thirds of the
limited partner shares on his side, with the votes of Badgett,

Harold Alfond of Dexter Shoes, team counsel Al Curran, and himself lined up against Sullivan. The handling of the Lynn-Fisk fiasco — ending up with only Frank Tanana, Joe Rudi, and Jim Dorsey — had made the Red Sox the butt of one joke after another. "They are the laughingstock of the American League," Harrelson said at a January talk at the University of Massachusetts–Boston, in which he also called Sullivan "incompetent." (By noon the next day, Sullivan had a tape of the speech.) By May, there was discussion among the limited partners about trying to oust Sullivan, which, though it didn't happen, was the beginning of what would be a long and bloody war.

Houk claimed that when he took the job, Sullivan had told him that he might lose some of his best players. If the Dodgers had not reneged on the Lynn trade, the transition might have been easier, for Houk would have had Steve Howe in his starting rotation (two years later, Houk wondered whether Howe's well-publicized drug problems would have occurred had he moved East from southern California) and a blossoming star in Mike Marshall at first base. Instead, to replace Fisk, Burleson, Lynn, and Butch Hobson, he had Carney Lansford for third base, Mark Clear in the bullpen, Glenn Hoffman to move over to shortstop, Rick Miller to put in center field, and a scrambled catching derby that left him with Gary "Muggsy" Allenson and rookie Dave Schmidt.

Houk had a number of advantages coming in. He was well known and respected from his Yankee days. Yastrzemski flew up from Florida for Houk's press conference, saying that he was one manager he'd always wanted to play for because of the respect he carried through the game. The stories about The Major's toughness had spread for years. Of his war record and how he rose from private to major fighting at Bastogne and the Bulge and won everything from the Silver and Bronze stars to the Purple Heart. Of how he'd disarmed a gunman in a bar in Kansas City. Of how as a manager he'd jumped right into brawls and physically removed writers from his office (one, Phil Hersh, brought suit against him in Baltimore for allegedly slapping him because of an offhand remark Hersh had made in the *Baltimore Evening Sun*).

On the one hand, Houk met an important criterion for Sullivan: he wouldn't publicly rock the boat. He was a company man, loyal, positive, polished at handling the media. He was known as a players' manager, which meant that Houk made the game simple for the players. He'd take a loss, ask himself, "What did we get out of it?" and proceed from there. He never dwelled on defeat, and found a way to go through the next day on the upbeat. His approach always involved thinking about what things could happen so they could win. After 1978, fueled by the inherent negative thinking of the New England fans, the Red Sox players had taken the approach that the worst could and probably would always happen, so the infusion of Houk's consistent optimism — which he mixed with the them-versus-us challenge to the remaining players to prove wrong the members of the media who thought this was a dead team with all the heroes of the 1970s gone — breathed new life into the players. Houk kept his distance from players, always eating alone on the road, never being seen in any hotel bar. His private and public postures about players were often diametrically opposed, but he didn't believe in creating any problems for himself by showing up a player in the newspapers. "I'm not going to do the writers' jobs for them," Houk used to say. "They should know enough and have guts enough to write what the story is." While he kidded with the players and gave them the "have-a-couple-of-Budweisers-and-hang-with-'em" pat on the fanny, they respected both his distance and his hair-trigger temper. Even in his sixties, Houk could and would react angrily, and the instincts to fight were there. In all his time with the Red Sox, few players ever openly questioned him. One was pitcher Brian Denman, who felt Houk hadn't given him a chance when he sent him to the minors at the end of spring training in 1983. Denman was quickly set straight. Curiously, Houk respected players' legitimate toughness, as in the case of catcher John Ellis, whom he had managed with the Yankees. Houk called Ellis into his office to tell him he'd been sent down, and Ellis slammed the door, pointed to Houk, and shouted, "You aren't sending me down." "I loved the guy," Houk admitted.

Not that Houk didn't have quirks. He didn't like players taking extra hitting. "All it does is wear them out," he maintained, in direct contrast to the philosophies of Hriniak, Yastrzemski, Evans, Remy, and others. "You can either hit, or you can't." Many times on the road Houk would have traveling secretary Jack Rogers tell Hriniak and any players who wanted early hitting that the field wasn't available.

He was a pitchers' manager. He believed in a set lineup he could throw out there every day without having to worry about it. All he wanted to concern himself with was the pitching. He kept books, one measuring and rating performances, another reminding him how much relief pitchers had thrown not only in games but in the bullpen (a practice he learned from Yankee pitching coach Jim Turner in the 1950s). And it would be the bullpen his first two years that he wove into the mirage of this team challenging for the pennant.

The first step in 1981 was to move Evans into the second spot in the order, to utilize his ability to get on base, get more power at the front of the order, and minimize his lack of RBI production (his career high had been seventy), all the while building Dwight up as a proven star. The second was to try to restore Mike Torrez, who was coming off a horrendous 9–15 season in which he had a 5.08 earned run average, allowed 256 hits in 207 innings, and was being unmercifully booed. Torrez had become predominantly a breaking-ball pitcher, and Houk made him stretch his arm back out by convincing him he was still a power pitcher and had to work off his fastball. Then, when the season started, he held him out of games at Fenway as much as possible (Torrez finished the season

8–1 on the road, 2–2 at Fenway). He released Skip Lock-wood, which was a popular contract-eating move considering the previous winter's fiascos, dumped Dick Drago to Seattle, and went North promising that the pitching staff would be better with two new starters (Tanana, rookie Steve Craw-ford) and the addition of Clear, and that the rest of the team was going to be a "lot better than people give us credit for."

The season didn't start out the way he promised. In fact, Opening Day was Haywood's Nightmare. Ironically, they opened the season at home with the White Sox, which meant Fisk's homecoming and the public reopening of all the wounds that Sullivan and Fisk had inflicted upon one an-other. Fisk, who a year later wore a T-shirt that read "Haywood and Buddy Suck" every time he faced his old team, was extremely bitter about Sullivan and what he felt was a vindictive exile. Sullivan, in turn, irrationally detested both Carlton and Linda Fisk to the point of excessively talk-ing about them, and some of the sycophants throughout the organization chimed in against him. Sullivan also was bitter at White Sox owners Eddie Einhorn and Jerry Reinsdorf, for they had signed Fisk as their first big public relations coup when it appeared that the other clubs' quiet disinterest would guide Fisk back to Boston. So, with that undercurrent and all the publicity that went with the Sixth Game poster boy's return, what happened? John R. Tunis couldn't have scripted it better. The Red Sox led 2–0 in the eighth inning, with Allenson hitting a home run, when Fisk came up and pulled a Stanley sinker into the screen for a three-run homer that gave Chicago an eventual 5–3 victory. "I felt like waving up to Haywood and Buddy's box and telling them that that one was for them," Fisk later admitted, "but even that might have given them some satisfaction."

Houk's first month had its ups and downs. Zimmer re-turned with the Texas Rangers on April 20, and to a shower of boos lost his first two games to two of his least favorite pitchers, Torrez and John Tudor, before seeing Eckersley hammered 16–8. Soon thereafter, however, it seemed as if the direst of predictions about the Red Sox would come true. They went to Texas, lost 10–0, 9–0, 5–0, and didn't even get a runner to third base. To make things worse, they then came home and were swept four straight by the Twins; in the seven consecutive losses, they scored a total of eight runs, and were headed off onto a nine-game road trip.

Within three weeks, the Red Sox owners were to meet, and the club was 7–12. But from that point Houk's construction of the bullpen came through. In the ensuing period of thirty-one games, taking them to June 5 in Oakland, the relievers had eleven wins and eight saves and the Red Sox went 21–10. In that time, Clear had six wins, five saves, and a 1.03 earned run average. Burgmeier, Stanley, and Campbell had an additional five victories, so while the only complete-game wins they got in that time were by Eckersley (three) and Tanana (one) they were able to sneak into the first week of June only two games behind the first-place Yankees. The offense gave them thirty-three homers in those thirty-one games, ten by Evans, but Houk's bullpen — as it would do for six weeks the next season — had stolen respectability.

The June 11 strike probably came at an opportune time. When Eckersley had a 3–1 lead with two out, one on, and two strikes on Tony Armas June 7 in Oakland, the miracles ran out. Armas fouled off an 0–2 pitch and belted a two-run homer, and Clear gave up an eleventh-inning homer to Dwayne Murphy for the 4–3 defeat. At that point, Carney Lansford was DHing; his shoulder was so bad that he couldn't throw, and the morning of the final prestrike game, he visited an Anaheim chiropractor who told him that he was having severe back problems as a result of one leg being shorter than the other. While the strike probably kept Rice from running up his usual hot weather numbers, it also kept the pitifully thin Red Sox pitching from having to face the home-run months when the winds blow out in Fenway. The strike enabled Houk and Sullivan to point out how close they were.

"We were only four games out in the first half, and we took it down to the final weekend," Houk argued at season's end. That the "seasons" were fifty-six and fifty-two games long and that Boston finished fifth overall were moot points. They had, technically, contended. "If I could know when the season started that we'd be in contention on the first of September, I'd take it," Sullivan said. "If you're in it, you never know what'll happen. You've also given the fans something to cheer about."

They were able to get help out of their farm system. When Allenson tore a thigh muscle in May, Rich Gedman came up from Pawtucket and, after starting off 1-for-17, was such a surprise that he ended up the *Sporting News* Rookie of the Year. Gedman was only twenty-one and had caught fewer than three hundred games, but he was a natural hitter. Opposing pitchers, not knowing him, began pitching him out over the plate, and Gedman took them off The Wall, sprayed line drives, and in sixty-two games hit .288 and slugged .434 — better than Fisk, better, in fact, than any American League catcher other than Cleveland's Bo Diaz. Needless to say, it helped that there was no second time around for pitchers against such an inexperienced hitter. The other call-up turned hero was left-handed pitcher Bobby Ojeda. He came up after the strike as the leading pitcher in the International League, and between then and the time they were eliminated the final Friday night, he won six games as a starter; Bruce Hurst, who came back from Pawtucket September 2, won two starts and the rest of the starters combined were 7–11. Ojeda also provided one of the season's highlights, going into the ninth inning with a no-hitter on September 12 in Yankee Stadium (where a no-hitter hadn't been pitched since Don Larsen's perfect game in the 1956 World Series) before Rick Cerone led off the ninth with a double that ticked off the glove of the diving Evans. Ojeda was such an intense and competitive individual that he could not talk for an hour after the game. Whatever chance they had of catching the

Brewers ended when Ojeda could start only one more game after the Yankee Stadium performance. He came down with severe headaches, which later turned out to be a symptom of a rare blood disease that bothered him for more than a year, missed his last three starts, and took the club's best pitcher out of the rotation.

After beating the Brewers two out of three September 21–23 and trailing by only a game, they lost six out of eight and were eliminated. As usual, it was the Indians — the only American League East team with a winning record against Boston in the 1970s — who began the downfall. Cleveland came in on a Thursday night, September 24, and started a twenty-eight-year-old rookie named Tom Brennan, whose bizarre motion, in which he lifted his leg and stopped like some Richard Simmons exercise, earned him the nickname The Gray Flamingo. The Flamingo and Dan Spillner beat them. The Red Sox did win the next night to gain their final first-place tie, but lost on Saturday to their 1978 amigo Rick Waits. On Sunday they were crushed. Evans came through as he did all season, dramatically tying the game at 7–7 with a two-out, ninth-inning homer off Indians reliever Sid Monge, and took his place for the tenth inning to a five-minute standing ovation. Clear, however, walked in the deciding run in the eleventh. After a last series with the Brewers, Boston was one and a half games out with three to play, and, appropriately, on a Friday night in Cleveland, they were eliminated by an 11–5 drubbing.

Houk's proud statements about what the team had accomplished camouflaged the overall fifth-place finish. They *had* been in it, even if as soon as they had a chance to win, the bullpen and the entire team went down ingloriously. His daily exhortations that they *could* win gave them a refreshing capacity to come back from the damnedest situations. In 1981, they led the majors with sixteen wins in their final at-bat, and through 1982 led in come-from-behind victories. The most poignant moment was September 16 against the

Yankees in Boston, when they trailed 5–0 with two out in the eighth inning and rallied for eight runs, the final three coming when Rick Miller hit a 3-and-0 pitch from Yankee reliever Dave LaRoche into the Boston bullpen. It was Miller's seventh home run in seven seasons, left them a game behind first-place Milwaukee, and sent people out of Fenway humming the Lovin' Spoonful's "Do You Believe in Magic?"

Some of what had happened the previous winter was forgotten, too. Fisk hit only .263 with seven home runs and the White Sox collapsed out of the race. Lynn hit .219 with five homers for the Angels, who similarly were out of it. Meanwhile, Lansford led the league at .336, Miller hit .291, and Clear was 8–3 with nine saves. Sullivan had juggled and survived. "We didn't win with that other team and it was on the down side," he said, which was probably true. And between the strike, Houk, and the failure of the other players to produce out on the horizon, his inability to adjust to the system to get his due for the worth of Lynn and Fisk wasn't yet apparent.

Houk basically stole respectability in 1982. He had a starting pitching staff that other than Dennis Eckersley (who was 11–5 in July when his shoulder wore out) and John Tudor (who was 7–2 the last two months to finish 13–10) was something out of expansion. Sullivan had steadfastly refused to enter the free-agent market for veteran starting pitchers, citing his famous "We know something about Tommy John" line and ignoring others who were available. He stood by his policy of "going with the kids," ignoring the difficulty of bringing young pitchers up in Fenway. Joel Finch and Bobby Sprowl would have been front-line pitchers had they been given time to develop. So might have Keith MacWhorter, who, after being brought up one month out of double-A, wild-pitched in a run trying to give an intentional walk. Soon thereafter, Harrelson asked Podres if he'd worked with MacWhorter on an off-speed pitch; Podres replied, "He don't belong in the big leagues. Why bother?" Ojeda and Hurst were dispatched to the minor leagues, ridiculed. With the help of Pawtucket (eventually Cardinals) pitching coach Mike Roarke, they both pulled themselves together, and when they got to Boston, Houk was there to pat them on the back. Sullivan was afraid of the gamble free-agent pitchers represented, and when he got severely burned with Lockwood, he threw up his hands entirely.

So, in 1982, Houk had starting pitchers so bad that they got into the sixth inning in less than half their 162 games. They got into the seventh a pitiful 52 times. Ojeda's blood disease had left him so sick that he found his knees buckling in elevators, got embarrassed, got hit in each shin by line drives, and finally ended a 4–6, 5.63 season when he dislocated his right shoulder falling in the bathtub. Hurst came down with chips in his elbow and didn't win a game after early July. Torrez was 9–9, 5.23, and Houk lost all patience with him.

Torrez had usually been one of those pitchers who always had runs with which to work; in 1980, '81, and '82, he won only five games in which the Red Sox scored less than five runs. He also was one of those players who had an excuse for everything. On May 27 in Seattle, he gave up two home runs in the first, another in the third, and left down 8–0. In the second inning, the Mariners' Julio Cruz had singled, and when he took off on a hit-and-run and Hoffman covered, Bobby Brown slapped the ball right behind Hoffman because Torrez put the ball out over the plate. Then Brown took off for second and Manny Castillo hit a high hopper over the mound; Hoffman played it perfectly, stretching from the second-base bag until Brown beat the hopper, then coming off and getting Castillo at first. After the game, Torrez told reporters, "If Hoffman had just been able to make those two plays, I'd have been all right."

Despite the pitiful pitching, Houk juggled his bullpen brilliantly. Clear was virtually unhittable from mid-April through early June, and Houk rode him for six wins and eleven saves by mid-June. Houk got two wins and three saves out of Luis Aponte by the end of May, and had Burgmeier (7–0) and Stanley coming in from the first inning on. Stanley won twelve games, saved fourteen, broke Bill Campbell's re lief record with 168⅓ innings pitched, and was 9–1 with three saves in the eighteen games — in which the Sox were 14–4 — in which he pitched four or more innings. By June 22, they were 42–26 and five games in front. From that point, when Clear's streak ended and the depth of the starting pitching became increasingly important, they were 48–48 until sweeping the final three games in Yankee Stadium, finishing six games out.

Houk had his skirmishes. Torrez threw his arms in the air and continually looked back at the manager as he left the mound after being yanked in a September game, and Houk privately told reporters, "If he's back, I won't be." Tony Perez was called in on April 16 and asked to waive his no-trade and go to the Dodgers for a minor-league outfielder named Mark Bradley, refused, and had a tenuous relationship with Houk the rest of the year. Houk's patience with Chuck Rainey grew short. At the end of the year, all three were gone: Torrez was traded for a minor leaguer the Mets said wasn't a prospect, Perez was a free agent, and Rainey was sent to the Cubs for Doug Bird.

Yet Houk somehow managed his team to eighty-nine wins and third place. When the season was over, Lansford, who was going to be the next generation's star after coming over for Burleson, was traded after .336 and .301 seasons because they couldn't agree on a contract. That Dr. Arthur Pappas advised against signing him because of varied physical problems didn't matter to the public; the Red Sox had apparently again traded a player because they couldn't deal with the system.

In Lansford's case, this may not have been true. Dr. Pappas did feel that a five-year $6 million investment in the third baseman was not wise, and he had recommended strongly that they re-sign both Fisk and Remy. But the Sullivan-Leroux regime had always been confused by the new system. They played the game their first year with Torrez, Drago, Brohamer, and Burgmeier, and they did go out and re-sign Rice and Eckersley while reaching into the free-agent market for Lockwood and Perez between the 1979 and 1980 seasons. But at that point, they seemed to freeze. Haywood listened to the more conservative members of his owners' and organizational circle who actually believed the inflationary cycle would be broken. He believed that in 1980 and 1981, as the owner-player Basic Agreement was expiring, the players were making so much money they would not stick together and the owners could force them to accept some form of meaningful free-agent compensation that would finally restrict their movement. So he believed in the strike; it was important for the industry, and it was important for those owners whose imagination — not to mention wallets — had been left behind by the George Steinbrenners and Ted Turners, who had sent salaries sailing from an average of $42,500 in 1975 to $143,000 in 1980. Once again, Sullivan and most of the owners underestimated Marvin Miller and the players; by 1984, that $143,000 had risen to $330,000.

By the time the new Basic Agreement was to be negotiated in 1980, the owners had hired a tough negotiator from General Electric named Ray Grebey. They felt that their former Player Relations Committee chairman, John Gaherin, was a nice man who buckled in to Miller and the players because of the twilight zone the game was in the first three months of the 1976 season after the Messersmith-McNally decision. They longed for the way it had been five years earlier, before Messersmith-McNally, when they held the gun, there was no such thing as an open market, and players took what was offered or became plumbing executives. So they hired Grebey and told him to break the union, which they thought wouldn't be that difficult.

From the moment the players hired Marvin Miller out of the steel business in 1966 the owners badly underestimated his ingenuity and his mettle. Some felt that Miller came in with a master plan for piecing together one item after another — grievance arbitration followed by salary arbitration followed by a test of the reserve system — but Miller himself denied that. "With a three-man office," he said, "we scrambled to meet each day's demands." He understood just how annoyed management got with his confrontational style, and in the early years, with the help of his brilliant lawyer (and later agent) Dick Moss, built up the process by which the Messersmith-McNally decision could trigger the financial wars. While Miller slowly drained pension benefits out of the owners, he got them to agree in 1969 to grievance arbitration with an independent arbitrator, the process by which the reserve system was eventually overturned by Peter Seitz. In 1972, the players struck for the first nine games of the season, clearly showing owners that they could and would stick together, thus winning the pension dispute at issue. That same year, twelve months after the Curt Flood case had been turned away under a fifty-year-old shelter provided by Justice Oliver Wendell Holmes protecting baseball from federal antitrust legislation, Miller won the concession of salary arbitration to begin at the end of the 1973 season. Again, at the time, salary arbitration didn't seem like such a big deal. After the 1973 and 1974 seasons, it should be remembered, players like Texas first baseman Jim Spencer were going into hearings fighting over the difference between $43,000 and $47,000. Less than a decade later, under the single-figure process similar to that used in public employee disputes, at the end of the 1983 season Dodgers pitcher Fernando Valenzuela would be awarded a yearly salary of $1 million by an arbitrator.

Miller and Moss had been hoping that some player would test the system. Sparky Lyle almost did after the 1973 season, Pittsburgh's Richie Zisk after the 1974 season. It was after that season, when Charlie Finley reneged on some insurance payments due Catfish Hunter, that Hunter showed what a player might get on the open market: he filed a grievance, was made a free agent by Seitz, and got $3.35 million from the Yankees. So, when the Dodgers refused to give Messersmith a no-trade clause in negotiating his 1975 contract, the veteran pitcher decided to play it out and test what Miller and Moss felt could be tested; ironically, when the Dodgers brought Messersmith back in 1982 for a brief trial at the end of his injury-plagued career, they gave him the no-trade provision. McNally had been traded by Baltimore to Montreal during the 1975 season and had quit midway through the season because he felt he couldn't pitch anymore, but he hadn't signed and so added his name to the challenge.

The players claimed that the reserve clause was good for exactly what it said, "the period of one year." The owners claimed that it was self-perpetuating, and that once that year was up, the clause automatically renewed itself for another year. The owners' attorneys kept insisting they'd win, so while some in management suggested at the December 1975 winter meetings that perhaps they should try to negotiate some settlement on a new system, including a form of free agency, with Miller and the players, the suggestions were ignored. Six weeks later, Seitz had overturned their protectionist world, and both players and owners were on their own.

The system agreed upon in July 1976 established that players had to have six full major-league seasons before they could become free agents, which, since most players spent three to five years in the minors, meant that a team had control over a player for nearly a decade if it so desired. By 1979, several owners felt that when Bowie Kuhn ordered a halt to the owners' lockout in March 1976, he killed the negotiating work of the Player Relations Committee. "Miller and the owners were willing to give in, and Kuhn pulled the rug out from under us," claimed Frank Cashen, who had moved from the Orioles to the National Brewery before returning to be chief operating officer of the Mets. Others pointed at some of the other items in the new agreement that fanned the inflationary fire, such as the seemingly innocuous right of a player traded in the middle of a long-term contract to demand a trade at the end of his first year with the new club. That was just another gun the players — and, of course, the agents — had at the owners' temples. The right to demand a trade forced renegotiations. The owners ignored the hand-in-hand effects of arbitration and free agency; at the time of the '76 agreement, salary arbitration had been suspended, but once it went back into place in 1978, the salaries created by the free-agent bidding wars were rungs for all other players with two years' service to pull themselves up.

From the time that Grebey and Miller sat down in November 1979, it was obvious that the main issue was free-agent compensation. There were the side and monetary issues — pension, minimum salary, and so on. But the owners wanted meaningful compensation for free agents, both to try to keep the smaller markets competitive (by 1981, the Yankees' local TV deal of $6.5 million per year nearly equaled the Twins' gross). If a club (say, the Yankees) signed a player (say, Dave Winfield), they wanted the Padres to be reimbursed with their choice of all but either twelve or fifteen players out of the New York farm system, two draft choices, and a bundle of cash to help replenish their system in some way. The players steadfastly refused even to discuss any form of compensation. "We're not giving back any rights we've already won," Miller insisted. "At no time has a union turned the clock back. Anyway, this isn't exactly a struggling industry. If it were, why is it that every time a team is sold, it's for an increasingly greater figure?"

The players voted in spring training to set a May 23 date for a possible strike. Walking out in spring training would accomplish nothing. The owners wouldn't be hurt seriously until the time around Memorial Day when the weather was warm and the gates were increasing. The two sides stonewalled right down to the final hours. Players were alerted that the strike was a virtual certainty; Giants players refused a flight to New York, certain that they would be stranded trying to get back. For two weeks, players had vied to get on the disabled list, figuring they'd get paid. When the Red Sox outfielder Sam Bowen was traded to Detroit for pitcher Jack Billingham a week before the deadline, Bowen told the Tigers he was hurt. "I'm damaged goods," Bowen said to Tigers general manager Jim Campbell, "and if Mr. Sullivan tells you otherwise he's shushing you." The Tigers told the Red Sox to keep Billingham and forget Bowen. Sullivan and Pawtucket manager Joe Morgan claimed that Bowen wanted to make sure he got paid, even if it was a triple-A salary.

However, at 2:30 A.M. May 23, the two sides reached an agreement. They agreed on an 85 percent increase in pension benefits, a raise in minimum salary from $21,000 to $35,000 (a windfall for several rookies), a 100 percent increase in payments for disabled players, a new life insurance policy, and increased hospital benefits. The owners got an increase in the limit on consecutive playing dates from nineteen to twenty days. What they agreed upon at 2:30 A.M. they could have agreed upon over salad and Perrier in November. The way they averted the strike in 1980 was to put the compensation issue off for a period of one year. Owners said that they had wording in the agreement concerning compensation, which was a major step forward. The players promised that compensation would never be more meaningful than a high school or college player.

The 1981 deadline was June 11, and as that day approached, no progress had been made. The players had stored a war chest for more than two years; the owners had their strike insurance. The players by then had agreed only to some sort of pool concept for compensation, suggesting that each team put its thirty-seventh, thirty-eighth, and thirty-ninth best players into a pool from which the team losing a free agent ranked in the top 5 percent of all players at his position could select. The owners continued to demand direct compensation for any free agent in the top 50 percent: the signing team could protect fifteen players. They upped it to eighteen, period.

Some owners still didn't believe the players would go out. Houk talked to Sullivan the morning of the 11th. They were planning to send Steve Crawford (0–5) to Pawtucket and recall Bobby Ojeda, but if there was going to be a strike, Houk wanted to option Crawford so he'd be pitching, and stick with the twenty-four-player minimum until he needed Ojeda. Sullivan told him he didn't think there'd be a strike. Later that night, the strike was official, and the next night, confused players scrambled to pay their ways back home.

At 7:05 P.M. PDT Friday night, Carl Yastrzemski and Jerry Remy climbed into a writer's rental car headed for Los Angeles International Airport and the redeye back to Boston. "O.K.," Yastrzemski asked. "What's the story?"

California player representative Don Baylor was on the car radio. "The owners won't budge; they've forced us out," Baylor explained to the talk-show host. "If the owners feel so strongly about compensation, why doesn't George Steinbrenner give the Padres his sixteenth-best player for Dave Winfield?"

"It doesn't explain anything," Remy said as the car rolled along the freeway. "Nothing does. Everything seemed so normal playing the game last night. Then, as soon as it was over, the media came charging in, asking what it's like to be on strike. I'd thought about it, sure. But not realistically. What could I say about something I know nothing about?"

The Red Sox player representative, Burgmeier, was at the airport explaining the situation to the players flying home. "There's no way of knowing how long it'll last," Burgmeier told them. "It's up to the owners. The players are not going to accept anything that restricts the movement of free agents and thus eventually would roll back salaries. They're paying the salaries. They're offering them. We're not going to give them artificial means to roll them back, not when they won't open the books. No union can."

"What is Bowie Kuhn doing in all this?" Yastrzemski asked Burgmeier.

"Working on the singer for the All-Star Game," Burgmeier replied.

As the plane took off, Remy made jokes. "I wonder if my wife can get her old job back at Zayre's in Fall River. Can I play in the Newport Sunset League?"

Then he turned serious. "I try to think about how this affects me," Remy said. "I'll be a free agent at the end of this season. Of course, I want to have all the possible options. Meanwhile, I'll survive. I have my savings, although no one in a career with as short a life span as this wants to tap his savings. If this is what it takes, I'll get everythinig back at the end of the year. If the owners break the union, I don't know what'll happen except that I'll still survive. I didn't come from millions, you know."

Remy, Burgmeier, and most of the other players went back to their Boston homes. They ran, worked out, and got together three or four times a week to hit and throw. Crawford went home to Oklahoma and worked out with an American Legion team. Yastrzemski went to Harwich and worked with son Mike's Cape Cod League team.

At first, there were diversions. The national media zoomed in to Pawtucket for the end of the thirty-three-inning game with Rochester, decided when a career minor-league first baseman named Dave Koza singled in Marty Barrett. There was scattered coverage of the minors, and most teams sent their managers, coaches, and scouts to the minors; the Red Sox were the exception, as their people were pulled off the road, Houk and Sullivan never drove the thirty minutes from their homes to Pawtucket, and after Pesky and Hriniak spent five days in Bristol working with the double-A players, they were told to go home.

But, as the strike dragged on, the players didn't budge. The owners had underestimated Miller's ability to spread them out physically and keep them together spiritually. Meanwhile, it was the owners who began to splinter; Baltimore's Edward Bennett Williams and Texas's Eddie Chiles met with Kuhn to try to get Grebey to soften his stance. Kuhn's position demonstrated just how split the owners were. While pundits suggested that "if Bowie Kuhn were alive today, he'd do something about the strike," he was powerless to do anything about it. All he could do was beat the drums for baseball, as his office was powerless and out of the negotiation process. In effect, Grebey was the most powerful man in baseball — as long as the majority of owners backed him.

"People always ridicule the owners because they never have been able to stay together and the players always do," Oakland owner Roy Eisenhardt explained. "But it's not that simple. The players are a monolithic group with one apparent interest. The owners are twenty-six monolithic groups, with distinctly different financial interests. It's practically impossible for George Steinbrenner and Calvin Griffith to view overall industry economic issues in the same terms. The only way they'd be comparable would be if owners handed them something like fifty percent of the gross and told them to divide it up. Then you'd see a different owner-player power structure. But, as it's set up now, Miller has the completely dominant upper hand on whoever represents the PRC and the owners."

Which is exactly as it turned out. In early August, the owners finally agreed to the pool concept of free agents. By a complicated set of statistical criteria, all players were ranked; those in the top 15 percent were Type A, those in the top 15 to 25 percent were Type B. A team losing a Type A player would receive a player (from a pool of players left unprotected by twenty other teams), the signing team's top draft choice, and an extra choice. Most important as far as the players were concerned, the player compensation would come from a pool comprising all the players from twenty teams (five clubs were allowed to be conscientious objectors, which meant they were not allowed to sign Type A players but wouldn't have to contribute to the pool for three years), with each team being able to protect twenty-five players from its organization.

(As it turned out, in the first three years, the compensation choices turned out to be Joel Skinner, a class A catcher; Steve Mura, a journeyman pitcher who didn't even make the White Sox team, was sent to triple-A, was 3–0 and released; Danny Tartabull, a double-A infielder; Mets pitcher Tom Seaver; and Tim Belcher, a pitcher whom the Yankees had signed for $119,000 as the top selection in the January 1984 free-agent draft and inadvertently left off their protected list.)

When it was over, Grebey admitted, "Bob Boone [a California catcher] said after the players' executive board meeting in February that if the owners want compensation, there will be a strike. He was right. We got some additional compensation, which is a windfall. But essentially, it was a million-dollar strike over a ten-cent issue."

The owners had failed to break the players' union, so they failed to get any artificial restraints on the open-market process. That meant that with salary arbitration as powerful as it was, the only restraints would have to be gentlemen's agreements among owners on the signing of players. Some agents, even the noted Pittsburgh attorney Tom Reich, feared "some backlash from the owners." Their fears weren't realized. While Grebey tried to get clubs to allow teams that wanted their own players to have the best crack at re-signing them and tried to keep a sort of offer tote board to keep one another abreast (St. Louis's Whitey Herzog let it slip when he told agent Alan Hendricks "We know what he's been offered" in negotiating for Joaquin Andujar), there wasn't any lessening effect. Ron Guidry returned to the Yankees, but for more than $900,000 a year. Journeyman relief pitcher Ed Farmer got $500,000 a year from the Phillies. Dave Collins, a spare-part outfielder whose skills were limited to running ability and enthusiasm, got $2.4 million for three years from Steinbrenner.

By then, Sullivan had admitted his shortcomings in dealing with the agents' world. "They control the game," he said, "and it's hard for some of us to accept that." So Harrington, as director of the Yawkey Foundation, took over the negotiations and kept Remy away from Oakland for $2.6 million for five years.

If Harrington had been around in 1979, they'd have re-signed Fisk and Burleson for less than that. But in 1979 and 1980, Sullivan was still thinking that things had to even off. The figures didn't, but right on through 1982, the Red Sox juggled and survived, in large part thanks to Houk, Evans, and Houk's use of the bullpen.

And when the illusion of respectability was finally shattered completely in 1983 as the Red Sox stumbled to their first losing record since 1966 and a sixth-place finish, fans still came to watch. They came not because the team was a contender any longer — no one really believed that. Fisk, Lynn, Burleson, Tiant, and Lee were gone. So, for that matter, were million-dollar free agents Campbell and Torrez, as well as transient Sox stars like Carney Lansford and Tony Perez.

The Red Sox drew fans — at home and away — all through 1983 because people wanted a last look at number 8, Carl Michael Yastrzemski, whose unparalleled toughness had enabled him to survive like some WPA building through decades of seasons to play more major-league baseball games than anyone who ever lived.

He was the last of a breed, not only because no one is likely ever again to play over twenty years for the same team (he played twenty-three for the Red Sox, more than anyone ever played for any team) but also because he is the last great Depression athlete. He grew up being taught survival, without television, and for him the '60s revolution meant the change of managers from Mike Higgins to Dick Williams. He was

willing to pay whatever price was necessary to succeed, be it
the hours in the library to earn a B average and the presi-
dency of the 1959 freshman class at Notre Dame or, three
months shy of his forty-fourth birthday, the hour's worth of
batting practice at 9:30 A.M. in the Minneapolis Metrodome,
which resulted in a 2-for-4 day against Albert Williams. He
was the man asked to replace Ted Williams, and he did. He
did it not because of any duende, for while Williams was a
Hemingway character, Yaz was *Popular Mechanics*. He was
just another blue-collar worker out of Studs Terkel.

His assembly line of records is that of a Marciano, not an
Ali. Never did he hit for the average Fred Lynn hit as a
rookie. His lifetime batting average is less than that of Reggie
Smith, his slugging percentage a few points lower than Ron
Santo's. No one ever batted *under* .300 more full seasons than
Yastrzemski. He reached .300 six times, as often as Jim Rice
and Pete Runnels and two less times than Cecil Cooper, and
he knocked in one hundred runs five times, as often as Jackie
Jensen, two less times than Del Ennis. But he was always
there, to vanquish or be vanquished, day in, day out, averag-
ing 151 games a season until he was past forty because, as
trainer Charlie Moss once observed, "He's too tough to know
pain or fear."

"I wasn't blessed with great tools," he liked to say, but the
greatest — and most immeasurable — of all baseball tools
are the heart and will, and from that "tough Polish stock"
and isolated farm on Long Island, the three tools Carl Yastrzemski brought with him were quick hands, a leather heart,
and an indefatigable will. He wasn't particularly fast or
blessed with a great arm, but he won several Gold Gloves for
defensive excellence in the outfield. His average season for
twenty-three years was .285 with twenty homers and eighty-
one RBIs, yet he was so respected that no man who ever
played in the American League — not Ruth, not Williams,
not Reggie Jackson — was walked intentionally more than
Yaz.

If the late acerbic sportswriter Colonel Dave Egan could tarnish Williams's silver numbers for what he did in the "ten biggest games of his career," then we can gold-plate Yastrzemski's averages with what he did in the twenty-two games that he played for a pennant ('67, '72, '75), in a playoff ('78), in a league championship series ('75), and two World Series ('67, '75). In the twenty-two biggest games of his career, Yaz batted .417, slugged .702, hit a homer every fourteen times at bat, knocked in better than a run a game, and scored nearly as many. (In Jackson's seventy-one postseason games, Mr. October's average is .289, his slugging percentage .539, and he has hit a home run every fifteen at-bats).

Yet, despite all those years that Yaz sat in front of a locker full of army brown 'n' green clothes, puffing cigarettes and sipping salted beers out of aluminum cans, there was in this simple man a dogged air of Greek tragedy. The flaw in Yastrzemski's career was that despite the .417 big-game average and .702 slugging percentage, the 1967 Joe Hardy Impossible Dream year, the diving stops off Jackson and throws to cut down Bob Allison in the cause of winning, he never achieved the one thing he wanted to go with the respect he earned. All he wanted was one World Series championship ring, and after going out with the worst team he had played on since the days of Dennis Bennett and George Smith, he left without that cheap piece of jewelry. Worse yet, while he retired

The 22 Biggest Games of Yastrzemski's Career

	OPPONENT	G	AB	H	HR	R	RBI	BA
October 1–2, 1967	Minnesota	2	8	7	1	2	6	.875
1967 World Series	St. Louis	7	25	10	3	4	5	.400
October 3–4, 1972	at Detroit	2	6	2	0	0	1	.333
1975 playoffs	Oakland	3	11	5	1	4	2	.455
1975 World Series	Cincinnati	7	29	9	0	7	9	.310
October 2, 1978	New York	1	5	2	1	2	2	.400
TOTALS		22	84	35	6	19	25	.417

Yaz's slugging percentage for those 22 games was .702.

with honor and riches and glory and justice, he did so knowing that some night he will wake up remembering three pitches from three men named Gibson, McEnaney, and Gossage, and his ensuing three swings that produced the final outs of the 1967 and 1975 World Series and the 1978 American League East playoff. The reward for playing longer, harder, and perhaps better than anyone in that club's history will be to wake up in the middle of the night in 2007 reliving one of the three fatal missed fractions of an inch.

In 1967, Jim Kaat threw a pitch to (at) Yaz that was "as good a knockdown pitch as you'll ever see come from Jim Kaat — eight inches behind the head," according to Ken Harrelson. Next pitch: base hit.

In 1978, as the Red Sox were in the process of climbing from three and a half games back to catch the Yankees, Toronto's Balor Moore, a pitcher with a reputation as a headhunter, faced Yaz. There were two on and the Blue Jays were leading by two in the eighth inning when he threw a pitch behind Yastrzemski's head. Then, in Harry Callahan style, Moore threw yet another one, harder, right at Yastrzemski's head as he fell backward. "That," Yaz said afterward, "was as close as I can recall to being killed." He got up and dusted himself off. Moore threw a 2–2 slider for which he thought he had Yastrzemski set up. But Yaz hit it off the center-field fence and raced safely to third with a slide and a cloud of dust. He called time, took one step toward the mound, and spit in Moore's direction.

The most recent similar incident came in 1982 in Anaheim. It was the top of the ninth inning, California leading 4–2. Jerry Remy was at third and Dwight Evans at second with two out and left-hander Angel Moreno pitching. Moreno tried to push Yastrzemski off the plate with an 0–2 brushback ("No one could throw a beanball at Yastrzemski. His eye-hand coordination and feet were too quick, which is why he got hit so few times in his career," says Gene Mauch, Yaz's minor-league manager). Yaz sprawled in the dirt, got up, called time, and slowly began adjusting himself. "It was one of the most amazing things I've ever watched. I'm just glad I had a good view to see him," Remy said the next day. "His face was cold. There was none of the excitement that there would be in most of us. He got out of the box, went through all his hitches, pulled himself together, all the while with his lips moving, talking to himself. Most of us would get mad or excited in that situation. He got even." Yastrzemski lined the next pitch six inches from Moreno's head into center field, scoring the two runs and sending the game into extra innings for an eventual Boston victory. "Don't ever throw at that man," Mauch told Moreno afterward. "There are few more fearless men who ever played. That's like staging a two-bullet shoot-out, only after you've missed with your shot, Yaz never misses with his."

By his own admission, Yastrzemski had gone through what he says "must be nine million stances and adjustments." In his younger days, he'd go 0-for-4 on a Saturday afternoon and, sure enough, he'd be out there as the typewriters clicked away upstairs, taking extra batting practice.

"The man has great mental toughness," Walter Hriniak marvels. That mental toughness was translated into the ability to apply himself for hours to make what he felt was the necessary adjustment without getting tired. Perhaps no Hall of Fame hitter ever used so many stances or was less stylish at the plate. The discipline sometimes manifested itself on the spot, at the plate. As a self-proclaimed "lousy breaking-ball hitter," he could discipline himself to take and take and take until he got a fastball in the area he wanted. Mauch, his manager in the Little World Series in 1959 in Minneapolis, pointed out that Yaz didn't often miss his one shot.

Translated into everyday life, his toughness made him seem a hard man. One time he was negotiating with Jack Satter of Colonial Provision about an endorsement contract on Fenway Franks. They had worked out the money; then Yaz said he needed a car for his wife, Carol. When Satter agreed to that, Yaz added that it had to be a new one each year. Finally, Satter went along. But Yaz still wasn't satisfied.

"O.K.," Yaz finalized, "but what if you die?"

He went to dinner at Sam Snead's Boca Raton house, and in the late hours of the night Snead mentioned that he was selling. Yaz asked how much. Snead said he didn't know for sure, and mentioned a value area. Yaz wrote him out a check to hold the sale, but when Snead called him back sober the next day, he told Yaz that the real estate people said the price was more than double what he'd thought.

Yaz took him to court and won the house.

He never could stand to lose, not at cards ("He'd cheat if he had to," says former bridgemate Larry Wolfe), not at tennis ("I had him five-love once, looked up and heard him mumbling, 'I'll still beat him,' and he did," says State Treasurer Bob Crane), not at anything. He'd never admit that he couldn't do anything, which is why sometimes he ran the bases in kamikaze fashion. He especially couldn't stand to lose to injury or time, which is why he steadfastly never gave in to age or pain. In twenty-three years he was on the disabled list but once, suffering through strained ligaments in his knee, torn ligaments in his ankle, a tear in his shoulder, a tear where his wrist and hand come together, a fractured rib, and a congenital back problem that would be painful enough to put him in traction at 9:30 A.M. but not enough to keep him from sliding into second with a double at 8:07 P.M. When he hurt his knee in a home-plate collision in May 1972, doctors in California told him he had to have surgery and that he was out for the season. "I want one more opinion," he told them, flew home, got it put in a special cast, was back in the lineup thirty-one days later, and nearly led the Red Sox to the Eastern Division title.

He used to say that after playing beside his father for the Bridgehampton White Eagles, he learned not to give in to age. When the old man was forty, he outhit Yaz. The old man's shoulder was so bad he could barely throw to first, but he'd refuse to talk about it. Or admit it. Or admit that once in a while the pitcher would relay his throws. So Carl the son never gave in or admitted it either, just as in the summer of 1983 he didn't give in to retirement, because to talk retirement and stand there receiving flowers around the country would be an admission that he was done and that, with the game on the line, he was beyond jumping on Bill Caudill's 2–1 fastball. "It's not age, because my hands are still there. I'm just screwed up mechanically," he said that last spring when he struggled. He was right.

Sometimes his refusal to concede anything to age worked against him — in his forties he couldn't bounce back so easily. He found that out in '82; after a terrific first half of the season as the DH, he became the oldest man ever to start in center field. He hit .144 with five RBIs in ninety-seven at-bats in August after the experiment, tainting what would have been an above-average year with numbers something like .300–20–82 at age forty-three if he had just stuck to DHing.

He accomplished some remarkable feats denying age. Three months shy of thirty-seven, he hit three home runs in a game in Detroit in May 1976, then went to New York and, in his next game, hit two more. In 1977, at thirty-eight, he became one of the five oldest players ever to knock in one hundred runs. In September and October of 1978, at thirty-nine, he had six homers, knocked in nineteen runs, and rocketed that memorable home run off Ron Guidry in the playoff. The records — the 400 HRs/3000 hits, the twenty straight years of 100 games, the twenty-two seasons with 100 hits, the 3308 games played — are those of a man who survived pain, age, and fastballs thrown at his head, and survived with the purpose of beating whomever he had to to win.

In some ways, the hardest part for Yastrzemski might have been his youth with the Red Sox. The first six years of his Boston career were filled with controversy, with clashes with managers Johnny Pesky and Billy Herman and with unfulfilled promise as the next Ted. He was surrounded by a country club team known as the Jersey Street Jesters, for whom beating anyone was the last purpose in life. That, more than any injury, made baseball very difficult for Yastrzemski. Then came Dick Williams and '67, and we found out what Yaz's limits under pressure were. There were none. In a span of four years, he won a Triple Crown and two batting titles and missed a third by less than .001, hit 40 or more homers, knocked in more than 100 runs, and thrice walked more than 100 times. In 1970, he hit .329 and lost the batting title to Alex Johnson on the last day, hit 40 homers, scored 125 runs, drove in 102, walked 128 times, stole 23 bases, and won a Gold Glove.

And he got booed. Though Yastrzemski performed to his '67 greatness at the turn of the decade, the team could not recapture its magic, and when Dick Williams was fired, it was Yaz who became the symbol of the inmates-running-the-country-club myth. When he hurt his wrist in 1971, he didn't publicly whimper, although "I couldn't roll my wrists and generate any power whatsoever." He suffered in silence as Billy Conigliaro blamed him for his brother's problems in 1971, then suffered again in silence the next year when a rookie named Carlton Fisk accused him and Reggie Smith of a lack of leadership. He was booed so unmercifully that he used to wear cotton in his ears in left field ("The fans didn't really mean it"). Talk shows begged for him to be traded. He couldn't even vent his frustration by smashing baseballs into bullpens, because the wrist was so bad — so bad, in fact, that he went more than a year (until late July 1972) without a home run. But in September 1972, with a chance for the Red Sox to win the pennant, he hit .350 with ten of his twelve homers, only to see the Red Sox fall short in Detroit when Luis Aparicio fell rounding third base.

The early 1970s were hard times for him, with the booing, the controversy (one *Sports Illustrated* story fingered him as the core of the "Team That Eats Managers"), the friction.

Even though he had an outstanding year in 1974, hitting .301, scoring ninety-three runs, and finishing second to Cleveland's Oscar Gamble in runs produced in the Eastern Division, his public posture didn't really change until 1975. By his own admission, it was about that time that he became less intense, the product of watching his mother and his uncle in their brave struggles with cancer. His mother was given "a few months" to live, and she fought it for more than three years, long enough to watch her son turn the Oakland playoff series around with his artistry off The Wall in the second game and his diving stop of Jackson's shot in the third. "Tough stock," beams Yaz when he recalls her.

The strength that his family gave him helped him endure those hard times, and then came Rice and Lynn to take away the spotlight. "I was never comfortable in the spotlight. Having them come along and get the attention really helped me," he said. Right down to his comical attempts to tip his hat his last time around the league, Yastrzemski never did feel comfortable as the Main Show.

Yastrzemski wasn't the leader in the manner of a Willie Stargell or an Andre Dawson. He didn't go around tapping people on the shoulder. He wasn't the rah-rah type. He didn't appreciate managers making him the captain. But in 1975, when the team came out of a 10–23 spring training, it was Yastrzemski who called a clubhouse meeting on Opening Day and chastised his teammates for "sitting around waiting to be beaten" after the collapse of '74, during which they were seven and a half games ahead of the Orioles on August 29 and finished seven games back. Baseball isn't a charge-up-San-Juan-Hill sort of game; in fact, much of it is essentially selfish. If every teammate had applied himself like Yaz, that would have been leadership enough.

Journalists have described him as stoic. But in fact he was often a clubhouse clown. "I expected some kind of statue," said Gary Allenson when he got to the big leagues, "and found kind of a goofball." He'd light fires under Dennis Eckersley's chairs. He, Aparicio, and Gary Peters used to slash one another's clothes. He'd throw Marty Pattin's raincoat out the window of the bus. It took him years to get even with Bill Campbell, who would stuff Yaz's glove or dress shoes with green slime. But he finally did. In 1982, when Campbell had already signed with the Cubs, he came up to Boston on an off-day in New York. He was in the clubhouse at 2:30, an hour or so before Yaz arrived, and took some scissors and slashed a shirt and jacket hanging in Yastrzemski's locker. When Yaz walked in and found them cut, he asked around until he got someone to admit that Campbell was in town. He went into the hallway, called Ferguson Jenkins, also with the Cubs, and the next night when Campbell got to his locker after the game, he found his clothes slashed.

His teammates always ribbed Yastrzemski about his clothes. He had one suitcase that he kept in the clubhouse, and Vinnie Orlando sent its contents out with the daily dry cleaning. Once, in 1976, the team ceremonially burned his raincoat. "It wasn't my only one, unfortunately," he said with a laugh. Two years later, he walked into Bob Crane's office on a ten-degree February day in another tattered trench coat and told the state treasurer, "At least I know it works — I've had it since 1965." On one 1978 bus ride, Dick Drago discovered a grease spot on his leather jacket and was going to throw the jacket away. "Don't do that. I'll take it," said Yaz, who had the coat dyed the color of the stain and wore it for another year. Tom Yawkey never needed fine clothes, either.

Although he could give teammates hotfeet and laugh at his own dress, Yastrzemski has always understood the sources of power and success off the field. Some players hang around with car and jewelry dealers; Yaz hangs around with Tip O'Neill, Ed King, and Ted Kennedy, flies to All-Star Games with George Bush, and has given his trophies to every president beginning with John F. Kennedy. He is a political man, needless to say conservative. Yet he is a fiscal conservative, a made-it-by-his-own-bootstraps hard-liner who accepts aspects of social liberalism, probably because of his cousin in the hierarchy of the Catholic Church in Poland. Ask his business associates such as Dick Thissen and David Mugar about his business sense. "He has an amazing capacity to listen to everything, boil it down to the bottom line, and put it on the line," says Mugar, with whom he tried to purchase control of the Red Sox. "He is never afraid of making a decision, and he instinctively knows the importance of whatever he is doing."

He seemed to grasp moments on the field instinctively as well, be it his unforgettable catch of a Tom Tresh shot for Billy Rohr in 1967 or the home run off Guidry in 1978. That a fluke home run by Bucky Dent should overshadow Yaz's homer off Guidry epitomized Yastrzemski's career; his homer should have been the winning RBI, for if Boston's pitching had contained New York, the bottom of the ninth wouldn't have been.

As Gossage's pitch came to the plate at a speed of ninety-five miles per hour, it looked like a pitch the best pure fastball hitter of his time could hit and hit hard. But Rich Gossage's fastball was in a world beyond, and as Yastrzemski swung, the ball trailed ever so slightly in on him. He could not stop his swing. He took a step or two, stopped, turned, and watched as Graig Nettles caught his foul pop-up. The Yankees won, the Red Sox lost, and Yaz never got another chance at his series ring.

Two years later, Gossage threw a pitch in the third and final game of the playoffs that George Brett hit into the second row of the third deck to bring the Kansas City Royals their only pennant. "I think of Yaz," Gossage said afterward. "I'd like to think of these moments as the best against the best, not winners and losers. The pitch to Yaz ran a little more than the pitch to Brett. Don't ask me why, because I don't know. If time were called and we went back and I had to throw those pitches over again, George might pop up and Yaz might have hit the ball into the bleachers."

For that ninth and final inning of the Red Sox 1978 season,

most of the media had come downstairs. We were crouched in the aisle, looking out at Gossage. Rick Burleson was at third, Jerry Remy at second. Just then, Clark Booth said, "There's probably no one else in Red Sox history that they'd rather have in this spot at this time than Yaz."

"There is no way," I replied, "that he won't get a hit."

Every time we see it now on videotape, some of us wish we could somehow will ourselves into the Twilight Zone and that Yastrzemski would swing and miss that 1–0 Gossage fastball.

So that Carl Michael Yastrzemski could have another shot at one final swing.

The thing about Yastrzemski was that publicly he maintained a kind of cold posture. He always stood up to the responsibility of talking to the media, but his answers were ever-measured, political, and usually predictable, sounding sometimes like a recorded device. "I guess it was something I did from the time I came up," he explained. "I wanted the opposition to know I was a machine, that nothing could bother me."

Then when it came time for Yastrzemski to say good-bye, the machine broke down and cried. Through the first thirteen good-byes in each city around the American League, he'd been able to maintain his cool exterior. In fact, at one point in the middle of the season when he was hitting eight of his ten home runs in July, he began toying with the idea of coming back in 1984, and friends whispered that he thought Ted Turner would sign him and his son Mike; all it amounted to was Yaz's way of telling himself that he wasn't through and refusing to give in to time, and hence, pitchers. He gratefully refused to accept gifts, which meant turning down a special night in Anaheim complete with an offer of a boat or car from Angels owner Gene Autry, a handsome fifteen-hundred-dollar shotgun from the Kansas City writers, and a night from George Steinbrenner in Yankee Stadium that Remy suggested would include Frank Sinatra singing "My Way," in person.

He stepped out and waved to the thunderous ovations in each city, but teammates kidded him that he did it so stoically that he looked like a statue. One time, in Seattle, Remy stepped out of the dugout and tipped his cap to the cheers of the sparse crowd that wouldn't know Remy from Yaz from Chuck Schilling; Yastrzemski had already gone into the clubhouse, angry at himself for grounding out.

For most of the season, both the New England fans and the Red Sox anticipated Yaz's farewell, fanned by the legendary farewell of Williams captured by Updike ("Hub Fans Bid Kid Adieu"). "He'd say things. 'You're not really planning anything big, are you?' " public relations director George Sullivan later told writers. "He'd say, 'I'll just get up and say a few words, right?' " But after twenty-three years, the farewell had to be more. The first game the ticket department sold out was the October 2 finale with the Indians, and when it was announced that because of the concern about the last day being rained out they made Yaz Day the second to last day, it, too, was quickly sold out.

First, there was the ceremony with his teammates. "Unless you've been around a clubhouse a lot, you could never understand how much that meant to me," he said. "It's the Bond." And the Bond is a spirit that exists within the scruffy white walls of the clubhouse, between piles of T-shirts and rolls of tape. In a capitalistic game, it is the essence of pure communism, where Carl Yastrzemski's locker is the same size as that of Al Nipper. "This isn't a seven-thirty to eleven-thirty job I've been living out all these years. It's four to midnight for a night game, ten to six-thirty for the day, and it's in the clubhouse where what you go through together as twenty-five individuals really shows itself. It's where you see the frustrations, tears, fears. You see guys get injured, their careers pass in front of them. You see the ups and downs in their faces, twenty-three years of moments shared only with people who were my teammates, so what my teammates did struck me."

They gathered around him, Dwight Evans gave him a fishing rod, and half the players in the room cried. "I thought it was a gag when they started coming around me," Yastrzemski later said, for, true to form, while he signed autographs in front of his locker a half-hour earlier, Allenson had crawled through the surrounding assemblage, stuck a pack of matches to his shoe with bubble gum, and given him a hotfoot.

So Yaz had broken down once. Then came the first public ceremony. "I thought I had myself under control," he explained. "But it was more than I anticipated." He had told George Sullivan and Dick Bresciani that he intended to run around the field, and they approved his idea. He ran onto the field at quarter of two and the cheering was deafening for six minutes, as he tried to keep under control at a stage assembled for his family and guests. There were politicians and personalities, speeches and presents. A car. A boat. A Notre Dame freshman jacket. A letter from Ronald Reagan. Then he spoke, stepping back from the microphone to gather himself, choking on words and emotions and the symbolism of his moment of silence for his mother and Tom Yawkey. Then he finally said, "New England, I love you," and began running around the park. He touched hands, he looked in faces messy with emotion, and for the first of two days in his career, he allowed Carl Yastrzemski to be human and put the baseball player aside. He was 0-for-4 Saturday, the kind of 0-for-4 that usually sent him reeling to Hriniak, but instead he told friends, "I wanted to show my emotions. For twenty-three years, I always blocked everything out. I wanted to show these people all the emotion they've offered me all these years deeply touched me."

On Sunday, his final day, he continued the emotional blitzkrieg. Ralph Houk took the suggestion of the *Herald*'s Joe Giulotti and played Yastrzemski in left field, but there was no homer in his final at-bat. In fact, after he punched a single through the hole into left field in the second, it almost be-

Final American League Standings and Red Sox Statistics, 1981

	W	L	PCT	GB	R	HR	BA
EAST							
MIL	62	47	.569		493	96	.257
BAL	59	46	.562	1	429	88	.251
NY	59	48	.551	2	421	100	.252
DET	60	49	.550	2	427	65	.256
BOS	59	49	.546	2.5	519	90	.275
CLE	52	51	.505	7	431	39	.263
TOR	37	69	.349	23.5	329	61	.226
WEST							
OAK	64	45	.587		458	104	.247
TEX	57	48	.543	5	452	49	.270
CHI	54	52	.509	8.5	476	76	.272
KC	50	53	.485	11	397	61	.267
CAL	51	59	.464	13.5	476	97	.256
SEA	44	65	.404	20	426	89	.251
MIN	41	68	.376	23	378	47	.240
LEAGUE TOTAL					6112	1062	.256

MANAGER	W	L	PCT	
Ralph Houk	30	26	.536	(1st)
Ralph Houk	29	23	.558	(2nd)

POS	PLAYER	B	G	AB	H	2B	3B	HR	R	RBI	BA
REGULARS											
1B	Tony Perez	R	84	306	77	11	3	9	35	39	.252
2B	Jerry Remy	L	88	358	110	9	1	0	55	31	.307
SS	Glenn Hoffman	R	78	242	56	10	0	1	28	20	.231
3B	Carney Lansford	R	102	399	134	23	3	4	61	52	.236
RF	Dwight Evans	R	108	412	122	19	4	22	84	71	.296
CF	Rick Miller	L	97	316	92	17	2	2	38	33	.291
LF	Jim Rice	R	108	451	128	18	1	17	51	62	.284
C	Rich Gedman	L	62	205	59	15	0	5	22	26	.288
DH	Carl Yastrzemski	L	91	338	83	14	1	7	36	53	.246
SUBSTITUTES											
UT	Dave Stapleton	R	93	355	101	17	1	10	45	42	.285
D1	Joe Rudi	R	49	122	22	3	0	6	14	24	.180
SS	Julio Valdez	B	17	23	5	0	0	0	1	3	.217
2B	Chico Walker	B	6	17	6	0	0	0	3	2	.353
OF	Reid Nichols	R	39	48	9	0	1	0	13	3	.188
OF	Garry Hancock	L	26	45	7	3	0	0	4	3	.156
OF	Tom Poquette	L	3	2	0	0	0	0	0	0	.000
C	Gary Allenson	R	47	139	31	8	0	5	23	25	.223
C	Dave Schmidt	R	15	42	10	1	0	2	6	3	.238
C	John Lickert	R	1	0	0	0	0	0	0	0	—

**Final American League Standings and Red Sox
Statistics, 1981, continued**

PITCHER	T	W	L	PCT	ERA	SV
Dennis Eckersley	R	9	8	.529	4.27	0
Frank Tanana	L	4	10	.286	4.02	0
Mike Torrez	R	10	3	.769	3.69	0
Bob Stanley	R	10	8	.556	3.82	0
John Tudor	L	4	3	.571	4.56	1
Mark Clear	R	8	3	.727	4.09	9
Bob Ojeda	L	6	2	.750	3.14	0
Tom Burgmeier	L	4	5	.444	2.85	6
Steve Crawford	R	0	5	.000	4.97	0
Bill Campbell	R	1	1	.500	3.19	7
Chuck Rainey	R	0	1	.000	2.70	0
Bruce Hurst	L	2	0	1.000	4.30	0
Luis Aponte	R	1	0	1.000	0.56	1
TEAM TOTAL		59	49	.546	3.83	24

came comical. His final at-bat in the seventh inning, reliever
Dan Spillner threw two pitches right down the middle, only
home-plate umpire Rich Garcia had told the Cleveland
pitchers, "If he doesn't swing, it's a ball." Yaz took a third
pitch, and on 3–0, not wanting to end it all with a walk, he
spun unhinged at a batting-practice fastball up in his eyes
and popped up. He went to his position, came back in to an
ovation, stepped back out for another ovation, then when the
game was over came back out and ran around the park again.

Yaz had outdone Ted in his own way, outdone anyone
who'd ever played anything in this town in a way that will
forever be remembered. No one really cared that in his final
at-bat he popped up to someone named Jack Perconte, or
that his final home run in a major-league uniform (off Jim
Palmer, September 12) was erased when rain wiped out the
game in the fourth inning. Yaz didn't do anything worthy of
the ABC Evening News. The networks carried nothing of the
two days, for television needed action, not thoughts. Yaz
never was Ted. Through all the highlights they showed in his
farewell film, those that brought the greatest response from
the fans — besides his inspired protest of covering home

Final American League Standings and Red Sox Statistics, 1982

	W	L	PCT	GB	R	HR	BA
EAST							
MIL	95	67	.586		891	216	.279
BAL	94	68	.580	1	774	179	.266
BOS	89	73	.549	6	753	136	.274
DET	83	79	.512	12	729	177	.266
NY	79	83	.488	16	709	161	.256
CLE	78	84	.481	17	683	109	.262
TOR	78	84	.481	17	651	106	.262
WEST							
CAL	93	69	.574		814	186	.274
KC	90	72	.556	3	784	132	.285
CHI	87	75	.537	6	786	136	.273
SEA	76	86	.469	17	651	130	.254
OAK	68	94	.420	25	691	149	.236
TEX	64	98	.395	29	590	115	.249
MIN	60	102	.370	33	657	148	.257
LEAGUE TOTAL					10163	2080	.264

MANAGER	W	L	PCT
Ralph Houk	89	73	.549

POS	PLAYER	B	G	AB	H	2B	3B	HR	R	RBI	BA
REGULARS											
1B	Dave Stapleton	R	150	538	142	28	1	14	66	65	.264
2B	Jerry Remy	L	155	636	178	22	3	0	89	47	.280
SS	Glenn Hoffman	R	150	469	98	23	2	7	53	49	.209
3B	Carney Lansford	R	128	482	145	28	4	11	65	63	.301
RF	Dwight Evans	R	162	609	178	37	7	32	122	98	.292
CF	Rick Miller	L	135	409	104	13	2	4	50	38	.254
LF	Jim Rice	R	145	573	177	24	5	24	86	97	.309
C	Gary Allenson	R	92	264	54	11	0	6	25	33	.205
DH	Carl Yastrzemski	L	131	459	126	22	1	16	53	72	.275
SUBSTITUTES											
3B	Wade Boggs	L	104	338	118	14	1	5	51	44	.349
DH	Tony Perez	R	69	196	51	14	2	6	18	31	.260
3B	Ed Jurak	R	12	21	7	0	0	0	3	7	.333
SS	Julio Valdez	B	28	20	5	1	0	0	3	1	.250
2B	Marty Barrett	R	8	18	1	0	0	0	0	0	.056
OF	Reid Nichols	R	92	245	74	16	1	7	35	33	.302
OF	Garry Hancock	L	11	14	0	0	0	0	3	0	.000
C	Rich Gedman	L	92	289	72	17	2	4	30	26	.249
C	Roger LaFrancois	L	8	10	4	1	0	0	1	1	.400
C	Marc Sullivan	R	2	6	2	0	0	0	0	0	.333

Final American League Standings and Red Sox Statistics, 1982, continued

PITCHER	T	W	L	PCT	ERA	SV
Dennis Eckersley	R	13	13	.500	3.73	0
John Tudor	L	13	10	.565	3.63	0
Mike Torrez	R	9	9	.500	5.23	0
Bob Stanley	R	12	7	.632	3.10	14
Chuck Rainey	R	7	5	.583	5.02	0
Bruce Hurst	L	3	7	.300	5.77	0
Mark Clear	R	14	9	.609	3.00	14
Tom Burgmeier	L	7	0	1.000	2.29	2
Luis Aponte	R	2	2	.500	3.18	3
Bob Ojeda	L	4	6	.400	5.63	0
Brian Denman	R	3	4	.429	4.78	0
Steve Crawford	R	1	0	1.000	2.00	0
Oil Can Boyd	R	0	1	.000	5.40	0
Mike Brown	R	1	0	1.000	0.00	0
TEAM TOTAL		89	73	.549	4.04	33

plate with dirt after an atrocious called strike in 1975 — were defensive plays: the catch for Billy Rohr in '67 that seemingly was the day the music played again for New Englanders, a catch crashing against The Wall off Jim Essian in 1980 (which ended Yaz's season), the diving stop off Jackson in the '75 playoffs. So, on his final day, Yaz gave the fans the playing memory they wanted. When Cleveland third baseman Toby Harrah ripped a line drive off The Wall, Yastrzemski held it to a single.

Yaz outdid Ted or most anyone else because he passionately explained that he understood what makes the Olde Towne Teame what it is, as if he'd worked all those years in a mill on the Nashua River and paid his way in himself. "As I stepped out of the box that last time, I tried to look around at every sign and every face and say 'thank you' to the *people* of New England who make this the greatest place to play baseball in the world." Which is why he didn't want to ride around in a limo.

When he was replaced by Chico Walker and ran in from his position at the top of the eighth inning, he stepped over to the boxes and handed his hat to an eight-year-old in the first row. He stood in the street in shower togs and signed autographs. He bought champagne for the media and toasted them for their fairness, then remembered Harold Kaese and Ray Fitzgerald and Larry Claflin and George Bankert and Freddie Ciampa and others who passed away. He remembered times he could have made a bundle by going elsewhere, such as in the October 1976 expansion draft, when if he'd allowed Toronto to draft him, he'd have gone to the Yankees for megabucks and the Blue Jays would have received a twenty-six-year-old pitcher with a 1–1 record named Ron Guidry. He said, "You know what made today great? The ovation for Rice."

There were hundreds, perhaps even thousands, still out on Yawkey Way when Yaz came out of his final press conference in the dining room atop Fenway Park. He was signing autographs for some security guards and ballpark people on the roof, awaiting the elevator, when he heard the chanting, "We want Yaz," and looked down to the street. He stepped out to the edge of the roof and waved to the crowd with a papal gesture in his uniform pants, team undershirt, and shower clogs, then turned to George Sullivan. "I'm going down there," he said, and ten minutes later there were women and children and red-eyed truck drivers in a line stretched around the corner from Van Ness all the way to Boylston Street. They came through an entrance, two by two, and he signed one program or poster after another for forty minutes until there was no more line. When he had finished that, he came back into the park and signed autographs for people who get paid hourly wages to work in Fenway.

It was 6:22 P.M. EDT, dusk, when he'd finished signing what they had for him to sign. He pulled the cork out of yet another bottle of champagne, toasted the kids who work in the ballpark, and stepped atop the Red Sox dugout. He took a swig, then turned away to survey the park that had been his home for more than half his life. He raised the bottle toward the right-field bleachers (perhaps remembering the homer off Joe Hoerner in the '67 series?) and took a swig. He raised the bottle toward the center-field bleachers (a homer off Catfish, perhaps?). Toward The Wall (ah, Bob Allison, Sal Bando, Bert Campaneris). He turned slowly, looking up at the lights of the press box, where the last two writers of the season remained, then turned back for one last look at the park. He chugged the last half of the bottle, tossed it onto the field, turned around, and stepped off the dugout to go to the clubhouse to take off number 8 for the final time.

And made no attempt to hide the fact that he was crying.

NINE

1983-84

SQUABBLING
IN THE RUINS

*The infamous Coup Leroux finishes off the era for the
Red Sox with a dull thud, sending Boston tumbling to
its first losing season since 1966. The realities of the
game in 1984 dictate a new approach to building winning teams, an approach the Red Sox must learn if
they are to return to contention.*

SEVERAL OF THE MEMBERS of the 1967 team were already
in the press room atop Fenway Park. There were hors
d'oeuvres, two bars, and cameras from nearly a dozen television stations around New England. It was June 5, 1983:
Tony C. Night, in which the Red Sox had raised money to
help the Conigliaro family pay for the costs of keeping the
then-thirty-eight-year-old former slugger alive. After becoming the youngest player in major-league history to hit one
hundred home runs, Conigliaro had his career snuffed out
with an August 1967 beaning, then suffered a paralyzing
heart attack in January 1982 that left him in a coma. It was to
be a gushy, weepy, nostalgic evening, not only because of the
unfair and tragic nature of Conigliaro's ailments, but because
most of his teammates from the 1967 pennant winners had
flown in from around the country.

No one in New England needs to say anything more than

sixty-seven. It was a magical summer entitled "The Impossible Dream," in which a team that had finished a game out of last place the year before, that hadn't even flirted with respectability for over a decade, came riding in to a pennant. *Sixty-seven.* It meant stopping one's car outside the Callahan Tunnel because Reggie Smith was at the plate with the bases loaded, or having one's car battery go dead in a parking lot in Chapel Hill, North Carolina, right after Dalton Jones hit a tenth-inning home run in Detroit, or knowing — just knowing — that Yaz would get a hit with the bases loaded on that wonderful final October day. It made a folk hero out of a rookie left-hander named Billy Rohr, who in his major-league debut, in Yankee Stadium, retired the first twenty-six batters he faced. Never mind that after winning his next start, again against the Yankees, he never won another game for the Red Sox and was in the minors by mid-May. Billy Rohr was the symbol of the end of one era and the beginning of the next: an era in which there was more interest in the Boston Red Sox than at any time in their history. It might not ever be that way again. Because of the sophistication of the media, we probably know too much to go through the romantic stages of that season, from puppy love to plighting our troths, but for anyone born in New England before Hula-Hoops it was the baseball summer that will never be forgotten.

In the press room, Darrell Brandon was recounting Jose Tartabull's throw to Elston Howard that cut down Ken Berry, and Jones remembered Eddie Stanky calling Yastrzemski "an all-star from the neck down." Mike Andrews recalled the game in which they came back from an 8–0 deficit against the Angels, and Rico Petrocelli recalled the night Tony C. hit the home run off long-time nemesis John Buzhardt in the eleventh inning of a game against Chicago.

That '75 team was very good. So were the '45–'49 and '78 teams. But the '67 Red Sox represented baseball as romance, as Mark Fidrych did in 1976. And almost all that team had gathered in the Fenway press room by 4:00 P.M., on a day when fans could forget about Fisk and Lynn and agents and Buddy and Haywood and what used to be. "We have shared something with the greatest fans in the world that few players will ever experience," Andrews, then chairman of the Jimmy Fund (and later a telecaster), told Rohr and Brandon.

"The Red Sox have called a major news conference for 4:30," the Associated Press's Dave O'Hara announced as he charged into the room. Sure enough, a few minutes past the scheduled time, Buddy Leroux walked in with Dick O'Connell and Leroux's attorney (and limited partner) Al Curran and announced that he, Curran, and Kentucky coal baron Rogers Badgett had merged their (fifteen of thirty) majority of the limited partner shares, reorganized the general partnership, fired Haywood Sullivan, made Leroux "managing general partner" and reappointed O'Connell as general manager.

As Petrocelli, Jerry Stephenson, Dave Morehead, Jim Lonborg, George Thomas, and the other '67 heroes stood at the back of the room and watched in disbelief, Leroux and O'Connell explained their plans for nearly half an hour. As soon as public relations director George Sullivan — a Leroux appointee and aide — closed off that conference, publicity director Dick Bresciani — a Yawkey holdover — announced there would be yet another press conference in another twenty-five minutes. In between, Leroux called the employees together and informed them that he was the boss and that they should take all orders from him and O'Connell. He left the room; Sullivan stood up and announced that everyone should ignore Leroux, the takeover was a phony and he was in charge.

Then, when he finished with the employees, Haywood Sullivan, John Harrington, and their attorneys marched up to the press room, held their own news conference, claiming that the Coup Leroux was invalid, and declared that they would be in court in the morning to get an injunction to prove it.

It didn't really matter which side had desecrated the evening; Leroux claimed that the Sullivan-Yawkey-Harrington people forced it by firing Curran as club legal counsel and claiming that Leroux had triggered an automatic buy-out covenant in their partnership, while Mrs. Yawkey and Sullivan claimed this was typical of Leroux's crass, publicity-seeking priorities. The heart of a franchise perceived as the Olde Towne Teame had been singed for once and for all. As Tony Conigliaro lay in a coma and fans lined up to relive *sixty-seven*, Dumwood and Shoddy were mud-wrestling over a team that the league office had called the Flagship of the American League when they inherited it, only to strip-mine it into a discount furniture outlet out on Route 1 in Saugus.

What happened from that point on returned the Red Sox to their tawdry Jersey Street Jesters era before *sixty-seven*. When Leroux called his press conference, the club was 28–22 and in first place; after he left the room and the media descended on the field, the players' attention was completely diverted from baseball. Ralph Houk packed his belongings at his house in Wellesley and told his wife, "If Haywood doesn't get the injunction, we're on the road home to Pompano Beach." Players tripped over cameras trying to get to batting practice, and while some joked ("We don't want to win for Buddy," said Bob Stanley), they didn't seem to notice any more than the public did that they were swept four straight by the Tigers and en route to a 50–62 record the rest of the season that would leave them with their first losing season since 1966. From June 6, 1983, through June 6, 1984, they were 76–89.

Between that night and Yastrzemski's last hurrah, the warring sides spent their summer in Suffolk Superior Court, airing their dirty laundry in a long-running, trashy soap opera. The papers daily carried the juicy details of the gossipy testi-

mony. Harrington was pictured as an ambitious, conniving
con man. Jean Yawkey was pictured as a vindictive old maid,
and she in turn accused Leroux of being greedy. Leroux and
Badgett accused Sullivan of being a complete and utter incompetent. Haywood never did get to the stand, but he had
prepared a long list of accusations about Leroux. Cross-firing
memos were introduced in which Badgett charged Mrs.
Yawkey with embezzlement and Mrs. Yawkey in turn accused Badgett of concerning himself only with profit. David
Mugar, who had tried to buy Leroux's shares only to be
blocked by the Sullivan-Harrington-Yawkey side (triggering
the court battle), told of Harrington's deception and Mrs.
Yawkey's hollering at him about what was said on the air at
Channel 7, which he owned. It was revealed that while sitting in his Fenway office, Leroux had negotiated to try to buy
the Cleveland Indians, and from the Common to Fenway
stories flew into print (Jerry Remy, for example, recounted
that while he was under anesthesia after one knee operation
Leroux had called him and asked him to come to his Woburn
office to discuss his contract, provided he drop Kapstein).

What Harrelson had prophesied at UMass–Boston in January 1981 — "The Red Sox are the laughingstock of the
American League" — had come true. Yastrzemski, who in
this old-style Boston political war had been involved to the
point that he was Mugar's partner, kept people coming to the
park for the rest of the year. But when 1984 started, crowds
had fallen, their games on Channel 38 were gathering share
numbers like 1.2 and 1.9 — USFL numbers — and the effects
were clear. "Baseball isn't a life-and-death matter, the Red
Sox are," Barnicle had written in October 1977, but the Coup
Leroux had brazenly and graphically reminded the people of
New England what does and doesn't matter, a cynical contrast to the memory of Tom Yawkey standing in his box in his
Windbreaker watching Fisk run around the bases that October night in 1975. "This," wrote Superior Court Judge James
P. Lynch in rendering his decision that Leroux's takeover

was invalid, "is a high-stakes 'commercial' case, pure and simple. That it happens to involve conflict for control of a professional baseball franchise — considered by many to be a community asset — is almost coincidental. As has been seen, the issues involve business documents and financial strategy, with the primary emphasis on profit after taxes rather than pennants after playoffs (which should surprise only those still naive enough to view professional baseball as primarily a sport rather than 'big business')."

A week before Lynch issued his ruling, Baseball Commissioner Bowie Kuhn had resigned at an owners' meeting at a Boston hotel. A group of five National League owners had used the archaic voting procedures to block Kuhn's re-election the previous November 1 in Chicago. From that point on, attempts to soften the dissidents failed, as Ted Turner of the Braves, Nelson Doubleday of the Mets, Gussie Busch of the Cardinals, Dr. John McMullen of the Astros, and the Williams brothers of the Reds had a blood pact that they wouldn't break ranks. Their complaints against Kuhn stemmed from a number of issues. Turner was angry about his suspension over tampering involving free agent outfielder Gary Matthews; Busch was angry about the 1976 and 1981 agreements with the players and infuriated about the split season after the strike of 1981; the Williams brothers were upset about the split season, since the Reds had the best record in baseball that year and didn't qualify for postseason play because they failed to win either miniseason; Doubleday was angry because Kuhn had opened the camps in 1976, and most important, he, Turner, and the Cubs (owned by the *Chicago Tribune* and superstation Channel 9) also didn't want any form of revenue sharing interfering with superstation cable TV revenues; McMullen and George Steinbrenner wanted "a businessman" in the role of commissioner.

What happened after the Messersmith decision was that the center came apart and all the game's centrifugal forces disintegrated. Owners' egos clashed in the open market and owners eventually had to find ways to finance those egos for the first time. "The game" had given way to twenty-six needs in twenty-two markets, and *revenue* became the most important word in the industry. Kuhn's successor eventually was Los Angeles Olympics organizer Peter Ueberroth, not because of any baseball experience — Ueberroth had none — but because he was an expert in commercial marketing and seemed fearless. By 1983, the owners were looking for a commissioner who could sell the game to soft-drink and automobile and clothing and pharmaceutical companies for their use. Search committee chairman Bud Selig gave them a man ready to force owners to look in the mirror. "Nobody owns a baseball team because he loves baseball anymore. It's financial suicide," observed Minnesota owner Calvin Griffith, whose family had been in the game since the turn of the century. "Beginning with 1976, the game has been run by agents turning the Steinbrenners and Turners by their tails, and the rest of the owners have had to hustle in the street to keep their egos satisfied."

By the time Kuhn finally avoided embarrassment and stepped down, Player Relations Committee chairman Ray Grebey had been fired. Though Grebey had been brought in to hard-line the players and break the union, he couldn't, because he — like everyone before him — couldn't negotiate with a unilateral union with one interest when he represented twenty-six bosses with twenty-six interests. Grebey, according to some owners, was *too* hard-line and didn't understand a more sophisticated, enlightened approach to relations with the players. After 1976, John Gaherin was fired because he wasn't tough enough. "We've got to get baseball back the way it used to be," Bob Howsam told his fellow owners in March 1984. He sounded like Batista in 1959.

Howsam that July had come out of retirement for a second stint as Reds president. His original replacement, Dick Wagner, had been dismissed in a wholesale shake-up of the organization, a shakeup that Howsam said was tantamount to an admission that the Cincinnati Reds had misread the post-Messersmith era. Howsam — and, eventually, Wagner — had represented the old-guard hard line more arrogantly than any team in baseball. Wagner turned out to be a scapegoat, for all he did was follow Howsam's advice, then get carved out of his job by Howsam himself. Arrogance? They refused even to come to the free-agent re-entry drafts in New York. They dumped Tony Perez at the end of the 1976 season, partially because of his agent, Kapstein. They let Pete Rose, Joe Morgan, Ken Griffey, and others go, and when it was time for George Foster to make his megabucks, they traded him to the Mets for three players who were the equivalent of thirty cents on the dollar.

The Reds survived for a few years, winning the division in 1979 and having the so-called best record in baseball in '81 (they even had a parade in downtown Cincinnati to celebrate that unrewarded feat), but the failure to adjust to the era finally caught up with them the way it caught up with the Red Sox. In 1982, they collapsed into last place in the National League West. Another year in the basement and they fired Wagner and manager Russ Nixon and tried to overhaul their image.

One of Howsam's first moves was to repurchase Perez from the Phillies, even though Perez was nearly forty-two years old. "Trading him was the biggest mistake in the history of the franchise," Howsam admitted. Then he went and signed the Reds' first major free agent, former Pirates outfielder Dave Parker, and in August brought back Rose as player-manager.

Before Perez returned to Cincinnati, he played in his fifth World Series with the Phillies. That Phillies team had been ballyhooed as the regathering of Perez, Morgan, and Rose. They'd graced the cover of *Sports Illustrated* in March, but while each played his part at one time or another — Perez carried the Phillies the first five weeks after being released by the Red Sox — only Morgan played regularly in the final stretch in which Philadelphia went 26–5 to win the National League East. Rose was forced back into the postseason lineup because Len Matuszek, who had been recalled from the minors in September, was ineligible. They rolled over the Dodgers in the playoffs, then split the first two games of the World Series in Baltimore and returned to Philadelphia to try to win this final go-round together.

When the hundreds of members of the media learned that Paul Owens's lineup for the third game against Orioles left-hander Mike Flanagan had Rose being benched in favor of Perez, they encircled the Philadelphia dugout, waiting for Rose and his reaction to the benching.

Finally, he burst up out of the runway and through the dugout, brushing past the cameras and microphones and hundreds of writers two steps at a time onto the field and into a sprint for the outfield. As they blurted out questions about the lineup, he ran through the assembled media as if he were frozen in *Chariots of Fire.* Pete Rose wasn't in the lineup of the third game of the World Series against the Orioles, Pete Rose was angry, and Pete Rose was going to talk about it only on ABC with Howard Cosell. When he talked, he indicated that he was hurt and upset and embarrassed, and that while he had no choice but to accept the decision, he didn't agree with it, or Owens. In Pete Rose's mind, Pete Rose should have been in the lineup, not Tony Perez, and an audience of seventy million people knew it before the story was sent in to hundreds of national newspapers.

"That's Pete," Tony Perez said with a forced laugh. Perez himself was angry, because he was the man replacing Rose at first base against Flanagan, and Perez felt he had every right to play. "Pete sometimes forgets about the people around him, but that's all right. I know he hasn't thought about the other people involved, only that he isn't playing. But I'm not some kid out of A ball that's here for the first time . . ."

Baseball is, despite its team image, a highly individual and selfish game. "You learn to disguise how you feel when you go three-for-four and your team loses," Jerry Remy always said. "That's part of being a professional and knowing how to play. If Rose had gone one-for-four all those years and been rah-rah for his team, do you think he'd have the same effect on the game as going two-for-five?"

Rose had a tremendous influence on everyone around him because he played so hard and so devoutly, but he also played for himself and nobody else. He wanted his records and, naturally, he wanted his ego assuaged, and he couldn't stand being benched in front of seventy million people. "I'm not washed up," he crisply insisted as the series began, in reply to questions about losing his job to the twenty-nine-year-old Matuszek down the stretch. "You'll see." Rose was playing not only for the World Series and his ego, he was playing for free agency and the opportunity to play somewhere — anywhere — for two years so he could break Ty Cobb's hit record. He knew the Phillies would probably not bring him back, so he needed every chance he could to impress the market. Unlike the old days, he didn't have to impress the Phillies, only one of twenty-six teams. The free market had thus at last severed all bonds, even those among teammates.

The last stand of Rose, Morgan, and Perez was a three-game sweep by the Orioles in Philadelphia's Veterans Stadium, culminated by Baltimore left-hander Scott McGregor beating them in the final game throwing only fastballs and change-ups. When the series was over, the Phillies decided not to pick up their options on Rose and Morgan. Pete's third stop was Montreal, Morgan's sixth stop was to be Oakland. The Phils then sold Perez back to Cincinnati. The Phillies' Wheeze Kids, having served their purpose, were disbanded.

Yastrzemski and Bench retired at the end of 1983, Yaz refusing all gifts, pomp, and ceremony at each stop around the American League, Bench taking what he could get around the National as if he were on *The Price Is Right.* By the time the 1984 season had started, the only players — not counting Perez and Rick Miller, who left and returned — in place with the Red Sox and Reds from the '75 World Series were Evans, Rice, Concepcion, and Dan Driessen. When Baltimore released Jim Palmer in May 1984, there was only one player in each league with more consecutive service with original teams than Concepcion (thirteen years) and Evans (eleven years); Perez, Rose, Yastrzemski, and Petrocelli all had had more years with the Reds and Red Sox in 1975 than Evans's eleven years, twenty-two days at the start of the '84 season.

When Yastrzemski retired, he kept saying, "I can't believe that we didn't win two or three World Series with that team that came along in '75." As it turned out, Cecil Cooper, Fisk, Lynn, Burleson, Tiant, Juan Beniquez, Lee, and Miller had all played for teams that went into postseason play after '75; Yastrzemski, Rice, and Evans hadn't.

Petrocelli had worked briefly (and successfully) as a radio announcer. Bob Montgomery was doing the telecasts of Red Sox games. Not one member of either '75 pitching staff was still in the major leagues, although Tiant, Diego Segui, and Rogelio Moret were trying to hold on in Mexico, and Lee was active in a semipro league in Quebec. Dick Drago came around the clubhouse a lot; he was still pitching well in Mexico in 1982, but couldn't get even a tryout and retired to work for a suburban office furniture outlet. Doug Griffin was working in construction for Leroux in Winter Haven. Carbo had a hair salon outside Detroit, was doing summer camp work with Willoughby (they played in the Portland, Maine, Twilight League in '83), and was an extra in a baseball movie filmed in Atlanta in May 1984. Griffey and George Foster were the only other Reds from the '75 series still active, making $1.2 million and $1.95 million a year respectively. Lynn ($1.65 million), Burleson ($900,000), Fisk ($700,000), and Cooper ($950,000) all had made their fortunes before the Red Sox signed Evans to a three-year, $2.95 million contract that was to begin with the 1985 season.

In 1975, the Red Sox had one player — Yastrzemski — making more than $80,000. He was making $250,000 then,

$50,000 less than thirty-five-year-old third-string catcher Jeff Newman made in 1983, when he played a full season with the Red Sox and did not hit a ball off or over The Wall. The total Boston payroll in 1975 was approximately $1.25 million; there were at least a dozen individual players making that around baseball by 1984, and the Red Sox payroll had increased to nearly $10 million, which put them in the lower half of the league! Where in '75 there wasn't one player on a multiyear contract, the Red Sox had sixteen on multiyear pacts in 1984. Where, in June 1976, they simply swapped the contracts of Carbo, Bobby Darwin, and Tom Murphy with Milwaukee, in May 1984, when they traded Eckersley (and minor leaguer Mike Brumley) to the Cubs for first baseman Bill Buckner, they had to get each player to agree to waive his "rights." Eckersley had a no-trade clause; the Cubs gave him a $175,000 bonus — more money than the yearly salary of all but a half-dozen players in the big leagues in '75. Buckner had to approve any deal because he was a 10/5 man (meaning ten years' major league service, the last five with the same club); the Red Sox agreed to add an extra year to his present pact that ran through 1986, which included a $300,000 buy-out, which is more than anyone in the American League made in '75. Where, in 1975, the only extras in the Red Sox contracts included a single room on the road, the contract the Red Sox inherited on Buckner read as follows:

1984 — $660,000
1985 — $710,000
1986 — $750,000

In addition, Buckner had incentives as follows: $25,000 for appearing in 150 games, $25,000 for making the All-Star team, $25,000 for being the MVP of the league championship series, $50,000 for being World Series MVP, $50,000 for being the league MVP, $40,000 for finishing second in the MVP balloting, $30,000 for finishing third, $20,000 for finishing fourth, and $10,000 for finishing fifth.

Sullivan and his new general manager, Lou Gorman, felt they had to make the deal for Buckner. "We have to do something to regain the fans' confidence," Gorman admitted. Attendance was plodding along at a rate that, coupled with the 36–5 start of the '84 Tigers, gave promise of a falloff of nearly half a million. TV ratings were pitiable, and attempts to market their cable network had placed it in as many eastern Massachusetts homes as Rembrandts. The concessions were dead, which wasn't lost on limited partners Harry M. Stevens Concessionaires. Sullivan was being compared to the Bunker Hill Monument, Gorman to Charlie McCarthy, and, meanwhile, they were still awaiting a ruling by the Massachusetts Court of Appeals on the appeal of Leroux and Badgett.

The Buckner trade opened the floor to the same sort of questions as the Evans signing had in January. But past mistakes had led to a flood of credibility questions. When they let Fisk, Lynn, and Burleson go, Sullivan said they hadn't won with that team and he had to rebuild another one. Then he let Lansford go; no matter what the reasons, it seemed to be the same old story. So, when they finished in sixth place, twenty games behind Baltimore, they couldn't go trade Evans, especially after he had so openly vocalized his concerns about the direction of the ball club. Fans never really gave Tony Armas his just due, for while he batted only .218, he was second in the league in homers with 36, knocked in 107 runs, and probably earned a Gold Glove, although he was never awarded one. On the other hand, the promises of spring had fallen — Newman didn't hit, Fidrych was released by Pawtucket, John Henry Johnson won and saved a combined total of four games and ended up in disfavor with Houk. In spring training, 1984, Houk had asked the front office to release Newman and told the *Globe* and the *Herald*'s Joe Giulotti, "I want to find out about Johnson in a hurry, because if he doesn't do the job right off the bat, his ass is gone."

Back at the (appropriately) Valentine's Day ownership trial, Judge John Greaney concluded the proceeding by saying, "I strongly urge both sides to put aside their differences, get together and try to do something about the pitching." Everyone in the courtroom laughed, but the statement from a judge — a man so serious that he once locked up all the teachers in the town of Franklin for ignoring his order to return to work — demonstrated just how much a part of New Englanders' lives the Red Sox are. The late Humberto Cardinal Medeiros took the opportunity at a recess of the College of Cardinals in 1978 to find Boston television journalist Clark Booth and ask him how the Red Sox had made out the previous day.

In early 1984, the Orioles were chic the way the Red Sox had been chic in the spring of 1975. ABC's *Good Morning, America* newsman Steve Bell broadcast live from their Miami spring-training base in March, and Barnicle could be seen on Channel 5's *Chronicle* wearing a Baltimore cap. The stability and durability of the Orioles organization was as admirable as that of the Celtics or Dallas Cowboys or Los Angeles Dodgers. Baltimore had the best record in baseball over the last five, ten, twenty, and twenty-five years, through two owners, four general managers, and a handful of managers; Hank Bauer, Earl Weaver, and Joe Altobelli had all managed world champions, after all, and the only threads that tied those teams together were one pitcher (Jim Palmer) and a developmental system geared to pitching.

When the Orioles won the 1983 world championship, they were run by a man, Hank Peters, who was generally respected as one of the two or three best executives in baseball. He had built the Kansas City A's from scratch, and the Kansas City A's became the Oakland A's and won three consecutive world championships and five straight divisional titles with the talent Peters put together before refusing to move to the West Coast. He took over the Orioles in 1976, at a time when the team that had won five American League East titles in six years through 1974 was undergoing a transition. Peters knew that owner Jerold Hofberger and the Orioles couldn't afford the immediate crush of the open market, as they averaged barely a million fans a year. So he adjusted, seizing the infamous June 15, 1976, trading deadline to ship three pitchers who were heading for free agency (Ken Holtzman, Doyle Alexander, Grant Jackson) to the Yankees for what would be a major part of his 1979 and 1983 pennant winners: Scott McGregor, left-handed reliever Tippy Martinez (the league's premier left-handed short man from 1979 to 1983), catcher Rick Dempsey, and pitcher Rudy May. The latter won eighteen games in 1977 and Peters quickly moved him on to Montreal for outfielder Gary Roenicke and pitcher Don "Stan the Man Unusual" Stanhouse, who carried them to the 1979 World Series.

By 1983, Peters and new owner Edward Bennett Williams neatly read the market. When Eddie Murray clearly established himself as the team's best player and leader, they got him signed to a five-year contract and went about the task of tying up all the other good players after Murray, with the scale based on Murray being the team's highest-paid player. Sullivan had tried to do that in Boston by signing Rice to a seven-year, $4.9 million contract in 1979, but, unlike Peters, put off dealing with his other priorities.

By 1983, teams like Detroit and Toronto were climbing to the top rungs of the American League ladder. Both clubs were run by extremely bright young executives — Detroit's Bill Lajoie, Toronto's Pat Gillick — who had come to grips with the post-Messersmith system. Lajoie and Gillick, like Peters, were scouting and development people who understood that the only hedge against the system is to have a constant influx of one's own talent rising from the minor leagues, and that when a team comes up with championship players, it must tie them up. Lajoie wasted no time getting his young stars, like Lance Parrish, Alan Trammell, Lou Whitaker, Jack Morris, and Dan Petry, signed for four- to seven-year deals,

while making the judgment not to risk a long-term investment on Steve Kemp and Jason Thompson. Gillick did the
same with all of Toronto's key players, like Dave Stieb, Willie Upshaw, Lloyd Moseby, Damaso Garcia, Jim Clancy, and
Alfredo Griffin. By 1983, George Steinbrenner's neglect of
the Yankee farm system had left him as desperate as a junkie.
He had to pay million-dollar prices for every available free
agent, but by 1983 the free-agent market contained for the
most part only veterans whose course had been run elsewhere — players like Rose or thirty-seven-year-old Darrell
Evans — and not the key skill position personnel that Steinbrenner had used to fill in with the talent core he had pur-
chased when he bought the Yankees in 1973. Steinbrenner
had a seemingly boundless market off which to mortgage his
need to keep the Yankees competitive. But he, too, had lost
to the new system because he didn't understand the fiscal and
talent necessities of the developmental part of an organization until turning the club over to Branch Rickey disciple
Clyde King in May.

A decade after Andy Messersmith and Dave McNally altered baseball, what was different about running a baseball
team was that executives were out in the open market like
other business executives. The old system provided safe-
guards; the new system forces teams to scout and develop talent and executives to make decisive million-dollar judgments,
decisions that general managers in 1975 never had to make,
decisions that from 1976 to 1984 took the Red Sox from the
next great team after the Reds to litigation and the second
division. When the Orioles went up for sale, they ended up
with Williams. The Red Sox ended up in Suffolk Superior
Court. When they went for free agents to complete their
1977–78–79 team, they got Mike Torrez and Bill Campbell;
the Yankees got Rich Gossage and Tommy John. They
couldn't make up their minds in 1980 and lost Fred Lynn and
Carlton Fisk.

The Red Sox seem tragically flawed, like Bernard Mala-

Final American League Standings and Red Sox Statistics, 1983

	W	L	PCT	GB	R	HR	BA
EAST							
BAL	98	64	.605		799	168	.269
DET	92	70	.568	6	789	156	.274
NY	91	71	.562	7	770	153	.273
TOR	89	73	.549	9	795	167	.277
MIL	87	75	.537	11	764	132	.277
BOS	78	84	.481	20	724	142	.270
CLE	70	92	.432	28	704	86	.265
WEST							
CHI	99	63	.611		800	157	.262
KC	79	83	.488	20	696	109	.271
TEX	77	85	.475	22	639	106	.255
OAK	74	88	.457	25	708	121	.262
CAL	70	92	.432	29	722	154	.260
MIN	70	92	.432	29	709	141	.261
SEA	60	102	.370	39	558	111	.240
LEAGUE TOTAL					10177	1903	.266

MANAGER	W	L	PCT
Ralph Houk	78	84	.481

POS	PLAYER	B	G	AB	H	2B	3B	HR	R	RBI	BA
REGULARS											
1B	Dave Stapleton	R	151	542	134	31	1	10	54	66	.247
2B	Jerry Remy	L	146	592	163	16	5	0	73	43	.275
SS	Glenn Hoffman	R	143	473	123	24	1	4	56	41	.260
3B	Wade Boggs	L	153	582	210	44	7	5	100	74	.361
RF	Dwight Evans	R	126	470	112	19	4	22	74	58	.238
CF	Tony Armas	R	145	574	125	23	2	36	77	107	.218
LF	Jim Rice	R	155	626	191	34	1	39	90	126	.305
C	Gary Allenson	R	84	230	53	11	0	3	19	30	.230
DH	Carl Yastrzemski	L	119	380	101	24	0	10	38	56	.266
SUBSTITUTES											
UT	Ed Jurak	R	75	159	44	8	4	0	19	18	.277
2B	Marty Barrett	R	33	44	10	1	1	0	7	2	.227
2S	Julio Valdez	B	12	25	3	0	0	0	3	0	.120
SS	Jackie Gutierrez	R	5	10	3	0	0	0	2	0	.300
OD	Reid Nichols	R	100	274	78	22	1	6	35	22	.285
OF	Rick Miller	L	104	262	75	10	2	2	41	21	.286
OF	Lee Graham	L	5	6	0	0	0	0	2	1	.000
OF	Chico Walker	B	4	5	2	0	2	0	2	1	.400
C	Rich Gedman	L	81	204	60	16	1	2	21	18	.294
C	Jeff Newman	R	59	132	25	4	0	3	11	7	.189

Final American League Standings and Red Sox Statistics, 1983, continued

PITCHER	T	W	L	PCT	ERA	SV
John Tudor	L	13	12	.520	4.09	0
Bruce Hurst	L	12	12	.500	4.09	0
Dennis Eckersley	R	9	13	.409	5.61	0
Bob Ojeda	L	12	7	.632	4.04	0
Bob Stanley	R	8	10	.444	2.85	33
Mike Brown	R	6	6	.500	4.67	0
Oil Can Boyd	R	4	8	.333	3.28	0
Mark Clear	R	4	5	.444	6.28	4
Doug Bird	R	1	4	.200	6.65	1
Luis Aponte	R	5	4	.556	3.63	3
John Henry Johnson	L	3	2	.600	3.71	1
Al Nipper	R	1	1	.500	2.25	0
TEAM TOTAL		78	84	.481	4.34	42

mud's Roy Hobbs in *The Natural*. But they also were simply unlucky. If the Dodgers had given Messersmith the no-trade provision he wanted in 1975 and the reserve system hadn't been overturned for another three years, the Red Sox might well have won a World Series or two.

If Tom Yawkey had only lived for three more years . . .

If Fred Lynn and Dwight Evans hadn't gotten hurt and Luis Tiant had held out in 1977 . . .

If Bill Campbell and Rick Burleson hadn't gotten hurt in 1978 . . .

Ever since they had the best team in baseball from 1912 to 1918 and were sold to a Broadway producer named Harry Frazee, disaster shadowed them. Just when they built the next dynasty in 1946, Tex Hughson, Earl Johnson, and Dave "Boo" Ferriss hurt their arms. Frank Baumann was eighteen years old and better than Herb Score when they were both in the American Association in 1954; Baumann got called into the army, got heavy, and hurt his arm. In a span of less than ten months from August 1967 to June 1968, the careers of a twenty-two-year-old slugger (Tony Conigliaro) and two of the league's best pitchers (Jim Lonborg, Jose Santiago) were, for all intents and purposes, snuffed out.

When all of a sudden on that October morn in 1975 the ball crashed off the mesh attached to the left-field foul pole, it didn't really seem to matter what would happen later that day. With George Frederick Handel blaring out over the Fens and church bells pealing on the Charlestown, New Hampshire, green and Carlton Fisk gamboling across the outfield grass, it didn't matter that the Reds would twenty-two hours later win the seventh game. The Reds could have that one today. The Red Sox had the Sixth Game and all the tomorrows.

What they didn't know was that the game that followed the Sixth Game was the last one played under the old rules, and tomorrow never came.

Postscript

*B*Y MID-MAY 1984, the Red Sox had bottomed out. They were fighting the Indians for last place, buried in the television ratings, and struggling to get people into the ballpark. Slowly but surely, however, they put the past behind them and started forward. They had brought in a general manager in Lou Gorman so that Haywood Sullivan would stop trying to be owner and baseball man simultaneously. Gradually, the structure of the team changed. An exciting, flashy rookie named Joaquin Gutierrez took over at shortstop. Rich Gedman, at twenty-four, blossomed into an everyday catcher who could throw and hit for power. Jerry Remy got hurt and an Eddie Stanky clone named Marty Barrett took over second. Gorman traded Dennis Eckersley to the Cubs for Buckner, who was the final stabilizing force in the infield.

The fact that the Tigers ran off to such a great start and that the Red Sox were virtually eliminated by May 25 probably helped them, because it allowed Ralph Houk to put out the youngest starting rotation in the league — Bruce Hurst, Bobby Ojeda, Oil Can Boyd, Al Nipper, and Roger Clemens — and let them get their education without pressure.

Simultaneously, the personality of the club began changing, as the new leadership in the persons of Jim Rice, Tony Armas, Mike Easler, and Gutierrez began to take hold. In the two months following the Buckner trade, the Red Sox had the best record in the American League, and got people interested again, after having been on a downbound train for five years. McNamara and a young, enthusiastic coaching staff took over in October.

"People could see that the best we could be was a third-place team," said Rice. "The spark came when Gutierrez took over at shortstop. Then came the Buckner deal, which showed that they would pick up a high-salaried player. Then the pitching began developing. Suddenly, we were going up-hill again. Give the fans of New England a glimmer of hope, and they'll jump right in behind you. Most teams have to win first. All the Red Sox have to do is give the fans hope of a next year."

APPENDIX A

Salaries

Red Sox Salaries, 1975 (Average: $56,347.
Major League Average: $44,676.)

Fisk	$80,000, one year
Cooper	$35,000, one year
Doyle	$80,000, one year
Petrocelli	$90,000, one year
Burleson	$32,000, one year
Montgomery	$38,000, one year
Heise	$30,000, one year
Griffin	$45,000, one year
Yastrzemski	$175,000, two years
Lynn	$18,000 (plus $20,000 bonus)
Rice	$18,000, one year
Carbo	$48,000, one year
Tiant	$165,000, second of a three-year contract
Wise	$90,000, one year
Lee	$80,000, one year
Cleveland	$65,000, one year
Moret	$30,000, one year
Willoughby	$35,000, one year
Drago	$50,000, one year
Segui	$35,000, one year

Red Sox Salaries, 1979

Fisk	$195,000, fourth of a five-year, $900,000 contract
Montgomery	$80,000, one year
Scott	$200,000, third of a five-year contract
Remy	$100,000, third of a five-year contract
Burleson	$125,000, fourth of a five-year, $625,000 contract
Hobson	$110,000, second of a five-year contract

Brohamer	$100,000, second of a three-year contract
Duffy	$80,000, second of a two-year contract
Wolfe	$30,000, one year
Rice	$700,000, first of a seven-year, $4.9M contract
Lynn	$175,000, fourth of a five-year, $1.65M contract
Evans	$150,000, third of a three-year contract
Yastrzemski	$375,000, second of a two-year contract, plus extension
Torrez	$540,000, second of a seven-year, $2.57M contract
Eckersley	$175,000, third of a three-year contract
Hassler	$65,000, one-year renewal
Stanley	$145,000, first of a three-year, $480,000 contract
Campbell	$165,000, third of a five-year, $1,075,000 contract
Burgmeier	$120,000, second of a two-year contract
Renko	$120,000, one year
Drago	$120,000, second of a two-year contract
Wright	$50,000, first of a two-year contract

Red Sox Salaries, 1984

Rice	$640,000, sixth of a seven-year contract
Armas	$725,000, third of a four-year contract plus $400,000 signing bonus and incentives
Evans	$320,000, third of a three-year contract. Signed 1985–'86–'87 contract for $2.9M
Nichols	$225,000, first of a five-year contract, plus incentives
Miller	$275,000, first of a two-year contract
Easler	$608,000, second of a three-year contract, plus incentives
Buckner	$660,000, third of a four-year contract
Barrett	$70,000, plus incentives
Jurak	$80,000, plus incentives
Hoffman	$185,000, one year
Boggs	$375,000, one year, plus incentives
Remy	$425,000, plus incentives
Stapleton	$325,000, second of a two-year contract
Gutierrez	$40,000, one year
Allenson	$175,000, one year
Newman	$275,000, third of a four-year contract
Gedman	$175,000, plus incentives
Hurst	$185,000, first of a two-year contract, plus incentives
Ojeda	$185,000, first of a two-year contract, plus incentives
Boyd	$65,000, one year, plus incentives

Clemens	$42,500, one year
Nipper	$42,500, one year
Stanley	$450,000, third of a four-year contract, plus incentives
Clear	$475,000, second of a four-year contract, plus incentives
Johnson	$185,000, one year
Brown	$75,000, one year, plus incentives

Average Major-League Salaries

1967	$19,900
1972	$34,092
1975	$44,676
1976	$51,501
1977	$76,066
1978	$99,876
1979	$113,558
1980	$143,756
1981	$185,651
1982	$241,497
1983	$289,194

Red Sox Average Salaries

1979	$145,692
1980	$184,686
1981	$223,252
1982	$247,513
1983	$264,883

Haywood Sullivan's Dealings, 1977–84

1977

Signed RHP Mike Torrez
Signed RHP Dick Drago
Signed INF Jack Brohamer
Traded RHP Don Aase and $300,000 to California for 2B Jerry Remy
Traded INF Steve Dillard to Detroit for RHPs Mike Burns and Frank Harris
Traded RHP Ferguson Jenkins to Texas for LHP John Poloni
Traded 1B Jack Baker to Cleveland for OF Garry Hancock

1978

Signed LHP Tom Burgmeier
Traded LHP Rick Kreuger to Cleveland for SS Frank Duffy
Traded C Bo Diaz, 3B Ted Cox, RHPs Rick Wise and Mike Paxton to Cleveland for RHP Dennis Eckersley and C Fred Kendall
Sold RHP Jim Willoughby to Chicago (AL)
Sold RHP Reggie Cleveland to Texas
Sold OF Bernardo Carbo to Cleveland
Traded LHP Bill Lee to Montreal for INF Stan Papi
Obtained OF Mike Easler from Pittsburgh. (Deal was paper, a favor to get Easler back through waivers and onto the Pittsburgh roster. Easler was sent back, as planned, on March 15 for OF Sandy Hill, OF Gene Gentile, and RHP Martin Rivas, so he never really belonged to Boston.)

1979

Signed RHP Steve Renko
Traded OF Dave Coleman to Minnesota for 3B Larry Wolfe
Sent cash and a player to be named later (Allen Ripley) to San Francisco for OF Jim Dwyer

Traded 1B George Scott to Kansas City for OF Tom Poquette
Traded RHP Peter Ladd and LHP Bobby Sprowl to Houston for 1B Bob
   Watson
Traded C Mike O'Berry to Chicago (NL) for 2B Ted Sizemore
Signed 1B Tony Perez
Signed RHP Skip Lockwood

1980

Traded INF Stan Papi to Philadelphia for C Dave Rader
Sent cash to Detroit for RHP Jack Billingham
Sold Brohamer to Cleveland for $20,000
Traded SS Rick Burleson and 3B Butch Hobson to California for 3B
   Carney Lansford, OF Rick Miller, and RHP Mark Clear

1981

Traded OF Fred Lynn and Renko to California for LHP Frank Tanana,
   OF Joe Rudi, and RHP Jim Dorsey
Traded Drago to Seattle for RHP Manny Sarmiento
Sold Poquette to Texas
Sold Sarmiento to Pittsburgh

1982

Traded RHP Mike Smithson to Texas for LHP John Henry Johnson
Traded 3B Carney Lansford, OF Garry Hancock, and RHP Jerome King
   to Oakland for OF Tony Armas and C Jeff Newman
Traded RHP Mike Torrez to New York (NL) for 3B Mike Davis
Traded RHP Chuck Rainey to Chicago (NL) for RHP Doug Bird

1983

Traded LHP John Tudor to Pittsburgh for OF-DH Mike Easler

1984

Traded RHP Luis Aponte to Cleveland for RHPs Mike Poindexter and
   Paul Perry
Traded RHP Dennis Eckersley and INF-OF Mike Brumley to Chicago
   (NL) for 1B Bill Buckner
Obtained LHP Ed Glynn from New York (NL)

Red Sox in the Free-Agent Market
Red Sox Signings
1976:   Bill Campbell, RHP, 5 yrs., $1,075,000
1977:   Mike Torrez, RHP, 7 yrs., $2,507,249

Jack Brohamer, INF, 3 yrs., $320,000
Tom Burgmeier, LHP, 2 yrs., $250,000
Dick Drago, RHP, 2 yrs., $250,000
1978:   Steve Renko, RHP, 1 yr., $120,000
1980:   Skip Lockwood, RHP, 2 yrs., $778,000
Tony Perez, 1B-DH, 3 yrs., $1,100,000

Red Sox Free-Agent Losses

1977:   Rick Miller, OF (signed w/California)
1978:   Luis Tiant, RHP (signed w/New York)
Fred Kendall, C (signed w/San Diego)
Bob Bailey, DH (did not sign)
1979:   Bob Montgomery, C (re-signed)
Bob Watson, 1B (signed w/New York—compensation was RHP Mike Brown)
1980:   Dave Rader, C (signed w/California)
Jim Dwyer, OF (signed w/Baltimore—compensation was C Kevin Burrell)
1981:   Bill Campbell, RHP (signed w/Cubs—compensation was OF Kevin Romine)
Jerry Remy, 2B (re-signed)
Frank Tanana, LHP (signed w/Texas—compensation was 1B Sam Horn)
Joe Rudi, OF (signed w/Oakland—compensation was 1B Jeff Ledbetter)
1982:   Tom Burgmeier, LHP (signed w/Oakland—compensation was INF-OF Mike Brumley)
1983:   Doug Bird RHP (was not signed)
1984:   Gary Allenson, C